'*Transgressive Design Strategies for Utopian Cities: Theories, Methodologies and Cases in Architecture and Urbanism* is an extraordinary book on the theory of architecture with an emphasis on the theory of urban design. Transgressive design articulates the active relationship between architecture and power. It is an inclusive approach to eliminate discrimination within spaces.

Transgression has not been considered well in architectural education. It is a complex concept, and when it is related to urban design, it gets even more complicated. Since this book handles the concept of transgression through philosophy, architectural theory and architectural/urban design, it fills a gap in knowledge and gives a full sense of transgressive design in architecture and urban design.

The mark of this book in the minds of its readers will be a deep understanding of transgressive design with all its dimensions – objective and subjective. This is something better than other types of learning because it provides a stronger understanding which might free many minds and enable them to practice transgressive design'.

Prof. Dr. Yonca Hurol
Department of Architecture, Eastern Mediterranean University,
Famagusta, Northern Cyprus

Transgressive Design Strategies for Utopian Cities

This book critically examines the philosophy of the term 'transgression' and how it shapes the utopian vision of contemporary urban design scenarios.

The aim of this book is to provide scholarly yet accessible graphic novel illustrations to inform narratives of urban manifestos. Through four select case studies from the UK, Cyprus and Germany, the book highlights the paradoxes and contradictions in architecture and provides detailed evaluation of the limits and contemporary forms of sustainable urban regeneration. The book proposes an 'utopian urban vision' approach to social, political and cultural relations, trends and tensions – both locally and globally – and seeks to inspire an awakening in architectural discourse. The book argues that the philosophical undermining of transgression is the result of a phenomenon from a different perspective – its philosophical background, social construction, experimental research process and design implications on the city. As such, the book provides a critical examination of how architectural design interventions contribute to sustainable urban regeneration and gentrification and can impact local communities.

This book provides a significant contribution to both undergraduate and postgraduate students, as well as early career researchers working in architecture, planning and sustainable urban design. It offers effective guidance on adopting the state-of-the-art graphical illustrations into their own design projects, while considering contradictions between architectural discourse and the philosophy of transgression.

Bertug Ozarisoy is an architect and expert in building energy modelling in Cyprus. His research focuses on understanding the theory between architecture and energy policy design in conjunction with exploring the impact of passive cooling systems on domestic energy use and households' thermal comfort. He is interested in environmental design and the development of novel design applications throughout his architectural practice. He has ten years of experience in intensive teaching, academic research and architectural practice. He was involved with the BSc (Hons) Construction Management programme at the University of East London between September 2016 and 2018. He has developed teaching skills to demonstrate significant intellectual input to students' technical drawings and monitor their learning adaptability and integration to the Construction Technology and Materials module. Currently, Dr. Bertug Ozarisoy is a postdoctoral researcher at the Middle East Technical University (METU) Northern Cyprus Campus where he teaches two post-graduate taught courses, which are entitled 'Deep Energy Retrofit' and 'Environmental Design and Engineering', as part of his postdoctoral research in the Sustainable Environment and Energy Systems (SEES) programme. He is also the first author of many scholarly articles relevant to the building engineering field. He has been mostly involved with research projects in the Sustainable Development of the Built Environment (SDBE) and Sustainable Development Goals (SDGs) in Europe.

Hasim Altan is Professor of Sustainable Design and Architectural Engineering in the Faculty of Design, and Director of the Research Centre at Arkin University of Creative Arts and Design (ARUCAD) in Kyrenia, Cyprus. He is a Chartered Architect (RIBA) and a Chartered Engineer (CIBSE) with over 20 years of academic and practice experience in the field of Architecture, Engineering and Construction (AEC) in the Built Environment in UK, Europe, Middle East and North Africa (MENA) regions. He sits on several editorial boards and reviews project proposals for the European Commission, UK Research Councils and Qatar National Research Fund (QNRF) of the Qatar Foundation. Since 2004, he has, singly or jointly, secured and directed 32 research grants worth over £21 million. He is a founding member of the International Network on Zero Energy Mass Custom Home (ZEMCH), which has so far organised eight international conferences, several design workshops, and numerous technical visits. As well as having supervised 17 successful PhD students, Prof. Dr. Altan has published over 280 refereed international journal and conference papers, technical reports, edited books and chapters and editorials in related fields.

Routledge Research in Architecture

The *Routledge Research in Architecture* series provides the reader with the latest scholarship in the field of architecture. The series publishes research from across the globe and covers areas as diverse as architectural history and theory, technology, digital architecture, structures, materials, details, design, monographs of architects, interior design and much more. By making these studies available to the worldwide academic community, the series aims to promote quality architectural research.

Sverre Fehn and the City: Rethinking Architecture's Urban Premises
Stephen M. Anderson

Exteriorless Architecture: Form, Space and Urbanities of Neoliberalism
Stefano Corbo

Transgressive Design Strategies for Utopian Cities: Theories, Methodologies and Cases in Architecture and Urbanism
Bertug Ozarisoy, Hasim Altan

Architecture and Affect: Precarious Spaces
Lilian Chee

Modernism in Late-Mao China: Architecture for Foreign Affairs in Beijing, Guangzhou and Overseas, 1969-1976
Ke Song

The Spatialities of Radio Astronomy
Guy Trangoš

For more information about this series, please visit: https://www.routledge.com/Routledge-Research-in-Architecture/book-series/RRARCH

Transgressive Design Strategies for Utopian Cities

Theories, Methodologies and Cases in Architecture and Urbanism

Bertug Ozarisoy and Hasim Altan

NEW YORK AND LONDON

Cover design credit: Utopia towards hybridity 2022 © Bertug Ozarisoy

First published 2023
by Routledge
605 Third Avenue, New York, NY 10158

and by Routledge
4 Park Square, Milton Park, Abingdon, Oxon, OX14 4RN

Routledge is an imprint of the Taylor & Francis Group, an informa business

© 2023 Bertug Ozarisoy and Hasim Altan

The right of Bertug Ozarisoy and Hasim Altan to be identified as author of this work has been asserted in accordance with sections 77 and 78 of the Copyright, Designs and Patents Act 1988.

All rights reserved. No part of this book may be reprinted or reproduced or utilised in any form or by any electronic, mechanical, or other means, now known or hereafter invented, including photocopying and recording, or in any information storage or retrieval system, without permission in writing from the publishers.

Trademark notice: Product or corporate names may be trademarks or registered trademarks, and are used only for identification and explanation without intent to infringe.

Library of Congress Cataloging-in-Publication Data
Names: Ozarisoy, Bertug, author. | Altan, Hasim, author.
Title: Transgressive design strategies for utopian cities: theories, methodologies and cases in architecture and urbanism / Bertug Ozarisoy, Hasim Altan.
Description: New York, NY: Routledge, 2023. | Series: Routledge research in architecture | Includes bibliographical references and index.
Identifiers: LCCN 2022047429 (print) | LCCN 2022047430 (ebook) | ISBN 9781032152158 (hardback) | ISBN 9781032152172 (paperback) | ISBN 9781003243069 (ebook) Subjects: LCSH: City planning--Philosophy. | Sustainable urban development. | Architecture and society. | Transgression (Ethics) Classification: LCC NA9050 .O93 2023 (print) | LCC NA9050 (ebook) | DDC 711/.4--dc23/eng/20221026
LC record available at https://lccn.loc.gov/2022047429
LC ebook record available at https://lccn.loc.gov/2022047430

ISBN: 978-1-032-15215-8 (hbk)
ISBN: 978-1-032-15217-2 (pbk)
ISBN: 978-1-003-24306-9 (ebk)

DOI: 10.4324/9781003243069

Typeset in Sabon
by Deanta Global Publishing Services, Chennai, India

Access the Support Material: www.routledge.com/9781032152158

 Printed in the United Kingdom
by Henry Ling Limited

To my family, for their unconditional support, and my aunt Dt. Serife Gurkan, for her financial support throughout my research journey and academic career. This book is also devoted to my beloved aunt Sevilay Salkok.

Memories from the exhibition launch event at the University of Westminster, September 2014. My aunt, (Dt. Serife Gurkan) standing in front of the utopian urban vision map for the transgressive city model in Nicosia, Buffer Zone, Cyprus.

Bertug Ozarisoy

Contents

List of Contributors	xviii
Preface	xx
Acknowledgements	xxii

Introduction	1

BERTUG OZARISOY AND HASIM ALTAN

PART 1
From Theory to Practice: Envisioning Utopian Urban
Design Strategies   7

1	**Analysis of the Context in Eleven Terms**	9

BERTUG OZARISOY

Introduction   9
Manifesto for the Utopian Urban Design (i): Why
    Cyprus?   11
Manifesto for the Utopian Urban Design (ii): Why
    Nicosia?   12
Manifesto for the Utopian Urban Design (iii): What Is the
    Green Line?   13
Manifesto for the Utopian Urban Design (iv): Why the United
    Nations Buffer Zone?   14
Manifesto for the Utopian Urban Design (v): Why the Ledras
    Street Checkpoint?   14
Manifesto for the Utopian Urban Design (vi): Why the Peace
    Hall?   16
Manifesto for the Utopian Urban Design (vii): Why the Event
    of Creative Possibilities?   16
Manifesto for the Utopian Urban Design (viii): What Is the
    Cypriot Identity?   17

xii *Contents*

*Manifesto for the Utopian Urban Design (ix): Why
   Cypriots?* 17
*Manifesto for the Utopian Urban Design (x): What Are the
   Issues of Cultural Identity of the City of Nicosia?* 18
*Manifesto for the Utopian Urban Design (xi): What Is the
   Representational Diaspora and the Language of the Green
   Zone?* 18
Conclusions 20
Notes 20
References 21

2   Searching a New Diaspora for the Buffer Zone   24
    BERTUG OZARISOY

    Introduction 24
    Speculation 26
    The Architecture of Transgression 27
    The Architecture of Violence 32
    The Space of Conflict 33
    Political Space: United Nations Buffer Zone 35
    Oppression and Occupation: Military Power 36
    Participatory-Led Design 37
    Hidden Power beyond Conflict: Participation 39
    Conclusions 41
    References 42

3   Political Discourse Acts as a Transnational Catalyst in the
    Decision-Making of Architectural Design Interventions   45
    BERTUG OZARISOY

    Introduction 45
    *Political Space as a Transnational Instrument of the United
       Nations Buffer Zone* 46
    *Scoping the Field and Setting Up the Counteractive
       Participant-Based Architectural Disseminations* 49
    *Setting Up the Research Design Approach for Reclaiming
       Architectural Discourse in the United Nations Buffer
       Zone* 50
    *Stages of Development in the Decision-Making of an
       Architectural Reconciliation Process* 51
    Creative Possibilities: Birds, Narratives and Artefacts 52
    Learning from the Exploratory Case Study Design and

*Its Implications on the Architectural Reconciliation
    Process 54*
Beyond Theory: Learning from the Transgression 56
A Manifesto: Multicultural Exchange and Unification 57
Conclusions 59
Notes 60
References 60

**4 Transgressive Design Strategies towards Utopian Urban
    Vision for Reclaiming Architectural Discourse**   **62**
BERTUG OZARISOY

Introduction 62
Transgression as a Way of Creating Urban Utopia 64
*The City of Nicosia as Base Case Urban Scenario
    Development 68*
*A Representational Diaspora and Language of the Green
    Zone 70*
Scoping the Field 72
*A Manifesto: Mapping Invisibility to Define a Utopian Urban
    Vision for Nicosia 73*
Mapping the Notion of Transgression and Vice Versa 75
The Key Design Principles of Creating an Urban Utopia 76
*Cultural Diasporas for Identifying Main Design Principles of
    an Urban Utopia 81*
City of Agriculture: Cultivating Green Communities 82
City of Trees: Celebrating Annual Food Festival 83
City of Birds: Echoes from the Green Zone 84
City of Watchtowers: Reinhabit Birds 85
Utopia Versus a New Green Zone 86
Conclusions 87
Notes 90
References 94

5 A Utopia   **97**
BERTUG OZARISOY

Introduction 97
Of Futures and Utopias 98
Visionary Utopian Urban Design Scenarios 100
Utopian Urban Vision of Nicosia 101
Utopia versus a New Green Zone 103

xiv   *Contents*

Symbolic Representation of a New Green Zone   105
Lifelines   108
Monumental Representation   110
Full Circle   111
Maximum Diversity   112
Intuitive Navigation   113
Cosmopolitan Nature   114
Public Spaces   116
Green Religion   118
Conclusions   121
References   124

6   **Representations of Diaspora, Cultural Identity and Difference**   127
    BERTUG OZARISOY

Introduction   127
Narrative Memories of Turkish Cypriots' Living and Their
    Domestic Space Use   128
History and Reasons for Immigration   129
Migration and Cultural Practices of Turkish Cypriots from
    Cyprus to London: Narrative Memories   129
Representational Space and Cultural Identity   132
Context of Change and Displacement   133
Cultural Practice of Turkish Cypriot Communities   134
Space Becomes a Way of Cultural Practice   136
Subject Participants' Interview Transcripts   137
The Poetics of Space   139
Hybridity as a Role of Cultural Practice   140
Critics on Cultural Practice and Space of the Turkish Cypriot
    Communities   141
Conclusions   143
Notes   145
References   147

7   **Housing and Policies in the United Kingdom**   150
    YOUNG KI KIM AND HASIM ALTAN

Introduction   150
Energy Consumption and CO_2 Emissions   151
Energy Efficiency of Housing Stock   153
Space Heating   154
Background on UK Policies   156
Scenarios for Carbon Emission Cuts from UK Housing   158

Contents xv

New Homes 160
Zero-Carbon New Homes by 2016 161
How Zero-Carbon Is Required or Encouraged 162
Code for Sustainable Homes 163
Construction of Zero-Carbon Houses 167
Fuel Poverty in the UK 168
Dwelling Characteristics and Efficiency 169
Existing Programmes and Policies 170
Government Funded Programmes 170
Conclusions 172
Notes 173
References 174

8 **Conclusions** 178

BERTUG OZARISOY AND HASIM ALTAN

Translations between Transgression and Utopia 178
Transgression and Radical Practices Are the Concept 179
Transgressions and Radical Practices versus Border 180
References 181

PART 2
**Learning from the Globe: Urban Regeneration, Brand
Identity and City Making** 183

9 **Introduction** 185

BERTUG OZARISOY AND HASIM ALTAN

*Transgression between Architectural Design and Urban
Regeneration Developments* 185

10 **Case Study 1: King's Cross Regeneration Development,
London, United Kingdom** 187

GUILLAUME DELFESC AND BERTUG OZARISOY

King's Cross: Past and Present 187
Mapping Existing Physical Conditions 189
*Design Proposals: Through Mapping, Prospective Analysis
and Drawings* 192
Greening the City 193
Urban Linkage: Reclaiming Urban Agriculture 198
Architectural Design Interventions: Courtyard Houses 200
References 203

xvi *Contents*

11 Case Study 2: Elephant & Castle Regeneration Development, London, United Kingdom   205

GUILLAUME DELFESC

Introduction 205
The Architecture of Luxury: Key Questions 207
Brand Identity versus Local Identity 209
Transgression between Luxury Brand and Architecture 210
The Birth of the Brand Street 212
An Interview with the Architect 213
The Shops 217
The Displacement between the Green Street and Walworth Road 217
Urban Regeneration in Elephant and Castle 219
Design Proposal: Through Mapping, Prospective Analysis and Drawings 221
The Elephant & Castle Shopping Centre: A Focal Point for London 221
A Manifesto – Urban Development Proposal: The New Elephant & Castle 224
Conclusions 226
Notes 229
References 229

12 Case Study 3: Berlin: The State of Power, Kreuzberg, Berlin, Germany   231

GUILLAUME DELFESC

Berlin: Past and Present 231
Existing Urban Conditions: Identification of Leftover Urban Space in Kreuzberg 233
A Manifesto: Conceptual Stages of a Mix-Use Development Project Proposal 233
References 236

13 Case Study 4: Undercliffe Social Housing, Bradford, United Kingdom   238

HASIM ALTAN AND YOUNG KI KIM

Introduction 238
Construction Detail 241
Heating System 244
Ventilation System 245

Monitoring Study 247
Indoor Environments 249
Energy Consumptions 251
Occupant Survey 253
Conclusions 255
References 256

14 Conclusions   258

BERTUG OZARISOY AND HASIM ALTAN

Introduction 258
Reviewing of Case Study Locations 259
A Future Outlook 260
Conclusion and Recommendations 261
References 261

Index   263

List of Contributors

Young Ki Kim obtained a BEng degree in the School of Architecture, University of Ulsan in South Korea (1995–2002). He holds an MSc degree (2005) in Environmental Design and Engineering from the University College London (UCL). He finished his PhD degree at the University of Sheffield with the title of thesis 'Adapting the UK Housing to Climate Change: Energy Consumption and Overheating'. He was a Research Associate, Teaching Fellow, and Computer Simulation Expert in the Building Environments Analysis Unit (BEAU) in the School of Architecture at the University of Sheffield (2007–2014). He was a Senior Executive Manager in the EAN Technology (2015–2017) in Seoul, and he achieved an LEED AP BD+C certification and was involved in several LEED certification projects in South Korea. He also achieved the BREEAM Assessor and was involved in the IKEA Korea BREEAM certification projects. His main role in the EAN Technology involved energy analysis, commissioning, sustainable building design, engineering consulting and project management. In 2017, he joined the University of Sharjah, Department of Architectural Engineering, as a visiting assistant professor, and he was involved in several design studios and graduate senior projects. In 2018, he moved to the United Arab Emirate University (UAEU) as an assistant professor, where he is currently working in the Department of Architectural Engineering at the College of Engineering.
ORCID ID: 0000-0001-5768-3816

Guillaume Delfesc is a French architect. He holds a BSc, MArch, and professional capacitation (HMONP) from the École nationale supérieure d'architecture de Versailles, France. He also holds an MA in Architecture, Cultural Identity and Globalisation from the University of Westminster, UK. Throughout his studies and professional experiences, he has been interested in the making of architecture in different contexts and regions. During his postgraduate studies at the University of Westminster he developed his master thesis project to link the existing communities with newcomers, in the context of a rapidly gentrifying area in London. There, he also explored the relationship between luxury and the built

List of Contributors xix

environment. Guillaume Delfesc has been a practising architect in France since 2014. He has work experiences in Japan, where he took part in the design of an hospital in Haiti as well as local projects. He was practising as an in-house architect for a luxury firm for a year between 2016 and 2017, where he worked on shop projects from design to completion. He now works in an architecture firm in Paris on large-scale domestic and international projects.

ORCID ID: 0000-0003-0204-3760

Preface

This book critically examines the philosophy of the term 'transgression' and how transgression shapes the utopian urban vision of narrating contemporary urban design scenarios. It explicitly illustrates a discourse of 'utopian urban vision' to extract a conclusion, and it interposes a specific lens through which to look at the future of the city. The objective of this book is to provide scholarly yet accessible graphic novel illustrations to inform narratives of urban manifestos. It aims for an 'utopian urban vision' approach to social, political and cultural relations, trends and tensions – both locally and globally. It also seeks to inspire an awakening in architectural discourse. The exploratory case study approach was adopted to reflect adaptive urban scenarios in the field of sociocultural notions to demonstrate interrelationships between architecture and urban theory. At the same time, the notion of urban regeneration is developed through a series of international case studies, some commissioned by government organisations, others speculative and polemic.

By contrast, this book argues that the philosophical undermining of transgression is the result of a phenomenon from a different perspective — its philosophical background, its social construction, experimental research process and design implications on the city. It is shown that these sociocultural norms offer a systemic vision of possible and potential manifestos, substantiated by the conceptual design of mapping architectural enrichment of this city and transcending visionary urban design proposals for rethinking the concepts in urban agency. It must be added that, unlike most radical practices and scientific research on new utopian city models, in this context, the specific function of both theory and documentation of the research would fulfil the knowledge gap of envisioning the future of local citizens. The use of select case material in the book helps to highlight the paradoxes and contradictions in architecture and enables detailed evaluation of the limits and contemporary forms of sustainable urban regeneration. This reference book proposal consists of novel graphical illustrations which provide a broad spectrum on designing utopian urban city models, hence, alleviating the issues of multiculturalism, crossings, displacement, migration and hybridisation. These norms enabled academics, students and researchers to understand urban manifestos effectively by entailing storyboards, conceptual sketches or any type of visual material for their core modules at the time of studying subject-specific undergraduate or postgraduate taught programmes in architecture and urbanism.

Dr. Bertug Ozarisoy
Famagusta, Cyprus

Prof. Dr. Hasim Altan
Kyrenia, Cyprus

Acknowledgements

Firstly, we would like to express our sincerest gratitude to the Faculty of Architecture and the Built Environment at the University of Westminster for offering a research environment for Bertug Ozarisoy and Guillaume Delfesc to pursue their postgraduate taught – Master of Arts (MA) in Architecture, Cultural Identity and Globalisation at the University of Westminster. Special thanks go to Assistant Head of School in Architecture and Cities, Mr. Samir Pandya, and Senior Lecturer Dr. Nasser Golzari for their continuous support throughout the authors' research journeys in the UK. Secondly, we would like to acknowledge and thank the following people whose help and encouragement made it possible for Bertug and Guillaume to receive the supportive and rigorous research culture during their MA research. They are Shahed Saleem and Yara Sharif. Finally, to Taylor & Francis for giving us the opportunity for publishing this reference book. We are greatly appreciative of Prof. Dr. Yonca Hurol at the Eastern Mediterranean University in Northern Cyprus for taking her valuable time to provide a book review about our book. Her thoughts could provide insight to the potential readers, particularly to the undergraduate and postgraduate taught students, to understand the invisible critical thinking approach of this book beyond its visibility in the field of architecture and urbanism.

Thanks to all.
Dr. Bertug Ozarisoy
Prof. Dr. Hasim Altan

Introduction

Bertug Ozarisoy and Hasim Altan

This reference book is neither a single perspective of the idea of creative possibilities of conditions nor a unified narrative; it is made of architectural investigations on different scales, locations, with different intensities and speeds. By extracting a selection of theoretical research and spatial experience of the context, it attempts to elaborate on several key concepts informing the overall architectural intervention scenarios and investigation of disjunction between utopia and dystopia to uptake delivery of decision-making criteria in the residential sector. The explored concepts in this research should be understood as a set of architectural fables, speculating about the seemingly impossible to articulate architectural narratives, the actual transformation of the existing contested urban conditions of limiting the use of space. It is thus also, and fundamentally so, an invitation to rethink the problem of political subjectivity not from the point of view of the notion of conflict but rather from the point of view of architectural discourse. This book could be an exemplar exploratory case study for other scholars in order to widen their knowledge on investigating more multidisciplinary case studies in the conflicted territories across the globe.

This research was conducted on the practice as a combination of architectural elements and a theoretical study on several key concepts on the case study locations in Cyprus, Nicosia – the last divided capital in Europe; United Kingdom – in the metropolitan city of London; and Germany – in the multicultural capital of Berlin. The mapping of both visible and invisible architectural elements was aimed to use spatial practice as a form of visionary urban development strategy in order to implement transgressive design strategies for policy making decisions in urban planning globally. This reference book is aimed to offer a new reading and narration of mapped reality beyond invisibility throughout the explorations of architectural fables and visionary documentation of utopian urban design scenarios. It seeks to activate the space around and between the collective memories and to create, through a renegotiation of the memories, a new topography of perceptual possibilities to unite communities.

This book illustrates emancipatory moments which project visions of a better life that question the organisation and structure of urban design

DOI: 10.4324/9781003243069-1

scenarios as we know them. The philosophical underpinning of this study could fit in the scope of investigating the architecture of transgression that is bound to a particular core module in architecture and urbanism. It also brings significant contribution to the postgraduate taught students' or early career researchers' projects in this field in order to provide effective guidance on adopting the state-of-the-art graphical illustrations into their own design projects while considering contradictions between architectural discourse and the philosophy of transgression. This book could bring significant contribution to the practitioners' professional works in architecture and urban design within the scope of exploring versatile social, political and cultural conditions.

Understanding the notion of transgression and its impact on urban development represents a crucial role in the discourse of architecture and the potential opportunities to improve the existing urban conditions or create new architectural design proposals which are considered beneficial in the decision-making process of urban redevelopment schemes. It is indispensable reading for practitioners and students in the field of architecture, architectural theory, architectural design and urban design. An inspiration to government agencies and nongovernmental organisations (NGOs) dealing with the conflicted territories. This book has great potential to contribute to professional or academic research projects in parallel with their course modules in order to guide them on understanding the significance of novel graphical illustrations' impact on their research projects.

The exemplar projects described in this book represent stages in that research programme, showing a commitment to the innovative design achieved in a commercially competitive context. The book also presents the theoretical base for a pilot scheme of urban regeneration projects in London – King's Cross and Elephant Castle – where these district-scale planning schemes have transformed the cultural identity of the city of London radically. The study looks to the future to explore correlations between architectural discourse and the notion of transgression. It could bring significant contribution to the other scholars who are working in the field of spatial practice in contested spaces in Europe and across the globe.

The overarching objective of this reference book is to help postgraduate taught students, early career researchers, academics, architects and urban planners to think critically on any STEM subject area by conserving the notion of transgression. This objective could be achieved by promoting design as the primary method for investigations into the dynamic relationship between architecture and urbanism. In this reference book, both theoretical and practice-based design projects are located in multicultural urban neighbourhoods, so it is deemed to demonstrate that culture is one of the important decision-making criteria while developing architectural fables in contested urban spaces. The study aims to explore themes such as social integration and exclusion, luxury, cultural transgression and architectural discourse. International sites were explored through a field trip to Cyprus,

Introduction 3

London and Berlin, where a range of urban regeneration projects were analysed to explore the notion of collective memory and coexistence in architecture and urbanism. Throughout the development of architectural fables, on-site observations were conducted. These extensive photographic documentation and field diaries enable the authors of this book to explore these multicultural and fragile cities by involving socio-spatial mapping exercises, as well as engagement with local citizens. Additionally, this reference book could bring significant contribution to student's design-led dissertation projects and other scholars' work. The case study projects mentioned in this reference book differ in nature but are all represented by a critical enquiry into the ways in which architecture and cities reflect, activate and circulate cultural meaning at various scales globally.

The exploratory case studies included in this reference book contain the utopian urban vision of contested spaces as a speculative architectural and urban project. It seeks to explore the radically evolved architectural transcripts and manifestos within the geopolitically shaped context of the city. It should be noted that this book is not just for the postgraduate taught students or early career researchers, as it also provides a general grounding in how to entail narrative stories into undergraduate students' design studio projects by using several methods of graphical illustrations such as rhizome mapping techniques. It provides guidance to students' design studio projects alongside the theoretical information explicitly discussed in architectural theory, transgression and urban design. At the same time, Part 2 (Learning from the Globe: Urban Regeneration, Brand Identity and City Making) of this book represents graphical illustrations relating to a pilot urban regeneration project in London and Berlin.

The notion of cultural identity has been shaped across a spectrum of languages and transcultural relations which may range from confrontation, indifference or mutual exclusion, to create an engagement depending on the social and cultural process and historical moments. The impetus for this design-led research is a curiosity about the term transgression and its application in today's globalised and fragmented world. This reference book has been informed by several complex sociocultural paradoxes into account, and through a redevelopment of exemplar contested urban conditions in order to provide effective delivery of visionary utopian urban design scenarios. This could bring significant contribution to the researchers who are working in the field of urban sociology to bring win-win situations to this extent.

In this reference book, the design superimposes a grid which is an iconic element in the history of architectural discourse throughout the fragmented urban territories. It was devised to respond to specific local conditions, particularly in the field of architecture and urbanism. This research concept began to restructure the city at an urban scale, creating new utopian urban design scenarios by using graphical illustrations in line with architectural fables and narratives. The graphical illustrations presented in this book

4 *Bertug Ozarisoy and Hasim Altan*

could fit in the scope of the transgression as a way of delivering a utopia. It must be stressed that the philosophical scope of this book would be beneficial to adapt the methodology in contested urban territories.

This book predominantly is aimed at three constituencies – undergraduate and postgraduate taught students and researchers: For those students whose environment requires them to produce architectural design proposals, manifestos or design-led studio projects – or could play an increasingly important role in the achievement of academic qualifications in the field of architecture and urbanism. This reference book could be used as an exemplar pilot project relating to the regeneration of conflicted cities with taking into account the case study locations namely, the fenced-off Varosha territory in the coastal city of Famagusta and the United Nations Buffer Zone in Nicosia, Cyprus. These case study locations will be supported by extensive photographic documentation and field survey into this reference book to inform readers about the history of research context and how utopian urban design proposals could interact within the subjectivity of architectural discourse.

In this reference book, the last divided capital of Europe, the city of Nicosia, was selected to inform a utopian urban visionary model. As a divided capital, Nicosia is 'cut' across its centre by a no-man's land, referred to as the 'buffer zone'. Rather than seeing the buffer zone as a transitional space, the proposed utopian vision informs the readers to transgress novel methodological urban design scenarios. Simultaneously, rather than a utopia based on a narrative of architectural design elements, the research aims to create a utopia based on multiple narratives, coexistence and openness. According to conceptual design scenarios developed through understanding the principles of architectural discourse and the term of transgression, this reference book could be used to guide the urban think-tankers towards understanding the translations between history and culture.

This reference book combines ways of using practice to provoke politics to reveal itself and act upon it, instigating the creative possibilities of conditions in architecture that the study seeks to explore in critical proximity with the local citizens. It also aims to transform the subject of 'Transgression and Power' to enter the third space, so to speak, into the respective idea of developing utopian urban visionary design guidelines to become part of the invisible forces that shape the built environment. Notably, this book could be an exemplary reference source for students' course modules and dissertation projects well beyond the European context. It also enables students to understand European architectural history and its interaction with the development of design-led research projects in urban design.

One of the unique features of the approach developed in this reference book is that it demonstrates novel graphical illustrations to inform the reader about visionary utopian urban design strategies. It is founded on the grounds of photographic survey, archival documentation and interviews with subject respondents to develop a novel methodological flow for the

Introduction 5

decision-making process of urban planning while taking into account the notion of transgression and its impact on architectural discourse, which is not well pronounced in architectural design education. It tackles the dilemma that understanding of transgression is complex and its interaction to devise urban design scenarios even more so. This is the reason that the research topic presented in this book could have great potential to fill the knowledge gap in architectural theory, and it enables the enrichment of graphical illustrations to the students, academics, professionals and practitioners in architecture and urban design.

As noted, the case study locations are predominantly located in Europe and the United Kingdom in order to inform the readers about different visionary urban design strategies that are taking place to interact with local communities in their everyday lives and changing the physical characteristics of these cities' under investigation. Although the study is limited to continental Europe and the United Kingdom, it could be generalised for other countries which have similar research agendas, such as investigating the significance of architectural discourse in contested spaces and designing visionary utopian urban design scenarios. The decision-making process of urban regeneration development projects, including cases studies dealing with the underlying phenomena of gentrification, is also discussed. This process can resonate with many readers from many cities around the world where these sustainable development goals are emerging.

With regards to the fulfilling the knowledge gap in the field of architectural design and theory, this study objective could fit the aims of potential readers in Europe, United Kingdom, North America, Australia and the Middle East, where students, academics, professionals and practitioners are unable to conduct on-field surveys in conflicted countries and understanding the planning process of urban regeneration projects may be hampered. Both the graphical illustrations and photographic survey presented in this reference book inform the readers on the research methodology undertaken for these projects and the conceptual design developed for visionary urban planning proposals. It must be stressed that this book presents novel graphical illustrations to inform the readers about visionary utopian urban design proposals. This is the reason that the contextual elements are investigated through the process of devising architectural buildings into the project, and the various aspects of European history are also considered as part of the development progress. This enables other scholars to read more about European architectural history without distorting their focus predominantly on the literature review and informing them by using novel graphical illustrations in architecture and urbanism.

The book consists of three major types of material: the philosophical investigation, a spectrum of design manifestos, which offers comparison domestically and globally, and in-depth context analysis of contested spaces and fragile urban territories. The combination of the three would potentially have a long-lasting shelf life. The content related to the physical context is currently the strongest. The design projects, methods and pilot case study locations demonstrated throughout the chapters may not be the timeliest material. There are rising trends of new technological and representational investigation in fictional architecture and urban design projects that students and practitioners are favouring more for the core learning in architectural and urban design studios.

Part 1

From Theory to Practice

Envisioning Utopian Urban
Design Strategies

1 Analysis of the Context in Eleven Terms

Bertug Ozarisoy

Introduction

This research project was undertaken on the Eastern Mediterranean Island of Cyprus, which is not a European Union (EU) member state. In the context of this research, the state will seek to resolve the difficulties of implementing effective revitalisation and urban planning schemes to unite Cypriots, nurture the enhancement of the cultural hybridity, and improve the physical urban conditions and the built environment, At the same time, this territory also contends with the detrimental political impact of being a *de facto*[1] state in terms of gaining international recognition to be allowed to implement EU directives for any type of industry and achieve holistic large-scale urban regeneration projects that have been recommended for the residential sectors in each EU country.

The island of Cyprus was a British colony from 1878 to 1960 (Argyriou, 2018).[2] Cyprus gained its independence from Great Britain in 1960, and the island became a republic, with Great Britain, Greece and Turkey serving as guarantor powers for their treaty with the constitutional system; this agreement was breached in 1963, however, when the Ozarks National Organisation of Cypriot Fighters (EOKA)[3] attacked Turkish Cypriot civilians (Sözen, 2004). The internal conflict was eventually subdued by the placement of United Nations troops on the island.[4] This situation continued until 1974, when the EOKA-B[5] group, with the support of the military junta[6] from mainland Greece, declared war by attacking the Greek Cypriots who opposed them, then attacking Turkish Cypriots with the intention of ethnic cleansing. Joining the island of Cyprus to mainland Greece was the aim of the ENOSIS[7] plan (Bryant, 2014).

As one of the guarantor powers, Turkey was asked to intervene to protect Turkish Cypriots and prevent the island from being overtaken by the military junta in Greece (Lacher & Kaymak, 2005). This intervention resulted in the division of the island, whereby the Turkish Cypriots were evacuated to the northern territory and the Greek Cypriots were moved to the southern territory. The island division was demarcated by the Green Line,[8] which is also known as the UN's 'buffer zone' (Bueno-Lacy & van

DOI: 10.4324/9781003243069-3

Houtum, 2019). The physical division of the island was mutually agreed upon and permanently put into place by the guarantors on 16 August 1974, but there were no plans or protocols for the organised resettlement of Greek and Turkish Cypriots (Yesilada & Anastasiou, 2004). According to the Voluntary Regrouping of Population Agreement, which was implemented on 2 August 1975, approximately 65,000 Turkish Cypriots moved to the north of the island, and an estimated 180,000 Greek Cypriots moved to the south of the island (Evcil, 2012).

In Cyprus, therefore, the disorganised resettlement of the Turkish Cypriots resulted in an initial settlement in temporary camps, then in abandoned houses in rural villages, while Greek Cypriots were evacuated to the southern territory (Tselika, 2019). These unplanned resettlements for the Greek and Turkish Cypriots led to a problem with the accommodations of these displaced populations in terms of low-quality social housing schemes in certain urban areas in the northern territory (Hoskara et al., 2009). This in turn resulted in housing shortages in five major cities and urban agglomerations in Northern Cyprus (NC): Famagusta (i.e., coastal), Nicosia (i.e., inland), Kyrenia (i.e., coastal), Trikomo (i.e., coastal and semi-mountainous) and Omorphou (i.e., mountainous).

Notably, the Eastern Mediterranean Island of Cyprus foresaw constraints brought about by its status as a *de facto* state in terms of its economy, construction industry and energy sector (Evcil & Vafaei, 2017). Due to the UN's buffer zone, the Greek and Turkish Cypriots were forced to be isolated from each other from 1974 to 2003 (Çarkoğlu & Sözen, 2004). But a significant step was undertaken by both political sides to end this isolation and initiate peace talks with the 'opening of borders' on 23 April 2003 (Sözen & Özersay, 2007). This was an important political event between these two communities, as this was the first time that these people were allowed to visit one another since 1974. The second step toward a possible resolution came about when the island was reunified with the establishment of a new constitutional system; the plan was called the 'Annan Plan' after Kofi Annan, who was the UN secretary at that time.

The aim of the Annan Plan was to put the unification of Cyprus into effect by establishing a new bi-zonal, bi-communal state, named the United Republic of Cyprus[9] (Sözen, 2005). This plan was put to a referendum vote in both entities on 24 April 2004; while 76% of the Greek Cypriots voted 'no' to the plan, 65% of the Turkish Cypriots voted 'yes' (Sözen, 2012). Following the unsatisfactory results of the referendum, the southern end of Cyprus, which lacked authority and control over the northern end of the island, retained the official title of the Republic of Cyprus (RoC) (Ersözer, 2017, p. 68); the RoC has its own, independent parliamentary system, and it became a full EU member state on 1 May 2004 (European Commission, 2004). In 1983, NC declared its own *de facto* parliamentary structure, which has no legal status in international law and is only officially recognised by Turkey (Gosh & Aker, 2006).

Analysis of the Context in Eleven Terms   11

Ongoing political factors have resulted in housing shortages and a lack of industrial regulatory bodies, in addition to a policy gap in the construction sector (Egemen & Mohamed, 2006). This created a domino effect in the residential sector, particularly in the ability of small and medium enterprises (SMEs)[10] to assume control of any vacant land to build mass-scale purpose-built housing-development estates across the island (Ünlücan, 2010). This property boom resulted in an abundance of housing stock in southern and northern Cypriot territories between 2002 and 2005 (Mehmet & Yorucu, 2008). Because no regulatory mandates were implemented during this rampant construction period, housing stock was constructed that neither adhered to the Energy Performance of Buildings Directive (EPBD) recommendations nor whose construction was regulated by the Cypriot authorities; this is the foremost reason that the current housing stock is vulnerable to changing climate conditions and prone to costly energy bills.

Manifesto for the Utopian Urban Design (i): Why Cyprus?

Cyprus has been chosen because it is the third largest island situated in the Eastern part of the Mediterranean Sea. It is positioned on the main route of travel and trade between the Middle East and Africa (Ozarisoy & Altan, 2017a). Due to its geopolitical position, Cyprus has been ruled by different civilisations going back for centuries – Lusignan, Venetians, Ottomans and British Empire. Hence every civilisation has left its own mark on the culture, ethnicity and diversity in the multidisciplinary formation of this fertile Mediterranean Island. As indicated, Cyprus has been conquered and ruled over by different civilisations for many centuries. This could result in the evolution of multicultural modality due to the fact that Cyprus is faced daily with a multitude of rapid changes and political and social turmoil on both the local and international levels. Hence, its cultural context and interaction of the many civilisations has resulted in a unique population formed by different cultural practices, which is the true narrative process of Cypriot identity.

In 1571, Cyprus became part of the Ottoman Empire. The island became ethnically mixed with a Muslim Turkish Cypriot minority and a Christian Greek Cypriot majority. In 1878, Britain took control of the island, and in 1914, Cyprus became an official British Crown Colony. From the beginning of British colonial rule, Greek Cypriots requested union (ENOSIS) with their ancestral peers in Greece. At that point, neither the British government nor Greece took any notice of these requests. In 1955, the armed struggle for independence from British colonial rule started. A large part of the Greek Cypriot community supported the campaign for the annexation of the island put forward by the National Organisation of Cypriot Fighters, a secret, armed movement under the leadership of the Greek military. As a result, Turkish Cypriots, alarmed by these threatening movements, countered that if the island were to be joined to Greece, then they should be permitted to live in a separate distinct part of Cyprus through *taksimi* (Turkish for 'partition', suggesting the partitioning of Cyprus into a Greek and Turkish state).

In the early 1970s, a second EOKA establishment engaged in subversive activities which threatened the continuing existence of Turkish Cypriots in the southern and northern parts of the island. The 'ethnic cleansing' of Turkish Cypriots and the Greeks' driven desire to claim Cyprus as a Greek nation has led to the Turkish army intervening in the summer of 1974, landing on the north side of the island and securing refuge on the north side of the island for Turkish Cypriots. Hence, this Eastern Mediterranean Island has been separated since 1974 due to the military intervention by Turkey. Today, the ongoing political 'Cyprus problem' has distinctly divided both Greek and Turkish Cypriots on the island. Due to being a de-facto state, the northern part of Cyprus has been left unrecognised by international committees and world countries. Whilst the entire island has been a European Union member since May 2004, the Turkish Cypriots have their sole right to claim for their existence and ownership, according to the European laws; therefore, this important matter is persistently pushed through the process of 'peace talks', which to date have failed.

Manifesto for the Utopian Urban Design (ii): Why Nicosia?

The present-day capital of Cyprus, Nicosia, sits in the middle of the Mesoarial plain surrounded between the Kyrenia mountain range and the Troodos Massif to the south. It is a cosmopolitan, multicultural city. The Byzantines, the Lusignans, Venetians, and the British colonial period have distinctively shaped the city (Ozarisoy & Altan, 2017b). The capital city has three accepted names: Nicosia – British, Lefkosia – Greek, Lefkoşa (Lefkosha) – Turkish. Throughout each civilisation, the city has been built on its multicultural layers which have also shown trademarks of history, culture and heritage, as shown in Figure 1.1. Additionally, the capital has been divided linguistically as well as literally by its three names. The traces of these tangible elements are the Venetian walls which surround the city and give its rich characteristics of the Cypriot identity. Hence it has remained the capital of Cyprus up to this day – where all the administration of culture, education, law and politics takes place. This capital city has diverse architecture, heritage and culture regardless of the political turmoil, conflict and physical division. It has preserved its unique architectural aesthetic and cultural identity belonging to different ancestral roots which have been ruled by many civilisations throughout centuries in this isolated and hostile Eastern Mediterranean context. Therefore, this city, the main architectural epicentre with its tangible heritage, trade and transportation of goods along the historic Silk Road, is also known as the last divided capital in Europe.

Nicosia has gained its identity of trade and agriculture going back centuries by way of the river Pedieos which runs across its epicentre. It had always been

Analysis of the Context in Eleven Terms 13

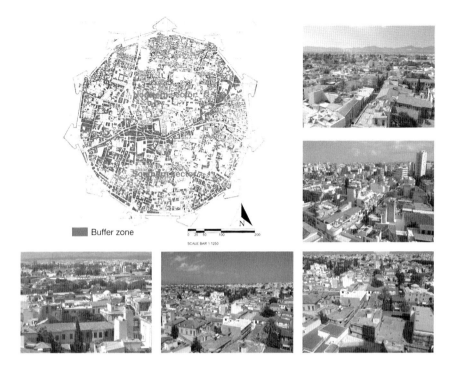

Figure 1.1 Map of the medieval old walled city of Nicosia and its urban tissue. Image credit: the author, 2022.

the first agricultural destination because of the water that flowed from this river. Beyond this rich historical character and cultural identity, Nicosia is the last divided capital in Europe today. The physical division of the capital city brings this research manifesto to focus on the current political and geopolitical situation where, through 45 years of conflict, the Turkish and Greek Cypriot populations have been forced to live separate from each other, whereas before they always lived and mixed with each other throughout the island.

Manifesto for the Utopian Urban Design (iii): What Is the Green Line?

The Green Line is the representation of the physical partition of Nicosia. Through memories of my field trip to the city, I describe that I remember thinking of myself when I last visited the kafenion (a coffee shop in Greek). It was located next to the checkpoint in the Ledras Street. It is a long walkway of transitional point between the Northern and Southern parts of the capital across the divide. I counted my footsteps to remember this unique location. It was only 52 steps to capture the scenery of mountain views.

A literal reminder of the residue of colonialism, this physical line dividing the centre of the capital is a motif that carries the weight of the entire division of the island. The Cyprus problem, the disputed nations and the centre of the divided capital(s) of Nicosia are all conflated into one image of time, space and conflicting national identities. Nicosia then may be seen as the epicentre of multicultural diversity, both a geopolitical territory and an imaginary landscape that represents the modality of Cyprus. The Green Line itself has its own unique character. There are the empty barrels and piled sandbags, the miles of wire fencing and the United Nations Buffer Zone; and checkpoints; and roads that end in the middle of nowhere, which is called the Green Line. It is not, in fact, a single but a double line. An area known as 'No-Man's Land' or the 'Dead Zone' exists between the two parallel fences monitored by the United Nations peacekeeping force.

Manifesto for the Utopian Urban Design (iv): Why the United Nations Buffer Zone?

Nicosia is divided into two separate entities (Turkish and Greek), using the traces of the river Pedieos – which does not exist anymore due to the landfill – dating back many centuries to the Lusignan and Venetians. Instead of the river, there is now a long street that has developed organically with its unique urban tissue and powerful architectural characteristic. This power takes into account the main commercial district of the city where the Cypriots and other nationalities would use this district as the main centre for shopping and entertainment outside of the walled city. During the conflict in Cyprus, the United Nations took over this part of the city, and it has since been in their control with no inhabitants living there. This has turned into a no-man's land called the 'buffer zone', as shown in Figure 1.2.

This abandoned space contains barricades, walls, wires, watchtowers and checkpoints. This forms the scene of military architecture, where the military is the main acting power. But as the architecture has been left to itself, nature has been allowed to take its course with decayed buildings invaded by shrubs and trees, leftover spaces overgrown with different types of vegetation. This self-made untouched nature reserve has provided unlimited resting and nesting space for different types of birds on their migration route. Hence this has led to the bird's multiplication without disturbance by outside factors. The natural beauty of the city is beyond this unique architecture created by all the misery of conflict.

Manifesto for the Utopian Urban Design (v): Why the Ledras Street Checkpoint?

Ledras Street checkpoint is located in the centre of the walled city and also the centre of the United Nations Buffer Zone. Beyond this strategic location, Ledras Street was called the longest street in the capital of Nicosia.

Analysis of the Context in Eleven Terms 15

Figure 1.2 Photographic documentation of border conditions across the divide. Image credit: the author, 2022.

It covers the distance between Eleftheria Square and Serai Square. It was always at the centre of the city's commercial district. This tells us that it was the centre of trade and movement throughout history. The other symbolic characteristic of this street is that it was closed for many years forbidding crossing between the two communities. There was just a temporary metal bridge people used to climb on to just watch over the two entities (Turkish and Greek). After the opening of the checkpoint, the two entities became accessible and the Ledras Street crossing checkpoint is the symbol of this because of its historical traces, rich architectural character and urban tissue. The opening of the Ledras Street checkpoint also symbolised the seeds of unification and the waning of political power in the conflict. This led to

16 *Bertug Ozarisoy*

a rapid increase in pedestrian movement and cultural conjunction between the Greek and Turkish Cypriots, resulting in easier access to both the northern and southern part of the walled city of Nicosia.

Today, the strategic location of the Ledras Street checkpoint has also provided a sense of curiosity in local citizens from both entities not just to meet and share cultural and intellectual ideas but also to see each other's living conditions and especially the 'taboo' area of the buffer zone, as everyone is curious as to what has happened to this untouched land during the last 45 years.

Manifesto for the Utopian Urban Design (vi): Why the Peace Hall?

The Peace Hall is located at the Ledras Street checkpoint and attached to the buffer zone border. This hall is run by the Nicosia Municipality and is open to people of both entities (Turkish and Greek). This easy access to the Peace Hall occurred after the Ledras Street checkpoint opened, enabling the bi-communal activities. The space represents the idea of place and unification between the physically divided Cypriot nationals.

The main aim of the Peace Hall was to create an interactive event place for the city located in the buffer zone to bring back the traces of feeling to the old historical city and Cypriot identity. Hence, this Peace Hall is a hybrid space allocated for local citizens where one feels the real Cypriot culture. Beyond this diaspora, the Peace Hall is used as an observation point for all people passing through the checkpoints. This is the best place to observe the changes in the Cypriot culture or the effect of forced separation of their views and opinions after the declaration of the Green Line.

Manifesto for the Utopian Urban Design (vii): Why the Event of Creative Possibilities?

The event of 'Creative Possibilities' is a participant-based research experience aiming to inform the Cypriots of a new utopian urban vision of Nicosia. The event is named 'Creative Possibilities' because we want to find a new name for the United Nations Buffer Zone. This is also to add that our vision is 'beyond division' because it sets out to explore invisibility through visibility of only one Cypriot identity. We intend to keep the traces and the natural architecture and habitat, as it is the reason I named the event 'Birds, Narratives and Artefacts'. We want to return to nature and reveal the past history of the city without destroying the existing urban condition and its architectural heritage.

In this event, I conceptualised 'Collective Memories and Narratives' as a tool to get people to talk about their past experiences in the city as they remembered it before and after the division of the island. I included the story of the artefacts because virtual objects help us to understand the Cypriot culture and practice as it was many years ago. The workshop 'Creative Map of Nicosia' helped the people to pinpoint themselves on a location on the map and to recollect their memories. Additionally, the workshop of the 'Future & Past, Matrix of Nicosia' was to support the idea of the utopian urban vision of the city. The workshop and exhibition were to create the 'Event City Model' to encourage people to participate in the design process and write and draw their own ideas of what they expect from the buffer zone in the future.

Manifesto for the Utopian Urban Design (viii): What Is the Cypriot Identity?

The island of Cyprus has been shaped by a complex multicultural history, division and by a geographical position that has caused perpetual ambiguity over the geopolitical borders of Europe, Asia and the Middle East. Any discussion of architecture, art, history and culture in this zone of justifying encounters between heterogeneous cultures and populations, is intriguing. The 'Cypriot Identity' has been shaped across a spectrum of languages and transcultural relations which may range from confrontation, indifference or mutual exclusion to creative engagement depending on the social and cultural process and historical moments.

Time compresses into a space, and the spatialisation of the temporal on island territory brings dissimilarities next to each other but also a mode of non-comprehension or charged cultural loss in the way of practice that opens for revision what may have been denied or apparently obsolete. A layered imaginative geography, in other words, governs the cultural differences related to cultural contests and national or ethnic divisions. The cultural practice of Cypriots within other communities may serve to replenish the layered intertextual resources of a culture such as de-territorialisation of one terrain to map another.

Manifesto for the Utopian Urban Design (ix): Why Cypriots?

Cypriots have been chosen because every person on the island of Cyprus whose ancestors were born and brought up in this community are known as Cypriots. The Cypriots are people who have evolved out of the mixture of many civilisations and who have ruled this island going back many centuries. Every civilisation left its own mark on cultural practice, identity and architecture. The genetics and the cultural practices are similar except for religion, ethnic and language differences.

Although going back in time in history there was an interchange in these differences for certain reasons. The differences between the two ethnic groups (Turkish and Greek Cypriots) have become more distinct since the division, as they have progressed in time with no interaction with each other. When the borders opened in 2003, they mixed and worked, especially the

18 *Bertug Ozarisoy*

young, who had contact with each other for the first time realising their similarities; but except for a few marriages, there was not much hybridisation. It is interesting to note that, beyond this multiversity and conflict between the two ethnic groups, there has been some loss in their goodwill and trust of each other. This research has been chosen to put together an idea which will enable the Cypriot community to live and work in harmony which has been denied to them for a long time through no fault of their own.

Manifesto for the Utopian Urban Design (x): What Are the Issues of Cultural Identity of the City of Nicosia?

The identity of Nicosia originates from the Venetian times because they brought their own architectural and cultural practices to Nicosia, and they had their political ruling administrative base there, hence it was made the capital of the island. To this extent, the Venetians used religion as the power to build churches and monasteries and engrave this religious power on the people they ruled in Cyprus. This research aims to look for a new Cypriot identity. As Nicosia is a source of multi-diverse cultural identity, it develops in an organic form and allows us to see traces from all cultures in a peaceful environment until the division and creation of the United Nations Buffer Zone. Today the buffer zone (no-man's land) adds another natural diversity to the city.

After the Venetians, the Ottomans took over the rule of the island, which caused the biggest impact to the changes in the Cypriot people by having two different religious and cultural practices (Greek Orthodox and Sunni Muslims) coming into conflict with each other. The Ottomans also had their political administration in Nicosia, and they converted the churches into mosques. This politically shaped the cultural practices and religion among the Cypriots because they were ruled by different civilisations for many years. The Cypriots of Nicosia became more similar and less diverse when the British Empire took over the island, ruling by political and military power. It should be noted that the British undertook massive redevelopment of Nicosia, which changed the urban fabric of the city by intervening with the Venetian and Ottoman architectures and eventually changing the cultural practices and identity of Nicosia. As noted earlier, this capital city was divided. Both entities (Turkish and Greek) were left isolated from each other, they carried on with their isolated lives until the Ledras Street crossing checkpoint opened. After it was opened, the cultural interchange started.

Manifesto for the Utopian Urban Design (xi): What Is the Representational Diaspora and the Language of the Green Zone?

The United Nations Buffer Zone represents a space which is under military rule, an authorised separation both physically and politically of the two entities

Analysis of the Context in Eleven Terms 19

(Turkish and Greek Cypriots), a space that is filled with military watchtowers and is out of bounds for the Cypriot people. This military power has taken over the architectural identity of the city by replacing it with watchtowers inside and outside the walls and on top of abandoned buildings – at the same time adding its own fabrications of walls with holes in front of these buildings, barrels and barbed wire outside the buildings, as shown in Figure 1.3. In

Figure 1.3 Contradictions between border conditions and nature. Image credit: the author, 2022.

the leftover space, the United Nations added their own watchtowers to enable them to observe the buffer zone twenty-four hours a day. This has led to the measurable impact of dramatic change in the architectural and cultural image of the city; hence, the Cypriot identity has been almost abolished in this space.

This physical change caused by the intervention of military power, has left voids and abandoned buildings just next to the Green Line, providing an opportunity for the creation of informal settlement areas along the Green Line by different ethnic migrant communities. This shows that, despite the isolation of the Cypriots, other cultures have been able to migrate and take over this abandoned area and give rise to different types of cultural activities, hence, replacing the original Cypriot culture of 45 years and changing the diaspora of the buffer zone.

Conclusions

The main reason for creating a new utopian vision and identity in this research is inspired by the term 'The Architecture of Transgression' because it is against any kind of radical practice which leads to changing the present situation of the space. According to architects, urban planners and NGOs, the best way of bringing together two ethnic groups is by re-reconstruction, revitalisation and restoration of the existing urban fabric by preserving the old cultural heritage values, bringing peace and harmony to the Cypriots. On the other hand, the theory of 'The Architecture of Transgression' looks at the other side of the image by taking into account the multidisciplinary role of changes in ethnic cultures and practices since the emergence of conflict. At the same time 'transgression' follows the traces of cultural practices from existing urban conditions and adapting it into its new no-man's land character.

The main reason for creating a new urban utopian vision and identity through 'The Architecture of Transgression' is because this research seeks to accommodate the changes in cultural practice and identity which has occurred in the last 45 years of living in segregation amongst the Cypriots. Furthermore, this utopia reveals the history, reclaiming the Green city as it was, to represent my own urban reconciliation vision beyond the division.

Notes

1 In law and government, '*de facto*' describes the constitutions that exist in reality, even though they are not officially recognised by laws. Northern Cyprus (NC) is a parliamentary system, which is the result of a unilateral declaration of replication by Cyprus. Notably, the EU security council condemned the declaration and called on EU member states to respect the independence, sovereignty and territorial integrity of the RoC.
2 Under the Cyprus Convention, Great Britain assumed administration of the island, which formally remained part of the Ottoman Empire until 1914. From this date until the independence of Cyprus in 1960, Cyprus was annexed by Great Britain as a consequence of war with Turkey.

Analysis of the Context in Eleven Terms 21

3 EOKA was a Greek nationalist guerrilla organisation, which was formed in Cyprus with the support of Greece. Their goals were the removal of Britain from Cyprus, elimination of Turkish Cypriots, and unification of Cyprus with Greece.
4 As a result of this outbreak of intercommunal fighting, the United Nations Peacekeeping Force in Cyprus (UNFICYP) was sent to the island for peacekeeping purposes.
5 EOKA-B was a Greek-Cypriot paramilitary organisation aimed at the annexation of Cyprus with Greece.
6 A 'junta' is a military or political group that rules a country after taking it over by force. As a consequence of this political event in Cyprus, Turkish Cypriots announced the formation of the Provisional Cyprus Turkish Administration in 1967. This sovereignty ended in 1983 when NC declared its own *de facto* parliamentary system. Today, the parliamentary system that was established in 1967 is recognised by EU security council; this law provides eligibility criteria for Turkish Cypriots who wish to have EU citizenship.
7 ENOSIS was the political union of Cyprus and Greece; many Greeks and Greek Cypriots were in favour of annexing Cyprus to mainland Greece and excluding Turkish Cypriots.
8 As a result of the outbreak of intercommunal fighting, the Green Line that divided communities in Nicosia was established. Currently, this physical line still divides the northern and southern territories in the RoC.
9 The United Cyprus Republic (UCR), which is what the new proposed state of Cyprus will be called, is a set of institutions that were inspired by convocational models drawn from EU member states. Currently, unification negotiations continue in an effort to determine which constitutional arrangements would allow the two communities to live together in amity when the physical division of the island is ended.
10 SMEs in NC are predominantly regulated by family- or privately owned construction companies. The 1998 withdrawal of social-housing schemes led to increased demand for construction projects built by the SMEs.

References

Argyriou, S. (2018). The imperialistic foundations of British colonial rule in Cyprus. *Cyprus Review*, 30(1), 297–316.

Bryant, R. (2014). History's remainders: On time and objects after the conflict in Cyprus. *American Ethnologist*, 41(4), 681–697. https://doi.org/10.1111/amet.12105

Bueno-Lacy, R., & van Houtum, H. (2019). The glocal green line: The imperial Cartopolitical puppeteering of Cyprus. *Geopolitics*, 24(3), 586–624. https://doi.org/10.1080/14650045.2018.1508014

Çarkoğlu, A., & Sözen, A. (2004). The Turkish Cypriot general elections of December 2003: Setting the stage for resolving the Cyprus conflict? *South European Society and Politics*, 9(3), 122–136. https://doi.org/10.1080/1360874042000271898

Egemen, M., & Mohamed, A. N. (2006). Clients' needs, wants and expectations from contractors and approach to the concept of repetitive works in the Northern Cyprus construction market. *Building and Environment*, 41(5), 602–614. https://doi.org/10.1016/j.buildenv.2005.02.021

Ersozer, F. (2017). The limits of Europeanisation and liberal peace in Cyprus: A critical appraisal of the European Union's Green Line regulation [PhD Thesis].

The Faculty of Humanities, School of Social Sciences, Politics, University of Manchester, United Kingdom. [Online]. Retrieved from https://www.research.manchester.ac.uk/portal/en/theses/the-limits-of-europeanisation-and-liberal-peace-in-cyprus-a-critical-appraisal-of-the-european-unions-green-line-regulation(57dba13d-095f-462b-9a8e-aa92de02517b).html [Accessed: February 2021].

European Commission. (2004a). Proposal for a Council Regulation on special conditions for trade with those areas of the Republic of Cyprus in which the government of the Republic of Cyprus does not exercise effective control, Brussels, 7.7.2004 COM(2004) 466 final, 2004/0148 (ACC). [Online}. Retrieved from https://eur-lex.europa.eu/legal-content/EN/TXT/PDF/?uri=CELEX:52004PC0466&from=EN [Accessed: February 2021].

Evcil, A. (2012). An estimation of the residential space heating energy requirement in Cyprus using the regional average specific heat loss coefficient. *Energy and Buildings*, *55*, 164–173. https://doi.org/10.1016/j.enbuild.2012.08.014

Evcil, A., & Vafaei, L. E. (2017). A comparative survey of the energy performances of dwellings across Cyprus. *Energy and Buildings*, *148*, 15–22. https://doi.org/10.1016/j.enbuild.2017.05.008

Ghosh, B. N., & Aker, S. L. (2006). Future of North Cyprus: An economic-strategic appraisal. *Futures*, *38*(9), 1089–1102. https://doi.org/10.1016/j.futures.2006.02.013

Hoskara, Ş. Ö., Tevfikler, B. Ç., & Ongul, Z. (2009). Legal frameworks and housing environments in North Cyprus. *Middle East Technical University Journal of the Faculty of Architecture*, *26*(1), 81–100.

Lacher, H., & Kaymak, E. (2005). Transforming identities: Beyond the politics of non-settlement in North Cyprus. *Mediterranean Politics*, *10*(2), 147–166. https://doi.org/10.1080/13629390500124341

Mehmet, O., & Yorucu, V. (2008). Explosive construction in a micro-state: Environmental limit and the Bon curve: Evidence from North Cyprus. *Construction Management and Economics*, *26*(1), 79–88. https://doi.org/10.1080/01446190701708272

Ozarisoy, B., & Altan, H. (2017a). Adoption of energy design strategies for retrofitting mass housing estates in Northern Cyprus. *Sustainability (Switzerland)*, *9*(8), 1477. https://doi.org/10.3390/su9081477

Ozarisoy, B., & Altan, H. (2017b). Energy performance development of non-regulated retrofit mass housing estates in Northern Cyprus. *Design Journal*, *20*(Suppl. 1), S1765–S1781. https://doi.org/10.1080/14606925.2017.1352697

Sözen, A. (2004). 5 A model of power-sharing in Cyprus: From the 1959 London-Zurich agreements to the Annan Plan. *Turkish Studies*, *5*(1), 61–77. https://doi.org/10.1080/14683849.2004.9687242

Sözen, A. (2005). The role of the European Union as a third party in resolution of external conflicts: The case of the Cyprus problem. *SSRN Electronic Journal*. https://doi.org/10.2139/ssrn.314822

Sözen, A. (2012). Heading towards the defining moment in Cyprus: Public opinion vs realities on the ground. *Insight Turkey*, *14*(1), 109–129.

Sözen, A., & Özersay, K. (2007). The Annan Plan: State succession or continuity. *Middle Eastern Studies*, *43*(1), 125–141. https://doi.org/10.1080/00263200601079773

Tselika, E. E. (2019). State housing, social labelling and refugee identities in Cyprus. *Cyprus Review*, *31*(1), 239–263.

Ünlücan, D. (2010). Characteristics of SMEs in North Cyprus: A small island. *Problems and Perspectives in Management*, *8*(3), 139–147.

Yesilada, B., & Anastasiou, H. (2004). Analysis of the bargaining space in the Cyprus negotiations: Prospect for peace in 2004? *Analysis*, 45–47.

2 Searching a New Diaspora for the Buffer Zone

Bertug Ozarisoy

Introduction

Throughout the existence of humankind, the general shape of world events has indeed changed. The dialectical, dialogical nature of politics and culture (West versus East, capitalist versus socialist) has given way to a chronological tendency called 'globalisation', which aims to establish a representative social and economic worldwide ideology. In addition, local issues are being absorbed by global issues, as is seen in the current pre-eminence of foreign policy issues in Cyprus over contested urban conditions, presented as a conflict inextricably binding local and global foreign affairs together. Sassen (2004) mentions that today's cities are characterised by a climate of crisis, the urban community is of a divided and unjust nature, its geography unpredictable in every sense, as shown in Figure 2.1.

These shifts and changes have had serious consequences for the way that we think about architecture: what it is, what it can and is supposed to do. The current political turmoil and global energy crisis impact how architects think about their work, and what they think is important to discuss (Ozarisoy & Altan, 2022). This is only natural, considering that architecture is, or inspires to be, a social practice and is attached to the society's convulsions and more orderly economic, political, cultural and intellectual transformations (Ozarisoy & Altan, 2021). This could bring us to question 'What does the future hold for the United Nations Buffer Zone?' At the very early stages of research capabilities, and well beyond the critical thinking of previous state-of-the-art studies, this question remains central in the pursuit of competitive insights by politicians, professionals and local citizens (Littlefield, 2013). The future of a complex organism such as a city, with countless participants involved in its continuous creation and the omnipresent possibility of unification ideology suddenly surpassing, represents an even greater challenge. Hence, the event of 'Creative Possibilities' builds upon a balanced framework of priorities to develop evidence-based design scenarios by conducting semi-structured interviews with local citizens at the Peace Hall, Ledras Street, Nicosia.

DOI: 10.4324/9781003243069-4

Figure 2.1 Graffiti on the wall, the Green Line, Nicosia. Image credit: the author, 2022.

Firstly, putting the possible condition of the future urban vision of the United Nations Buffer Zone under the notion of 'transgression' poses the key question: How might 'individuals' and 'groups' behave, desire and find motivation in the next decade?

Within this qualitative study, this is represented by means of the sociocultural practices which aid the construction of conceptual nature organised precisely in these two distinct categories: individuals and groups.

Secondly, the possible development of the city is schematically identified at a strategic level by operating a further subdivision within two distinct development scenarios as follows:

a) A first set of two parameters, identifying a conceptual vision of 'time' in terms of either acceleration into a transactional, globalised future versus a return to the historical roots of its past.
b) A second set of two parameters, identifying a longer-term focus on 'urban vision' or 'space', with opposite options pertaining to creating a conflicted space.

These two sets of binary parameters are only the first example of several operational references, tools and structures that were used in the event and

26 Bertug Ozarisoy

that will populate this for 'Unification of the United Nations Buffer Zone' in order to ensure comparability, cross-referential validity and provide a strong balance to the overall study. It must be added that, unlike most radical practices and scientific research on new utopian cities, in this context, the specific function of both theory and documentation of the research is not in themselves to set-fulfil the task of envisioning the future.

These offer a systematic vision of possible and potential manifestos, substantiated by the conceptual design of the United Nations Buffer Zone, which remains the fundamental tool for the study, maintaining its compactness and coherence across primary research, desk optimisation and design co-creation. It should be noted that participant-based research and critical thinking has the unique ability to stimulate synthesis and synergy. These above reflections seem essential in the context of a certainty expressed by the 'Creative Possibilities' participants at the Peace Hall.

In this complex and contradictory context, the notion of culture will certainly be an important element within a mix specifically designed to attract international and local knowledge participants, those uniquely capable of generating valuable intellectual assists as new citizens while managing the city for all, but at the notion of a sociocultural paradox.

Speculation

Before discussing the theoretical framework of the research and reporting on the event of 'Creative Possibilities', an introduction is needed to scope the field of this study, by capturing a number of key indications about how critical design, architecture and creative ideas are likely to evolve in the future, through political manifestos and in the awakening of current policies and programs. As noted earlier, critical design is the primary reference adopted throughout the exhibition and workshop at the level of practices and creative direction. It seems necessary to explore and envision how design itself might evolve in the future towards different constitutional models, towards an increasingly diverse and differentiating role in addressing participants' challenges and towards its very own future scenarios, as shown in Figure 2.2.

No field of inquiry is more exposed to intellectual doubt than the study of the future. Because of its nature – no future objects exist for scientific repeatable experimentation – the future is fluid and invasive in the eye of the social researcher. The field of the future of the United Nations Buffer Zone could be accepted as objects of enquiry is no exception. However, in contrast to lifestyle or consumer trend studies, they do offer the advantage that architecture and design processes naturally structure the critical vision of the city (Sheil, 2005). The moment of conception of participants' ideas and the completion of the related radical practices were reflected to identify urban manifestos, such as revitalisation of the historic urban quarters. In essence, an event is a natural timing for critical architectural visions to

Figure 2.2 Transgression versus contested urban conditions. Image credit: the author, 2022.

materialise ideas and concepts into manifestations, fictionally built places. Such timing works to the advantage of future scenarios because it offers a relatively established and technically necessary cycle of observation, investigation and analysis.

Additionally, the role of design intervention in the city is the object of close examination and deep analysis in countless academic and professional references; therefore, desk research in this field can offer a rich, textured image of the working mechanisms that regulate relationships across the field, taking into consideration the viewpoints of different participants recruited for the development of evidence-based urban design scenarios (Dovey, 2013). Available historical data range from studies of the conflict between two entities to qualitative action research for change among communities through direct, co-creative participation of citizens. From this wealth of consolidated information, by cross-referencing participant opinions based on research questions, it is possible to form a preliminary critical opinion regarding the terms of 'The Architecture of Transgression', 'The Architecture of Violence' and 'The State of Conflict'. These statements are the ideal platforms from which to elaborate insights to the future.

The Architecture of Transgression

Transgression would be the means to set a new kind of architectural ghetto for Tschumi and the key to develop a new state of consciousness for Bataille. Foucault in an article in homage to Bataille after his death would address the possibilities of transgression this way:

> Transgression prescribes not only the sole manner of discovering the sacred in its unmediated substance, but also a way of recomposing its empty form, its absence, through which [it] becomes all the more scintillating.
>
> (Tschumi, 1996)

> Transgression is a door to an unmediated and profound contact with reality; a kind of experience which hadn't a space of its own within traditional systems of representation and meaning.
>
> (Tschumi, 1996)

> Transgression is an action which involves the limit, that narrow zone of a line where it displays the flash of its passage, but perhaps also its entire trajectory, even its origin; it is likely that transgression has its entire space in the line it crosses.
>
> (Tschumi, 1976)

In his chapter entitled 'De-, Dis-, Ex-', Bernard Tschumi acknowledges a parallelism in architecture, arguing that the cities are the places of dispersion and disjunction of many often-invisible systems. He makes reference to Foucault in relation to what Tschumi calls the 'essential disjunction' that exists in the process of architectural production. Tschumi's continuing strategy has been to turn these dispersions and complexities into advantage. He argues that the architect's ability to see the underlying dispersions as new regularities of an urban context can contribute towards finding a new creative solution for a particular problem in urban design (Tschumi, (1996).

I was inspired by the ideas of Tschumi, where he advises how problems and disadvantages caused by architects to the community can be transformed into an advantage by an architect. Drawing from the ideology of Tschumi, I went on to form my own idea of transforming the present chaotic urban planning and architecture of Nicosia city into my visionary utopian urban 'Exchange'.

Transgression happens on the infinitely narrow space defined by the line that separates two worlds. The division line, though, must be traversable in order to be transgressed. From violence to conflict, regardless of the power, the border between them must be penetrable. If it were uncrossable, the 'unification' as such would not exist, as shown in Figure 2.3.

Transgression comes out of the possibility of crossing from one side to another, merging one substance with the other of two opposite states (Mosley & Sara, 2013, 5). The terminology of conflict has to exist through urban interventions. It cannot be merely a trace or a memory if it must produce the fragmentation of urban layers that we will call 'Unification'. It is in the same act of crossing, out of the pressure produced by the confluence of two realities, where transgression happens. As Foucault puts it:

Searching a New Diaspora for the Buffer Zone 29

Figure 2.3 Transgression versus cultural diaspora. Image credit: the author, 2022.

Transgression does not seek to oppose one thing to another, nor does it achieve its purpose through mockery or by upsetting the solidity of foundations. The philosophical underpinning of the transgression does not transform the other side of the mirror, beyond an invisible and uncrossable line, into a glittering expanse. Transgression contains nothing negative, but affirms limited being, affirms the limitlessness into which it leaps as it opens this zone to existence for the first time. But correspondingly this affirmation contains nothing positive: no content can bind it, since, by definition, no limit can possibly restrict it. Perhaps it is simply an affirmation of division; but only insofar as division is not understood to mean a cutting gesture, or the establishment of a separation or the measuring of a distance, only retaining that in which may designate the existence of difference.

(Foucault, 1976)

In the contested spaces, the definition of division is the conflicted speculation to justify the terminology of transgression. Division has not to be understood as an equivalent of contradiction. Transgression is built out of the absence of two worlds. First, unification is the experiential side of transgression, which is not sustained over contradiction. Second, contradiction would be the opposition of two entities that never converge, that preserve their relative positions in an eternal unresolved fight. In fact, contradiction is at the base of the pathway to the language of unification, precisely the form of thought transgression is challenging. Transgression offers us a new space, a new reality, which emerges from the manipulation of the conflict between the two opposites.

Foucault (1991) mentions that 'the role of the architect is restricted to large-scale movements in cities, public spaces and institutions rather than the private space of individuals'. He also critically analyses what about the architects who choose to be transgressive? Drawing from Foucault's arguments, the position of an architecture as transgressive is undoubtedly complex, multi-layered and, at times, a complete contradiction to draw archipelago in architecture and urbanism (see Figure 2.4).

Architecture is deemed to provoke utopian ideas (Doron, 2000, 2). Notably, this idea had become to describe the novel forms in architectural theory. It considers the definition of third-space which has been correlated with the space and form concurrently. Foucault also questions how to redefine the architecture in some abstract way? All this critical thinking on the re-conceptualisation of architecture is bringing together only the idea of 'The Architecture of Transgression'. To this extent, it is necessary to vividly define a desired space of place making in contested urban spaces (Denison & Ren, 2013, 38–43). This could result in making the task more difficult hence the desired space or set of spaces of a field can be anything but reductive because it must embody spaces in the complex variants of continuous transformation.

Foucault mentions the philosophy of 'Space, Power and Knowledge' to adapt this philosophy to architecture in a pragmatic, slightly disappointing version in these words:

> Whether through literal or phenomenal transgression, architecture is seen here as the momentary and sacrilegious convergence of real space and ideal space. Limits remain, for transgression does not mean the methodical destruction of any code or rule that concerns space or architecture. On the contrary, it introduces new articulations between inside and outside of the third space, between concept and experience. Very simply it means overcoming unacceptable prevalence.

On the other hand, Tschumi (1976) describes the term 'transgression' as an instrument which is capable of making two distinct theoretical experiences in architecture to offer a new design resolution for the development of the greatest architecture. It is a vision of architecture as an autonomous entity. Therefore, this ideology has not been mentioned by Foucault.

Searching a New Diaspora for the Buffer Zone 31

Figure 2.4 Architectural archipelago throughout the buffer zone, Nicosia. Image credit: the author, 2022.

32   *Bertug Ozarisoy*

According to Tschumi (1976), the principles of developing the utopia are not capable of collecting memories of citizens. In fact, he felt the ideology of exploring transitions between the real space and the ideal space in other worlds. For example, the critical thinking of the user's experience and the intellectual experience of architecture provide different perceptions on understanding the term of transgression. This could be offered to rethink the social dimension of architecture from a non-expert perspective.

With regards to Tschumi's ideology, the abstract term of transgression addresses a world that, in a sense, is a prelude to the present one, a world in transition from the dialectical to the monological. The dialectical world is a conflictual one, composed of different forces contending – not for exploring contested urban conditions. In the dialectical relationship, each side needs its opposite; that is, the perquisite for choosing the architecture of transgression as a communication tool. The aim of this study is not to destroy the opposition but to find parity within the co-existence of the archipelago in architecture and urbanism. The emerging situation of current political turmoil and global energy crisis has led to changes in the planning schemes of the cities. The aim is to propose the opposite which could affect the translations between co-existence and architectural diaspora.

In the new world's geopolitical structure, conflict is still an existing notion, but it constitutes an issue of eradication (Hejduk, 2007, 393–404). The aim is to smooth the way for a single point of view, a single way of thinking and living in contested territories such as the capital city of Nicosia. The term of conflict is seen as an almost autonomous necessity, not a matter of primary choice of each notion in the contested cities (Terkourafi, 2008, 60–96). Hence it can be brutal and arbitrary by its co-existence in the decision-making process. The methodology and its rationale of the study could contribute to the development of visionary urban design scenarios. To this extent, the term of transgression is the superscript of the project in order to explore the prophetic new architectural language by considering a global tendency. On the contrary, the terms of violence and conflict in this research still look for the dialectic, for the possibility of creative dialogue between opposing forces and most especially between destruction and construction as equally vital elements of co-existence.

The Architecture of Violence

Architecture is an object of power. It operates in the development of aesthetic beauty and spatial configuration of our living spaces on many technical levels. In Nicosia, the way of living has been transformed from the construction of the barricades through the Green Line and United Nations Buffer Zone to the front lines of urban nomads. This could result in the development of the psychological moulding of modernist space conformity. Tschumi (1976) describes that the very architectural image of placemaking is a documentation of power and expressionism. Designing a place is the utmost challenging learning process for the architects. It requires documenting the narratives and collective memories of inhabitants by using the traditional rhizome mapping techniques. This could lead to reclaiming nature for designing utopian urban visionary scenarios. Miessen (2007) articulates the integrity of power through his experimental interventions in the contested territories. He describes that the term of architecture of transgression articulates the spatial experience of users' living space better than the architectural parallelism, such as adopting the 'third space' or co-existence in architecture. At the end, he describes the significance of power in architecture as political consensus to collect narratives and collective memories for the utopia.

Miessen (2007) describes that architecture is the materiality through political explorations. The power of architecture is not limited with physical division nor an ethnic segregation. Therefore, it provides imaginary design scenarios that could contribute to the theoretical underpinning of the term of transgression. To this extent, the theory has proven that there is a strong correlation between the power of state and architectural transgression. This important manner is also justified by Tschumi in 1976. He explains that architecture is itself the power of state. He also describes that many socioeconomic and political legal or nonlegal forces are contested and spatialised, concentrated and formatted for a larger geopolitical terrain.

Tschumi (1976) indicates that architecture is violent. On the contrary, there are a number of contexts for observing these complex urban conditions while politicians defined that embodying politics could have only brought constitutional power to claim the politics in architecture by exploring social exclusion, community segregation and physical division of entities. Also according to Tschumi (1976), many various forms of knowledge can only be reshaped by its construction. It can also be a form of obliterating knowledge and people, such as in the case of violence.

From my point of view, architecture is also a technology depending on how it is used. I am not agonising over architecture in principle, but I only want to stress that many times it is hardly innocent in its philosophical nature. I am also a strong believer that the boundaries and powers of architecture could be extended well beyond those physical spaces which have been designed and built by architects. In summary, manifestos are embodied by spaces and cultural practices of local citizens. This could result in ending the restrictions and being a 'de-facto' state in contested urban spaces. All these explorations would be seemingly inconsequential archipelagos, conflicted spaces and default containers of power.

The Space of Conflict

Ford (2005) observes that spaces of conflict are more or less legal territories of violence. The question of the legitimacy of people's forced presence in contested spaces is not so relevant in the context. What is more interesting

34 *Bertug Ozarisoy*

about the problem is that political discourse constitutes societies that can be pronounced difficult in the architectural apparatuses, which could shape the development of utopian urban visionary scenarios. On the contrary, spaces of conflict have been created in a peculiar revanchist way of thinking. It is then important for the society that it hosts territories of violence where it represents institutional power, and they represent the cultural paradox in any transformative way as viable. It should be noted that their speculations are therefore intentionally and considerably aggressive to the context. This state of conflict is comparable to the one of the statements is that 'conflict exists because the taboo and violence in daily life represents violence to areas of existing confined space and time and that follow their own rules' (Bataille, 1997, 20–23).

The term of spaces of conflict is based on, as they exist in reaction to potential threats for the society. The philosophical underpinning contributes to the materiality of the state of conflict since the violence states that transgressors can be forced to move to a space of conflict. However, spaces of precaution temporarily apply the exact same schemes as spaces of conflict on people who did not transgress the conflict. Camus (1998) depicts in his novel *The Plague*, 'the city itself becomes a conflict for which the exterior becomes an abstraction'. One important architectural archipelago seems to stand in an ambiguous way between spaces of conflict and spaces of violence. On the contrary, Agamben (2000, 123–124) mentions that the border condition (Green Line) is the expressionist example of the state of the conflict's embodiment.

According to Agamben (2000), the transgression is required about the paradoxical status of the conflict in its quality as an extra-terrestrial space. It is a part of a territory which stands outside the normal rule of law but which is not, therefore, an external space. In his philosophical explorations, Agamben (2000) explores that the space of conflict includes partial involvement of virtual reality in the development stages of utopian urban visionary scenarios. Additionally, the state of conflict is captured in the order of the border and urban explorations. The right to declare a state of conflict is the basis of sovereign authority, and a border is the physical appearance of a division line. It also represents the state of conflict in its permanent form (Faustino, 2013).

The state of conflict is being embodied by two types of architecture. First, it is devoted to the purpose of violence over the transcultural border conditions which represents the state of expressionism. Second, it consists of the revolutionary physical change of the built environment. This is a potential establishment of a precautionary emergency state. It transforms domestic ways of living into detention and control. It should be noted that the state of conflict is supposed to represent a temporary political regime in an affluent society. However, it is noticeable that every state of conflict never completely disappears after having been established within a constitutional agreement. Nowadays, the society reflects the resemblance

Searching a New Diaspora for the Buffer Zone

of exceptional circumstances such as war and violence which have been unresolved in the past.

Political Space: United Nations Buffer Zone

Miessen (2008) identifies that contextual practice is a tool to explore contested urban conditions. This could be the philosophical definition of architecture by exploring transgression and politics. Architecture and politics need not only construct and present a context, but the transgression acknowledges itself as actively producing or fabricating the environment (Roberts-Hughes, 2017, 157–168). Understanding the revolutionary development of context and improving the transcultural explorations could result in city-making. This transformation of the understanding of context, and a set of conditions to a political production, could describe the invisibilities beyond the visibility. The description of transgression is not simply formal or architectural interventions, but it develops urban trajectories; therefore, these sets of architectural fables could imply interventions between visible and invisible elements.

Perfecting the politics of uncertainty, separation, seclusion and visual control, the no-man's land, checkpoints, walls, barricades and other security measures are also the last gesture in the development process of urban enclaves. Additionally, the physical and virtual extension of borders are the most recent global conflict. The architecture of the United Nations Buffer Zone occupation could be seen as an accelerator and an acceleration of other global political processes.

Foucault said, in his famous interview with Paul Rabinow, 'the forces of global political processes remain unpredictable in architecture' (Foucault, 1976, 45–47). One of the main reasons is that the transgression only articulates the active relationship between architecture and power, but it opens the possibility for including social exclusion, segregation and physical division. Foucault (1976) explores the importance of 'suprematism' to explore current conditions between architectural dissidence and oppression. In his transactions, Foucault (1976) indicates that liberalism and democracy are the main key factors which are aided to develop resilience in architecture. The liberalism also affected the integrity between the spatial form and layout development within the human-based explorations. Foucault (1976) also describes that an architecture of oppression might be one of the elements which makes resistance and opposition possible, but it is not in the philosophy of architecture itself where liberation from oppression is contained nor embodied.

According to Foucault (1976), architecture might be able to support the evolution of political institutions as the constitutional power, but it does not provide a guide map to control or determine it. However, it causes material and formal differentiations to develop an urban trajectory while exploring the boundary conditions across the Green Line. Altay (2013) indicates

36 *Bertug Ozarisoy*

that the institutional power is the state of notion itself to support physical conditions such as urban design scenarios. The political space depends not only on physical or conceptual form, but it relies on the context-spatial, political and temporal fragmentation in architecture.

Architecture is in control of some aspects of material form, minor relationships to the events through programme and a very indeterminate relationship in context through some relationship to the site (Sara & Littlefield, 2014, 295–304). It participates in producing political space, but it is unable to determine it. What we constantly need are other forms of institutions to prone the critical thinking of architecture and the notion of transgression in architecture. Hence, city-making is in contradiction to the notion of political explorations. It could develop a peaceful solution or any other form of conceptual thinking. The theory depends on the types of institutions and social patterns to support the participatory based design in urban planning. Additionally, the transgressive architecture supports the participants and produces the new future scenarios. Inherently, it draws the political ideology and architectural dilemma to support the 'unification' propaganda.

Architecture and any other spatial form therefore come into being through the participants point-view, rather than embody what the participants are or can imagine. This exposes all the problems inherent in thinking of architecture and power as applied practices in relationship to transgression, violence and conflict. The idea of unification is pulling away from the inherent messiness of intervening in the social realm working away from political issues toward notions of peace and it is profoundly conceded with a certain type of invisibility. This is the invisibility of permanence and image, which actively promoted the speculation to articulate any kind of final product in the urban reconciliation process.

Oppression and Occupation: Military Power

Military power is an act which is supposed to affect the everyday life of communities in such a way that the notion of conflict cannot be neglected by any other institutions. In this context, the state of the military must be experienced daily by Cypriots (Kliot & Mansfield, 1997, 495–521). It must be taken into account that buildings and cities are the most tangible element of civilization since even the written heritage. It consists of a nation's archive, and it requires an architectural container. On the contrary, it has happened that the evolutionary structure of civilization has fully disappeared from history. It has suffered from the combination of violence and conflict. Cypriots have experienced the first stages of occupation from the outbreak of military interventions. Hence this could be explained as a moment of spontaneous transgression.

Miessen (2007) indicates that the military occupation provided a new transcultural language between power and architecture. Hence, occupations had become a strategic military operation in architecture or practically and symbolically destroyed the organisational and cultural aspects of the United Nations Buffer Zone in a political attack on a population. Furthermore, architecture is provoked not only to protect from current entities but also in order to actively participate in the global machine of secularisation and segregation of social groups and individuals. In this context, architecture had been targeted and attacked; thus, it seems now normal that the current era of oppression materialises itself with architecture. However, this issue is not only characterised by the fear of conflict but by a global fear of otherness.

Participatory-Led Design

Miessen (2007) describes that any form of participation is already a form of conflict. In order to participate in a given environment or situation, one particular transnational element needs to understand the forces of conflict in the built environment. In this context, it seems urgent and necessary to promote an understanding of conflictual participation. It acts as an uninvited, agonistic and irritating theoretical underpinning into the fields of knowledge and experience (Philippou, 2007, 249–274). It could arguably benefit from spatial thinking and urban explorations. In this context, it is useful to think through a concept of conflictual participation as a productive form of interventional practice. Conflict refers to a condition of intellectual participation or state of opposition between two or more groups of people.

According to the semi-structured interviews via an e-mail in May 2022, Makrides recounts:

> These activities at the very end will eventually keep us apart and serve the maintenance of division instead of bringing us together because you simply serve and support the division, you talk about North and South, you talk about two communities, about sides, using the United Nations Buffer Zone for advantage (otherwise maintaining it) all these language terms surges to embed to our minds the existence of division and continue to learn to live with it. Lasting peaceful relations we had enough for forty-five years. We do not need any activities to serve this further as this to keep us apart. There are better ways and activities if you really want to unify this island.

On the other hand, subject respondent relates:

> Many thanks for the organisation of this peaceful event. It seems very noble, clever and engaging from the description. I look forward to seeing your work and joining you in your quest for peace.

Participation can also be described as a conflict of interests, aims or targets in the written transcript of transgressions in architecture. When we look at conflict as opposed to forms of participation, conflict is not to be understood as a form of provocative action or contrary provocation. It could be accepted as a cultural practice through which the participant plays a key role who insists on being an actor in the conflicted space they are facing. Thus, participation becomes a form of critical engagement, as shown in Figure 2.5.

According to Miessen (2006), when participation becomes conflict, conflict becomes space. In the context of spatial practices and participation, probably the most interesting aspect of the notion of the conflict overlaps with the cultural practice. Although, the participant-based workshop was more of a monologue than a conversation, it reveals the most important point of the event to explore transitions between space and culture. Because today's networking culture is based on consensus rather than conflict, it merely produces multiplications, but rarely new knowledge and experience. In this context, it could be useful to rethink the concept of conflict as a protagonist actor and producer of a productive environment rather than as direct physical violence.

In summary, the notion of transgression connects to the concept of the event as well as the need for a more hybrid mode of participation from the eye-of self-initiated practice versus the more well-established model of unification plan. Furthermore, increasing the fragmentation of identities and

Figure 2.5 Mapping spatial organisation layout for the event of Creative Possibilities, narrative and birds at the Peace Hall. Image credit: the author, 2022.

the complexities of the United Nations Buffer Zone, we are now facing a situation of unifying the communities to regenerate the city. This is crucial to think about a form of architecture, which allows for conflict as a form of productive engagement with transgression and power.

Hidden Power beyond Conflict: Participation

The participant-led co-design represents the unintended and unrecognised forms of knowledge, values and beliefs that are part of the participation process. The concept of methodology can be seen to exist alongside every participatory process for the Cypriots. This co-led design constitutes a large part of the community engagement. Examples of this include a variety of research methods and strategies that participants develop evidence-based urban design scenarios in order to reflect their way of thinking related to their everyday lives and experiences. This method focuses on the stages of actions that are developed by the participants. These activities consist of existing norms, showing creative ways of navigating institutional structures and subverting enforced cultural values and attitudes.

In this study, the event of 'creative possibilities' had been considered through a series of workshops with the local citizens and daily visitors. The workshops set a framework in which the communities investigate their own actions and forms of experiences and transfer the knowledge gained from their experiences towards other ends, such as the production of their memories on conflict and unification. Activating situations may go beyond common sense or explore memories, they will reflect on the legitimacy of a utopian urban vision, taking a critical position towards their own memories in order to act independently, think creatively and address the complexity of their own actions.

The workshop took place during the day while Turkish and Greek Cypriots and tourists were crossing the Ledras Street Crossing Checkpoint. The space of the 'Peace Hall' gave the participants varying degrees of publicness and privacy to expose their memories. Inherently, the event has been accepted as a sense of inclusion and exclusion, visibility and invisibility to explore existing urban conditions. The participants were given a prompt to decide what could be accessed and what remained for a selected audience.

In this context, the participants worked within a workspace developed specifically for the projects under the different concepts. Hence, the themes were shaped by personal experiences and memories. The space adapts them to their own imaginary world or provides opportunities through subtle distortion or adjustment. The exhibition was diverted by a large set of panels which were organised parallel to each other, creating the possibility of the separation of spaces, such as one more private and the other more open. The panels can be covered in layers of transparent blank papers and enable different kinds of activities that allow the participants to decide how public certain moments and parts of the project can be. The space was furnished

40   *Bertug Ozarisoy*

with a set of tables and chairs that are joined parts of existing furniture, which can be kept together or separated. These adaptable elements offer the participants multiple possibilities to change their environment.

When venturing out into the space, the participants observed the current notion of the United Nations Buffer Zone in the public and national scene. It tried to test it out by slightly changing the idea of 'Unification'. The themes are underlying with the transcultural juxtapositions where participants negotiate and resist the concepts through the series of workshops. The concept was set to confront the ideas and memories within the boundaries of the 'Peace Hall'. This experimental space organisation could lead to transferring this knowledge, understanding and learning for the Cypriot community. The event forms a model of how participation is negotiated in other areas of the concept of 'Unification', observing how participants deal with instructions and internalise them as well as subconsciously re-interpret them. How do norms and values control our knowledge and practices for Unification? How do these contribute towards the development of creative possibilities of conditions within social context? What is the meaning of the term 'The Architecture of Transgression' of thought that is embedded in the modes of participation? The step-by-step development of the event is outlined as follows:

- **Collecting Memories:** Each participant was asked to donate a memorable object from their home as a way of demonstrating their commitment to the project and as a sign of their participation. The objects were collected from their homes and exhibited in the space at Peace Hall, the individual experiences of the participants create an odd array of different kinds of organisation.
- **Drawing Exercise:** The participants were asked to interact with existing drawings on the panels in a way that goes against their own ideas under the variation of concepts.
- **Space Exercise:** It was set to expand in scale to encompass the building. The participants set off to investigate the structure of the workshop, finding ways to approach it that are different to the way in which they habitually navigate it. The participants looked for in-between panels or non-spaces, seeking the gaps within the building that offered opportunities for reshaping the critical theory of the 'Unification'. They physically stepped into them and documented their findings.
- **Sharing Ideas:** What would the equivalent notion of the 'Unification' in between Turkish and Greek Cypriots be as an action? The participants were invited to reflect upon what they have done and relate that to their own actions. They have shown parts of an archive of interviews in which participants share their own experiences. As many of these video clips were taken in Peace Hall (See **Video A** – Diaries from the event), the video sets off a discussion about participants' knowledge, in particular, between what is allowed or not within particular contexts.

- **Transferring into Actions**: The exhibition was accepted as a starting point for a brainstorming session in which the participants develop their own ideas of how to transfer the abstract thinking into other actions. The intention of this is for the participants to find their own particular concept of interest that raises questions surrounding the broader topic of the investigation.
- **Participant-Led Research**: Each participant developed their own drawing within the framework of the 'Creative Possibilities: Birds, Narratives and Artefacts'. These were started by interviewing participants to get their point of view or setting training sessions in order to see how one could develop new ideas.
- **Performative Situations**: The participants found ways to intervene in the process of the exhibition and workshop. Action includes, writing and their own memories, ideas on Unification and experiencing the space as a critical tool. Each creates a way of altering the participants to draw the ideology of the 'peace' and negotiate with the reshaping the future of the United Nations Buffer Zone.

Conclusions

This self-initiated project represents the stage in configuring a United Nations Buffer Zone through which we wish to be read. By making connections between what we do and what others such as radical practices do, we can begin to enable pluralist forms of exchange. Initiator comes from the position of wanting space of readership, as well as production. There is recognition of an absence, which the initiator can make visible. By bringing this role into situations, individual positions can fall to the wayside and illuminating the connections between participants.

As Hannula (2006) argues:

> Self-organisation is so-called third space. It is a peculiar concentration of time and energy in a particular place where the interests of the participants in that context are debated, constituted, defined, clarified, and defended. It does not belong to either A or B, but it is constructed spontaneously through the interaction between A and B. It is a meeting point at which both sides have found the capacity to listen to each other on the other's terms. It is based on acknowledging interaction that seeks to negotiate a sustainable compromise for existing alongside one another, not as a unity, but in plurality.

In contrast, Williams (1976) discusses that "Self-initiated projects are the life-blood of culture such as culture as understood in both material production and as a symbolic system of that production." He also indicates that self-organisation is about making things happen on one's own terms alongside like-minded positions. For example, artists, curators, writers,

42 *Bertug Ozarisoy*

or academicians who initiate projects with others can self-direct notions of both 'commonality' and 'connectivity' in relation to the scope of each theme. These two central terms act as inherent qualities within one's work: 'common' relates to the general idea of practice as a form of self-positioning alongside other like-minded positions while 'connected' conveys a belief that these other like forms of practice can take part in the same critical discourse.

As Jakobsen (2006, 11–14) claims in his co-penned essay, 'There Is No Alternative: THE FUTURE IS SELF ORGANISED', self-organisation is, amongst other things, 'a social process of communication and commonality based in exchange; sharing of similar problems, knowledge and available resources'.

As a shared space for participation and discussion, self-organisation enables a directed vocabulary to form based on one's own work. Every exhibition becomes a contingent moment in the evolution of a practice over time, where such momentary events function as self-regulated research tools for establishing links between practice as a space of negotiation and the individual position.

In fact, the exhibition and workshop, such as the private view or the after opening discussion session can end up as the most formal for all discursive exchanges. Conversations are the main stage of exchange in necessary moves towards more formalised critique and modes of participation through which diverse audiences can be widened beyond the mere convivial space of architectural diaspora and juxtaposition. The transformation of the discursive space into forms of exhibition, public events and public discussions also enables the configuration of a useful social network, which enables the initiator to activate a potential space for a network. It is called upon again in the future and for that network to grow over time.

From my point of view, the best motivation for the self-initiated project is the desire to contextualise one's work. In the concept of the 'Creative Possibilities', we must ensure that participants receive the best statements on the idea of the 'Unification'. By placing the participant-based research work alongside not only similar work but work seemingly unrelated from other disciplines such as radical practices on United Nations Buffer Zone. In this study, we aim to create new meanings that emerge from the juxtaposition.

References

Agamben, G. (2000). *Means without end*. Minneapolis, MN: University of Minnesota Press, p. 43.

Altay, C. (2013). Transgression in and of the city. *Architectural Design*, *83*(6), 102–109. https://doi.org/10.1002/ad.1682

Bataille, G. (1997). Architecture. In N. Leach (Ed.), *Rethinking architecture* (p. 21). London: Routledge.

Camus, A. (1998). *The plaque*. New York: Penguin Publications.

Denison, E., & Ren, G. (2013). Transgression and progress in China: Wang Shu and the literati mindset. *Architectural Design*, *83*(6), 38–43. https://doi.org/10.1002/ad.1672

Doron, G. M. (2000). The dead zone and the architecture of transgression. *City*, *4*(2), 247–263. https://doi.org/10.1080/13604810050147857

Dovey, K. (2013). Architecture the challenge of informal. *Architectural Design*, *83*(6), 82–89.

Faustino, D. (2013). In praise of transgression: The work of Didier faustino/bureau de mésarchitectures. *Architectural Design*, *83*(6), 120–123. https://doi.org/10.1002/ad.1685

Ford, S. (2005). *The situationist international: A user's guide*. London: Black Dog Publishing.

Foucault, M. (1976).Transgression. In N. Leach (Ed.), *Space, knowledge, power* (p. 371). New York: Penguin Publications.

Foucault, M. (1991). Preface to transgression. In F. Bolling & S. Wilson (Eds.), *Bataille: A critical reader* (p. 27). London: Wiley-Blackwell.

Hannula, M. (2006). '*Self-organisation: A short story of a family tree*', *self-organisation/counter-economic strategies*. Berlin: Sternberg Press, p. 207.

Hejduk, R. (2007). Death becomes her: Transgression, decay, and eROTicism in Bernard Tschumi's early writings and projects. *Journal of Architecture*, *12*, 393–404. https://doi.org/10.1080/13602360701614672

Jakobsen, J. (2006). *The future is self-organised*. London: Black Dog Publishing.

Kliot, N., & Mansfield, Y. (1997). The political landscape of partition: The case of Cyprus. *Political Geography*, *16*(6), 495–521. https://doi.org/10.1016/s0962-6298(96)00020-0

Littlefield, D. (2013). Ashes thrown to the wind: The elusive nature of transgression. *Architectural Design*, *83*(6), 124–129. https://doi.org/10.1002/ad.1686

Miessen, M. (2006). *Did someone say participate? An atlas of spatial practice*. Cambridge, MA: MIT Press.

Miessen, M. (2007). *The violence of participation*. Berlin: Sternberg Press.

Miessen, M. (2008). *East Coast Europe*. Berlin: Sternberg Press.

Mosley, J., & Sara, R. (2013). The architecture of transgression: Towards a destabilising architecture. *Architectural Design*, *83*(6), 14–19. https://doi.org/10.1002/ad.1668

Ozarisoy, B., & Altan, H. (2021). Developing an evidence-based energy-policy framework to assess robust energy-performance evaluation and certification schemes in the South-Eastern Mediterranean countries. *Energy for Sustainable Development*, *64*, 65–102. https://doi.org/10.1016/j.esd.2021.08.001

Ozarisoy, B., & Altan, H. (2022). Significance of occupancy patterns and habitual household adaptive behaviour on home-energy performance of post-war social-housing estate in the South-Eastern Mediterranean climate: Energy policy design. *Energy*, *244*. https://doi.org/10.1016/j.energy.2021.122904

Philippou, S. (2007). Policy, curriculum and the struggle for change in Cyprus: The case of the European dimension in education. *International Studies in Sociology of Education*, *17*(3), 249–274. https://doi.org/10.1080/09620210701543916

Roberts-Hughes, R. (2017). Transgression and conservation: Rereading Georges Bataille. *Journal for Cultural Research*, *21*(2), 157–168. https://doi.org/10.1080/14797585.2016.1239608

Sara, R., & Littlefield, D. (2014). Transgression: Body and space. *Architecture and Culture*, *2*(3), 295–304. https://doi.org/10.2752/205078214X14107818390513

Sassen, S. (2004). Afterword. In J. Gugler (Ed.), *World cities beyond the west* (pp. 371–386). Cambridge: Cambridge University Press.

Sheil, B. (2005). Transgression from drawing to making. *Architectural Research Quarterly*, 9(1), 20–32. https://doi.org/10.1017/S1359135505000059

Terkourafi, M. (2008). Perceptions of difference in the Greek sphere The case of Cyprus. *Journal of Greek Linguistics*, 8(1), 60–96. https://doi.org/10.1075/jgl.8.06ter

Tschumi, B. (1976). *Architecture and transgression*, published in architecture and disjunction, Bernard Tschumi. Cambridge, MA: MIT Press, 1996, p. 78. Originally appeared in oppositions 7, Winter 1976.

Tschumi, B. (1996). *Architecture and disjunction*. Cambridge, MA and London: The MIT Press, p. 83.

Williams, R. (1976). *Keywords: A vocabulary of culture and society*. London: Fontana Press, p. 90.

3 Political Discourse Acts as a Transnational Catalyst in the Decision-Making of Architectural Design Interventions

Bertug Ozarisoy

Introduction

Over time, the general shape of world events has changed radically. The dialectical, dialogical nature of politics and culture, such as West versus East and capitalist versus socialist, has given way to a monological tendency called 'globalisation', which aims to establish a dominant social and economic worldwide ideology (Miessen, 2008). In addition, local issues are being absorbed by global issues, as is seen in the current pre-eminence of foreign policy issues in Cyprus over domestic ones, presented as a 'conflict' inextricably binding domestic and global together. Sassen (2004) mentions that today's cities are characterised by a climate of crisis, the urban community is of a divided and unjust nature, its geography uneven in every sense.

These shifts and changes have had serious consequences for the way we think about architecture: what it is, what it can and is supposed to do. They impact how architects think about their work, and what they think is important to discuss (Hannula, 2006). This is only natural, considering that architecture is, or aspires to be, a social practice and is finely tuned to society's convulsions and more orderly economic, political, cultural and intellectual transformations. What does the future hold for the United Nations Buffer Zone? At the very edge of research capabilities and well beyond the critical thinking of precise studies, this question remains central in the pursuit of competitive insights by political players, professional actors and local citizens. The future of a complex organism such as a city, with countless participants involved in its continuous creation and the omnipresent possibility of 'unification' suddenly surfacing, represents an even greater challenge (Pollastri et al., 2016, 45–51). The event of 'Creative Possibilities' builds upon a balanced framework of priorities.

No field of enquiry is more exposed to intellectual doubt than the study of the future (Hejduk, 2007, 393–404). Because of its nature – no future objects exist for scientific repeatable experimentation – the future is in itself fluid and evasive in the eye of the social researcher (Shonfield, 2000). The field of the future of the United Nations Buffer Zone as objects of enquiry is no exception. However, in contrast to lifestyle or consumer trend studies,

DOI: 10.4324/9781003243069-5

46 *Bertug Ozarisoy*

they do offer the advantage that architecture and design processes naturally structure the critical vision of the city (Graham, 2008, 100–101). The moment of conception of participants' ideas and the completion of the related radical practices such as revitalisation of the historic urban quarters. In essence, an event is a natural timing for critical architectural visions to materialise ideas and concepts into manifestations and artificially built places (Given, 2005, 207–213). Such timing works to the advantage of future scenarios because it offers a relatively established and technically necessary cycle of observation, investigation and analysis.

Additionally, the role of design intervention in the city is the object of close examination and deep analysis in countless academic and professional references; therefore, desk research in this field can offer a rich, textured image of the working mechanisms that regulate relationships across the field, taking into consideration the viewpoints of different participants (Stepnik, 2020, 127). Available historical data range from studies of the conflict between two communities to qualitative action research for change among communities, with direct, co-creative participation of citizens (Miessen, 2006). From this wealth of consolidated information, by cross-referencing participant opinions based on research questions, it is possible to form a preliminary critical opinion regarding the terms 'the Architecture of Violence' and 'the State of Conflict'. These statements are the ideal platforms from which to elaborate insights to the future.

This research is neither a single perspective of the idea of creative possibilities of conditions nor a unified narrative; it is made of architectural investigations on different scales, locations, with different intensities and speeds. By extracting a selection of theoretical research and spatial experience of the context, it attempts to elaborate on several key concepts informing the overall programme, the event of 'Creative Possibilities'. The concepts in this research should be understood as a set of architectural fables, speculating about the seemingly impossible, the actual transformation of the structures of domination. It is thus also, and fundamentally so, an invitation to re-think the problem of political subjectivity not from the point of view of a 'Unify Nicosia' conception of a local citizen but rather from the point of view of architectural discourse.

Political Space as a Transnational Instrument of the United Nations Buffer Zone

Architecture as an object of power operates on many levels, from the construction of the barricades through the Green Line and United Nations Buffer Zone to the front lines of urban nomads, to the psychological moulding of modernist space conformity, as shown in Figure 3.1. The very architectural image itself is a document of power (Weizman, 2003). The design document and the collective objects, much like the map, by nature is an inscription of a form of power. On the contrary, Weizman (2007)

The Decision-Making of Architectural Design Interventions 47

Figure 3.1 Documenting the contested urban territory, Nicosia, Cyprus. Image credit: the author, 2022.

articulates better than most, it is the medium through which politics happens. In his seminal article, Weizman (2007) indicates that it is a political consensus to articulate many different design scenarios in a participatory research approach. Therefore, architecture is the materiality through which politics are rectified. It is not only how we physically negotiate the context but how one imagines it, for another, and perhaps how one can also reclaim it. In this regard it is inherently political (Agamben, 2000, 43). It is through architecture that so many socio-economic and political legal or nonlegal forces are contested and spatialised, concentrated and formatted for a larger geopolitical terrain (Hill, 1948, 19–23).

Architecture is violent. There are a number of contexts for observing this and, while defined by a politics, or embodying a politics, architecture is the embedding of social ordering and divisions and various forms of knowledge that can only be reshaped by its construction (Sheil, 2005, 20–32). It can also be a form of obliterating knowledge and people, such as in the case of violence (Miessen, 2007). Many scholars have mentioned the significance of participatory design process for identifying effective policy making

48 *Bertug Ozarisoy*

decisions to shape the future of cities (Birch et al., 2017). It must be high-lighted that architecture is also a technology, depending on how it is used. In this theoretical study, we are not aimed at demonising architecture but only want to stress that many times it is hardly innocent (Cunningham, 2001). The most updated studies in the field of architectural theory highlights the importance of adapting participant-based interventions into the practical discourse (Bataille, 1997, 21). The reason is that the boundaries and pow-ers of architecture extend well beyond those physical spaces that have been designed and built by architects, but also are embodied by spaces that end up in more or less fragile conditions in the urban environment; these would be seemingly inconsequential architectures, conflict spaces and default con-tainers of power.

A contextual practice, and this may be architecture or politics, need not only construct and present a context but also acknowledge itself as actively producing or fabricating an environment with which it engages (Shadar & Maslovski, 2021, 516–540). This transformation of the understanding of context, and therefore of the context itself, from a set of conditions to a political production, is to inscribe it with a new set of possibilities. What is being identified is not simply formal or architectural intervention but implicit connection, visible or invisible to the potential concept of struc-tures of power (Wimmelbcker, 2012, 407–432). Exploring the politics of uncertainty, separation, seclusion and visual control, the no-man's land, checkpoints, walls, barricades and other security measures are also the last gesture in the hardening of urban enclaves and are the physical and vir-tual extension of borders in the context of the more recent global 'conflict' (Beeckmans, 2014, 849–871). The architecture of the United Nations Buffer Zone occupation could thus be seen as an accelerator and an acceleration of other global political processes.

Foucault said, in his famous interview with Paul Rabinow, that the forces of global political processes remain unpredictable in architecture (Foucault, 1976). The reason this may be important here, even if predictable, is not only articulating the active relationship between architecture and power, but it also opens the possibility for it to be thought and exercised as new, differently, again and again. Foucault in a sense liberated spatial form, and with it the practice of architecture, from being conceived as belonging to inescapable orders of oppression (Foucault, 1977, 21). An architecture of oppression might be one of the elements which makes resistance and opposition possible, but it is not in the architecture itself that liberation from oppression is contained nor embodied: Architecture might be able to support a form of political institution, but it cannot control or determine it (Sharp, 2022). However, it can cause material and formal differentia-tions; but it is the other institutions that support physical condition that established the political space (Hejduk, 2007, 393–404). The political space depends not only on physical or conceptual form but on the context-spatial, political and temporal urban conditions.

The Decision-Making of Architectural Design Interventions 49

Architecture is in control of some aspects of material form, minor relationships to events through participant-led activities and a very indeterminate relationship in context through some relationship to site (Foucault, 1991, 15–16). It participates in producing political space, but it is unable to determine existing boundary conditions. What we constantly need are other forms of institutions to prompt the critical thinking of architecture and the notion of developing utopian urban vision design scenarios. This is a certain concept about architecture, and it is in contradiction to the notion of political issue (Pullan, 2011). It could install a peaceful solution, or any other form of conceptual thinking, depending on the types of institutions and social patterns.

In fact, the architecture supports the participants and produces the new future scenarios. It stages the political and the ideology of 'Unification'. Architecture and any other spatial form therefore come into being through the participants viewpoint rather than embody what the participants are or can imagine. These expose all the problems inherent in thinking of architecture and power as applied practices in relationship to transgression, violence and conflict (Kraff, 2019, 56–58). The idea of 'Unification' is pulling away from the inherent messiness of intervening in the social realm working away from political issues towards notions of peace and is profoundly conceited with a certain type of invisibility. This is the invisibility of permanence and imagination, which actively promoted the speculation to articulate any type of transgressive design strategies.

Scoping the Field and Setting Up the Counteractive Participant-Based Architectural Disseminations

Before discussing the theoretical framework of the research and reporting on the event 'Creative Possibilities', an introduction is needed to scope the field of this study, by capturing a number of key indications about how critical design, architecture and creative ideas are likely to evolve in the future, through political cycles and in the wake of current policies and programmes. As noted, participant-led design is the primary reference adopted throughout the exhibition and workshop at the level of practices and creative direction. It seems necessary to explore and envision how design itself might evolve in the future, towards different organisational models, towards an increasingly diverse and differentiating role in addressing participants' challenges and towards its very own future scenarios.

The event of 'Creative Possibilities' is a participant-based experience aiming to inform the Cypriots of a new utopian urban vision of Nicosia. The event is named 'Creative Possibilities' because we want to find a new name for the United Nations Buffer Zone. This is also to add that our vision is 'beyond division' because it sets out to explore invisibility through visibility. We intend to keep the traces and the natural architecture habitat, and it is the reason we named the event 'Birds, Narratives and Artefacts' – because

50 *Bertug Ozarisoy*

we want to return to nature and reveal the past history of the city without destroying the present.

In this event we included 'Collective Memories and Narratives' as a tool to get people to talk about their past experiences of the city as they remembered before and after the division. We included the story of the artefacts because virtual objects help us to understand the Cypriot culture and practice as it was many years ago. The workshop 'Creative Map of Nicosia' helped the people to pinpoint themselves on a location on the map and to recollect their memories. Additionally, the workshop of the 'Future & Past, Matrix of Nicosia' was aimed to support the idea of the utopian urban vision of the city. This workshop and exhibition were to create the 'Event City Model' to encourage people to participate in this design process and write and draw their own ideas of what they expect from the Buffer Zone in the future.

Setting Up the Research Design Approach for Reclaiming Architectural Discourse in the United Nations Buffer Zone

Adopting the co-design seeks to present a recognised form of knowledge, values and beliefs that are part of the participation process (Merrill, 2019). The concept of methodology can be seen to exist alongside every participatory process for both Turkish and Greek Cypriots.[1] This activity constitutes a large part of the community engagement. Examples of this include a variety of research methods and strategies that participants develop in order to access their own experiences.[2] This method focuses on the series of actions that are developed by the participants and it consists of existing norms, showing creative ways of navigating institutional structures and subverting enforced cultural values and attitudes.

In this context, the participants worked within a workspace developed specifically for the projects under the different concepts, as shown in Figure 3.2. In this participant-led design, the concept was to use personal experiences and memories and adapt them to their own use or benefit through subtle distortion or adjustment. The space was cloaked by a large set of panels that settled parallel to each other, creating the possibility of the separation of spaces, such as one more private and the other more open. The panels can be covered in layers of transparent blank papers and enable different kinds of activities that allow the participants to decide how public certain moments and parts of the project can be. The space was furnished with a set of tables and chairs that are joined parts of existing furniture, which can be kept together or separated. These adaptable elements offer the participants multiple possibilities to change their environment.

When venturing out into space, the participants observed the current notion of the United Nations Buffer Zone in the public and national scene, and they tried to test it out by slightly changing the idea of 'Unification'. Through looking at how the participants negotiate and resist the concepts through the series of workshops that they are confronted with in the space of the 'Peace Hall', as well as transferring these investigations into the

Figure 3.2 The spatial organisation of the Peace Hall. Image credit: the author, 2022.

Turkish and Greek Cypriots realm, the project forms a model of how participation is negotiated in other areas of the concept of 'Unification', observing how participants deal with instructions and internalise them as well as subconsciously re-interpret them. How do norms and values control our knowledge and practices for unification? How do these contribute towards the development of creative possibilities of conditions within social context? What is the meaning of the term 'The Architecture of Transgression' of thought that is embedded in the theory of participation?

Stages of Development in the Decision-Making of an Architectural Reconciliation Process

Each participant was asked to donate a memorable object from their home as a way of demonstrating their commitment to the project and as a sign of their participation. The objects were collected from their homes and exhibited in the space at the Peace Hall. In this participant-led design, the individual experiences of the participants create an odd array of different kinds of organisation. The participants were asked to interact with existing drawings on the panels in a way that goes against their own ideas under the variation of concepts. The space exercise was expanded in scale to encompass the building. The participants set off to investigate the structure of the workshop, including effective ways to explore existing urban conditions.

The participants looked for in-between panels or non-spaces, seeking the gaps within the building that offered opportunities for reshaping the critical theory of the 'Unification'. They physically entered them and documented their findings. What would the equivalent notion of the 'Unification' in between Turkish and Greek Cypriots be as an action? The participants were invited to reflect upon what they have done and relate to their own actions. They were shown parts of an archive of interviews in which participants share their own experiences. Many of these video clips were recorded in the Peace Hall.

Additionally, each participant developed their own drawing within the framework of the 'Creative Possibilities: Birds, Narratives and Artefacts'. These ranged from interviewing participants to get their point of view or setting training sessions in order to see how one could develop new ideas. The participants find ways to intervene in the process of the exhibition and workshop, as shown in Figure 3.3. Actions include writing, sharing their own memories and ideas on Unification, and experiencing the space as a critical tool. Each creates a way of altering the participants to draw the ideology of the peace-making and negotiate with the reshaping of the future of the United Nations Buffer Zone.

In summary, the exhibition and workshop, such as the private view or the after opening discussion session can end up as the most formal of all discursive exchanges. Conversations are the main stage of exchange in a necessary move towards more formalised critique and modes of participation through which diverse audiences can be widened beyond the mere convivial space of materialising the unification idea.

Creative Possibilities: Birds, Narratives and Artefacts

The event of 'Creative Possibilities: Birds, Narratives and Artefacts' is a participant-based community engagement which is intended to unify both Turkish and Greek Cypriots in the notion of architectural discourse. It also discusses, explores and anticipates the future of the United Nations Buffer Zone, Nicosia from the sociocultural, outdoor environment and critical thinking of the architecture perspectives (Pollastri et al., 2016). The related exhibition and workshop were set for three days from 10 to 12 June 2014 and included several interdependent activities including professional networking, qualitative research, event design and workshop. The following

The Decision-Making of Architectural Design Interventions 53

Figure 3.3 The collection of memorable objects from the subject participants and the olive tree welcoming participants in the Peace Hall. Image credit: the author, 2022.

sections of the study document the outcome of the participant-led event, which aimed to bring information from primary research and applicable workshops, ending with prototype design through to practical realisation of utopian urban design scenarios.

This event structure was divided into three sections – (i) Collective Memories and Narratives, (ii) Creative Map of Nicosia and (iii) Future & Past Matrix – covering the different stages of the programme as it was organised. The study presents the chronological order of activities from qualitative research to critical review of design concepts. For example, the event of 'Creative Possibilities' was intended as a multicultural, multidisciplinary opportunity to reflect, envision and possibly make the future happen. This research should be regarded not so much as a point of arrival but as the starting point for future elaborations on the various themes presented during the exhibition and workshop at the Peace Hall, Nicosia.

54 *Bertug Ozarisoy*

The study of the future of the United Nations Buffer Zone is not an enterprise that can be successfully addressed by one specialisation only; holistic thinking and the ability to connect different and diverse priorities and interests of multiple participants are essential features in this field study. It is the hope of the participants of this research that the result of their commitment and engagement within the realm of the future of the city might inspire further possibilities of urban conditions. Utopian urban vision manifestos were written with the ambition of mobilising the best energies of those who will have future scenarios in their hands, whether academic thinkers, professional practitioners or simply citizens.

The event of 'Creative Possibilities' has been envisioned, designed and built as a place for dialogues with leading practitioners, urban theorists and a number of cross-disciplinary contributors, who were invited to join the conversation in research interviews, in event panels and in workshop teamwork, with the focus on collaborative networking. The focus on the event exercises has been kept around Cypriots and city travellers, both settled ones and new migrants, with a research framework to ensure the presence of thematic areas of creative investigation. Additionally, this has been based on theoretical sociocultural drivers describing societal change towards the next decade. This approach provides a stage for moderated discussions and the systematic elaboration of ideas about the future, without the desire or intention to determine any specific outcome at conceptual and national levels.

Learning from the Exploratory Case Study Design and Its Implications on the Architectural Reconciliation Process

The aim of this event was to inform local citizens about our utopian urban vision for the Buffer Zone, Nicosia, as shown in Figure 3.4. It was set to inform people about our design proposal and create a collective environment from this exhibition to get their views about this utopian vision and their thoughts and imagination for the future of the Buffer Zone. This event was also participant-based to gather information on collective memories and narratives, inclusion of the creative mapping of Nicosia and the Future & Past matrix of Nicosia. We have tested our ideas under these three workshop themes. The aim of these three themes was to support our thoughts on future urban vision. We set up this event for three days at the Peace Hall, Ledras Street Crossing checkpoint, Nicosia. We chose this space for the event because this place is at the heart of the Buffer Zone which offers diverse possibilities with architectural discourse and juxtaposition.

This participant-led event at the Peace Hall could not be seen by only Cypriot participants but many other nationalities who just happened to be passing through the checkpoints and walked in and participated in this event. We were expecting this to happen because of the strategic location of the Peace Hall. Among the Cypriots who participated, the majority were Greek Cypriots. Hence, most people did not participate in these workshop[s], but we narrated to these people the aim of our project and our urban vision

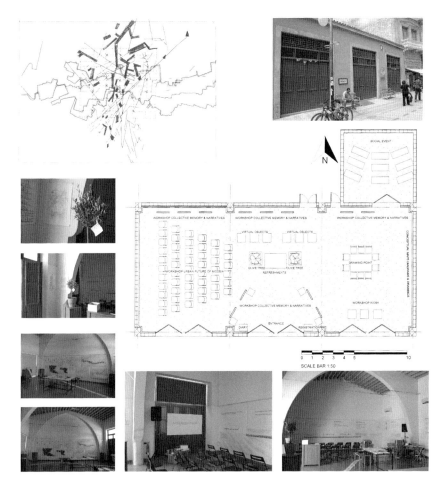

Figure 3.4 A perspective view of the model of a utopian urban vision of Nicosia – new public spaces will bring effective cultural practice between the two communities. Image credit: the author, 2022.

of the Buffer Zone. Notably, most people were interested in our utopian urban vision, and at the same time, the participants narrated to us their own experiences about Nicosia. Throughout the experience, we observed that the Greek Cypriots were more aware and interested in revitalising the Buffer Zone.

From the narratives and storytelling from the older generations, we came to understand how our visionary touched them deeply, awakening some of their childhood memories of a long time ago about the city of Nicosia. We learned at this event that the younger generations, particularly the generation born after the division of the island, had great difficulty understanding our utopian urban vision for the city because they have always seen it as it

56   *Bertug Ozarisoy*

is now – divided. The Buffer Zone has always been there, so they could not visualise anything different, as they have grown up thinking this is the norm. However, the Greek Cypriot younger generation showed more interest than their older counterparts. This pattern has been proved in the storytelling task which could enable us to establish effective communication throughout our discussion on utopia and unification.

Representatives of the Nicosia municipality agreed that this vision was the best way to create a new cultural practice and bring the Buffer Zone to life. They felt that their previous plan of adding cafes and bars for the younger generations was a mistake. It hadn't changed their thinking about the isolated world they lived in, and accepted as normal, or inspired ideas about what could be done to the city to transform it.

Beyond Theory: Learning from the Transgression

This research combines ways of using practice to provoke politics to reveal itself and act upon it. Instead of creative possibilities of conditions in architecture, we sought critical proximity to explore correlations between the local communities and stakeholders. This research seeks to inhabit the subject of the 'Transgression and Power' to enter, so to speak, into the respective idea of 'Unification' to become part of the constitutional agreement which shapes the built environment. Echoing Foucault's understanding of the event, it should be noted that the category of 'event' is an underscoring notion for architecture, as there is no architecture without programme, no programme without action and no action without event. With regards to the justification of philosophy in transgression, these phenomena are part of architecture, and architects need to engage on this level of analysis.[3]

In this research, we were inspired by Foucault's thinking of an event and Tschumi's architectural practice of an event. We used their ideas to understand and put into practice our own vision, because the context of Nicosia which we have chosen is unique in itself. Drawing from this ideology we went on to create our own event at the heart of the Buffer Zone. Although the form of research and practice is collective, relational and active, it would be beneficial to think of it as a 'catalyst'. It doesn't work in an ameliorative manner; it has never proposed any kind of radical reconstruction of architecture. It seeks to respond worldwide as a solution to alleviate conflict. It does not use architecture to reveal the existing hierarchy of the city or rebuild it. On the contrary, it has sought to establish a different balance between withdrawal and engagement, action in the world and research, fiction and proposal. This research should be interpreted as an attempt to articulate an architectural utopia as a political instrument for 'Unification'. This practice is not reactive to dominant forms of power; it has a different vision to look at (Tassinari et al., 2017, 52–57).

In a place like the United Nations Buffer Zone, there is a risk of becoming dependent on the frenetic rush of mainstream reporting. This research

The Decision-Making of Architectural Design Interventions   57

envisions the practice instead as an attempt to produce a space from which it is possible to operate in the here and now but with critical long-term transformative visions. Architectural proposals are a form of fiction. Their effects could be the opening of imagination. This research aims to find a place for architecture to act in the world and not in the service of a pre-existing agenda. The critical thinking of architecture has materialised in both built and political space and in the cultural collective imagination of participants in collaborative workshops and negotiations.

The transgression of architecture has been accepted as an on-going process of conflict, and it has led to a less than ideal world. This has not only to do with the violence that contaminates every aspect of our lives but also with determining the point in time from which speculation could begin. Conflicts create a sense of postponement. Architecture tends to await the conflict stage or to imagine it. However, this is an endless struggle to determine existing urban conditions, inclusion with different perceptions. The desirable conflict stage might offer the state of political affairs or constitutional unification of Cyprus. Notably, political ideologies are not defined by present practices but by the type of end state desired. Are you a one, two or three state solutionist? A partitionist? Hence only one of the Unified Nations Buffer Zone solutions are equally entrapped in their respective 'top-down' expert perspectives. This could result in the development of each referential logic, system and order. The only state we know is the state of conflict and struggle.

Thinking about politics through architecture helps us enter the problem from another direction. Our architecture is not about determining a utopia of the future, but simply starting from what exists: the current political situation and its material manifestation, the rubble 'unceasingly piled before our feet'. This research seeks to find and utilise cracks and loopholes within existing tensions of conflict and its power. In the event of 'Creative Possibilities: Birds, Narratives and Artefacts' as we were describing our utopian urban vision to the participants, they informed us that as this urban vision is open to discussion, they wanted to create their own free spaces there. The idea of these free spaces to the participants of our event came from their experiences of seeing and meeting the ethnic migrant workers from Asia of different cultures all coming together on their free days and creating their own free spaces in the city where they socialise, entertain themselves and set up markets for food, etc., hence creating a new type of cultural practice in the centre of Nicosia city.

A Manifesto: Multicultural Exchange and Unification

We need a new term for the United Nations Buffer Zone. Its name is so laden with its past that when we try to postulate a present Buffer Zone that may extend into an unpredictable future, we are flung backwards. In fact, the more we try to project forward, the more others will remind us of what the United Nations Buffer Zone has been and ought to be. The

58 Bertug Ozarisoy

term 'United Nations Buffer Zone' possesses inverse elasticity of meaning in relation to radical vision, as shown in Figure 3.4. Is there any future in the world of the 'United Nations Buffer Zone'? The work presented in this research is thus an invitation to undertake a critical architectural and political thought experiment: let's think about the current conditions of the world from the perspective of Cypriots; let's think of today's struggles, not from the point of view of conflict from that of a continued struggle of 'Unification'.

It is by now possible to identify the event of 'Creative Possibilities' as a participatory design process of urban foresight involving selected members of professional communities, such as academicians and politicians. The focus is on creative possibilities of conditions of the United Nations Buffer Zone design opportunities to address sociocultural and strategic challenges of future cities, always placing people at the centre. In order to do this, the event fully claims design as a hybrid approach. This enables us to connect in a fertile process of cross-referencing. The adaptation of conceptual scenarios at the prototyping level is a means of 'learning by doing' while producing the necessary assists for the visual documentation of each concept in the formats of photographic and video recording. In addition, the 'scenario' format of futures storytelling has been reconstructed with new hybrid mixes involving presentations, conversations and visualisations, hence co-developing narrative structures with participants and guests. The result has been accelerated prototyping assets. The prototypes were assembled by the workshop participants themselves, confirming that they are the actual protagonists of the idea of 'Unification of Nicosia'.

One of the key successes of the event lies in creating networking relationships over time and in the co-creative dialogue with citizens, professional experts, leading practitioners of the Nicosia Master Plan, architecture and planning. All participatory processes were conducted according to a specific qualities survey design, comparatively based on the Nicosia Master Plan. Data followed statements specifically designed for each of the workshop concepts within the general structure.

This research component of the event built upon a wealth of insights, information and opinions by adapting the same questionnaire format, hence creating a natural extension to those earlier research assets. The fact that the idea of 'Unification of Nicosia' is an area of study with particularly long cycles helped in the establishment of this ideal dialogue over time. This offers a unique opportunity to both validate and improve where appropriate by means of sharpening those earlier assets. Thus, it is possible to build a coherent and consistent stream of the future of the United Nations Buffer Zone. These two sets of binary parameters are only the first example of several operational references, tools and structures that were used in the event and that will populate this for 'Unification of the United Nations Buffer Zone', to ensure comparability, cross-referential validity and provide a strong balance to the overall study. It must be added that, unlike most radical practices and scientific research on new utopian cities, in this context,

The Decision-Making of Architectural Design Interventions

the specific function of both theory and documentation of the research is not in themselves to self-fulfil the task of envisioning the future.

These offer a systematic vision of possible and potential manifestos, substantiated by the conceptual design of the United Nations Buffer Zone, which remains the fundamental tool for the entire study, maintaining its compactness and coherence across primary research, desk optimisation and design co-creation. Again, participant-based research and thinking has the unique ability to stimulate synthesis and synergy. These above reflections seem essential in the context of a certainty expressed by the event of 'Creative Possibilities' participants. In this complex and contradictory context, the notion of culture will certainly be an important element within a mix specifically designed to attract international and local 'knowledge participants', those uniquely capable of generating valuable intellectuals assists as 'new citizens' while managing the city for all, but at the notion of a socio-cultural paradox. After our event of 'Creative Possibilities', we experienced the multilayered cultural practices of the Cypriots, and, drawing from this and our observation of the Buffer Zone itself, we put together a frame that is called a 'City of Hybridity' for construction of four different diasporas through a utopian urban vision of Nicosia: (i) City of Agriculture; (ii) City of Trees; (iii) City of Birds and (iv) City of Watchtowers. Direct findings are invisible elements of the Buffer Zone, but in our utopian urban vision, we are aimed to interpret these as visible urban design scenarios.

Conclusions

This study addresses the philosophy of the term 'transgression': how transgression shapes the utopian urban vision of Nicosia. The architecture of transgression is a polyhedral phenomenon which by its nature, escapes a synthetic definition. This does not provide a design of a 'utopian urban vision' to extract a conclusion; rather it interposes a specific lens through which to look at the future of the city and it will add another layer of information to the existing facts. This research seeks to highlight and negotiate existing positions and contradictions surrounding the apparent homogeneity of a globalised environment of the city.

Time compresses into space, and the spatialisation of the temporal on our island territory, brings dissimilarities next to each other but also a mode of non-comprehension or charged cultural loss in the way of practice that opens for revision what may have been denied or apparently obsolete. A layered imaginative geography, in other words, governs the cultural differences related to cultural contests and national or ethnic divisions. The cultural practice of Cypriots within other communities may serve to replenish the layered intertextual resources of a culture such as de-territorialising one terrain to map another. The genetics, the cultural practices (e.g., morals, food) is similar except for religion, ethnic and language differences. Although going back in time in our history there was an interchange in these differences for certain reasons. The differences between Turkish and

60 *Bertug Ozarisoy*

Greek Cypriots have become more distinct since the division as they have progressed in time with no interaction with each other. When the borders opened in 2003, they mixed and worked, especially the young who had contact with each other for the first time realising their similarities; but except for a few marriages, there was not much hybridisation. It is interesting to note that beyond this multiversity and conflict between the Turkish and Greek Cypriots there has been some loss in their good will and trust of each other. This research has been chosen to put together an idea which will enable the Cypriot community to live and work in harmony which has been denied to them for a long time through no fault of their own.

Notes

1 George Costantinou. 'The Birth of an Island', in *Monuments and Sites Cyprus*, ICOMOS, (1996).
2 Könings, Karen D., Catherine Bovill, and Pamela Woolner. 'Towards an Interdisciplinary Model of Practice for Participatory Building Design in Education.' *European Journal of Education* 52.3 (2017): 306–317.
3 Bernard Tschumi, B. 'Architecture and Transgression', in *Architecture and Disjunction*, Bernard Tschumi (Cambridge, MA: MIT PRESS, 1996) p.78. Originally appeared in *Oppositions* 7, winter 1976.

References

Agamben, G. (2000). *Means without end*. Minneapolis, MN: University of Minnesota Press, p. 43.
Bataille, G. (1997). Architecture. In N. Leach (Ed.), *Rethinking architecture* (p. 21). London: Routledge.
Beeckmans, L. (2014). The adventures of the French architect Michel Ecochard in post-independence Dakar: A transnational development expert drifting between commitment and expediency. *Journal of Architecture*, *19*(6), 849–871. https://doi.org/10.1080/13602365.2014.982146
Birch, J., Parnell, R., Patsarika, M., & Šorn, M. (2017). Creativity, play and transgression: Children transforming spatial design. *CoDesign*, *13*(4), 245–260. https://doi.org/10.1080/15710882.2016.1169300
Cunningham, D. (2001). Architecture, Utopia and the futures of the avant-garde. *Journal of Architecture*. https://doi.org/10.1080/13602360110048195
Foucault, M. (1976). Transgression. In N. Leach (Ed.), *Space, knowledge, power* (p. 371). New York: Penguins Publications.
Foucault, M. (1977). A preface to transgression. 1963, published in language, counter-memory, practice: Selected essays and interviews. Ed & Trans. Donald F. Bouchard. Ithaca, NY: Cornell University Press, 1977, p. 30. A Preface to Transgression was an essay in homage to his death friend Georges Bataille F.
Foucault, M. (1991). Preface to transgression. In F. Bolling & S. Wilson (Eds.), *Bataille: A critical reader* (p. 27). London: Wiley-Blackwell.
Given, M. (2005). Architectural styles and ethnic identity in medieval to modern Cyprus. In J. Clarke (Ed.), *Archaeological perspectives on the transmission*

and assimilation of culture in the eastern Mediterranean (Vol. 2, pp. 207–213). Nicosia: Council for British Research in the Levant, Moufflon Bookshop Publishing.

Graham, G. (2008). Art and architecture: A place between. *British Journal of Aesthetics*, *48*(1), 100–101. https://doi.org/10.1093/aesthj/aym048

Hannula, M. (2006). *'Self-organisation: A short story of a family tree', self-organisation/counter-economic strategies*. Berlin: Sternberg Press, p. 207.

Hill, G. (1948). *A history of Cyprus*. Cambridge: Cambridge University Press.

Hejduk, R. (2007). Death becomes her: Transgression, decay, and eROTicism in Bernard Tschumi's early writings and projects. *Journal of Architecture*, *12*, 393–404. https://doi.org/10.1080/13602360701614672

Kraff, H. (2019). A critical exploration of agonistic participatory design. *Design Journal*. https://doi.org/10.1080/14606925.2019.1684730

Merrill, E. M. (2019). Zaha Hadid's center for contemporary art and the perils of new museum architecture. *ARQ: Architectural Research Quarterly*, *9*, 123–125.

Miessen, M. (2006). *Did someone say participate? An atlas of spatial practice*. Cambridge, MA: MIT Press.

Miessen, M. (2007). *The violence of participation*. Berlin: Architectural Association School of Architecture Publishing.

Miessen, M. (2008). *East Coast Europe*. Berlin: Sternberg Press.

Pollastri, S., Cooper, R., Dunn, N., & Boyko, C. (2016). Visual conversations on urban futures. Participatory methods to design scenarios of liveable cities. In *DRS2016: Future-focused thinking*. 4, Design Research Society.

Pullan, W. (2011). Frontier urbanism: The periphery at the centre of contested cities. *Journal of Architecture*. https://doi.org/10.1080/13602365.2011.546999

Sassen, S. (2004). Afterword. In J. Gugler (Ed.), *World cities beyond the west* (pp. 371–386). Cambridge: Cambridge University Press.

Shadar, H., & Maslovski, E. (2021). Pre-war design, post-war sovereignty: Four plans for one city in Israel/Palestine. *Journal of Architecture*, *26*(4), 516–540. https://doi.org/10.1080/13602365.2021.1925946

Sharp, D. (2022). Concretising conflict. *Journal of Architecture*. https://doi.org/10.1080/13602365.2022.2029026

Sheil, B. (2005). Transgression from drawing to making. *Architectural Research Quarterly*, *9*(1), 20–32. https://doi.org/10.1017/S1359135505000059

Shonfield, K. (2000). The use of fiction to interpret architecture and urban space. *Journal of Architecture*. Routledge. https://doi.org/10.1080/13602360050214395

Stępnik, M. (2020). The house that lars built. The architecture of transgression. *Arts*, *9*(4), 127. https://doi.org/10.3390/arts9040127

Tassinari, V., Francesca, P., & Elisa, B. (2017). Storytelling in design for social innovation and politics: A reading through the lenses of Hannah Arendt. *Design Journal*, *20*(Suppl. 1), S3486–S3495.

Weizman, E. (2003). *A civilian occupation*. New York: Verso Publications.

Weizman, E. (2007). *Hollow land*. London: Verso Publications.

Wimmelbcker, L. (2012). Architecture and city planning projects of the German Democratic Republic in Zanzibar. *Journal of Architecture*, *17*(3), 407–432. https://doi.org/10.1080/13602365.2012.692610

4 Transgressive Design Strategies towards Utopian Urban Vision for Reclaiming Architectural Discourse

Bertug Ozarisoy

Introduction

'Utopia' is a word invented 500 years ago at the start of the modern age as a description of the ideal society by Tomes More. It is composed of Latin parts that taken together mean 'no place' or 'nowhere'.[1] We now use the word utopia to mean an impossible dream of perfection. The New Green Zone of Nicosia recasts the actual world, the changing world we already live in, as utopia – to make the impossible possible, as shown in Figure 4.1. What began as a cooperative community inspired by utopian ideals, is relentlessly put to an end by the powers of nature.[2] Neither utopian ideals nor higher urban visions can withstand the inevitable reality of existence. Our general understanding of the notion of utopia today is a token for a visionary concept of complete political and social ideas on cities (De Man, 1971, 157–161).[3]

In the field of architecture and urbanism, utopias have always been confronted with the same complexities and paradoxes inherent in the search for the translation of a visionary city model.[4] By means of mapping architectural discourse elements, it may well be the philosophy of transgression that provides the most valuable tool to imagine possible futures due to the inherent notion of progress in the discipline, which is naturally linked to the discourse on utopia (Weizman, 2009, 23–25).[5] In fact, the entire discipline is consequently focused on the future from basic process all the way to the inevitable configuration of social and political space (Kraftl & Adey, 2008, 213–231).

Utopia, on the other hand, is a concept we have created to instigate innovation and change; to 'make things happen' (Roberts-Hughes, 2017, 157–168). Within this logical twist, we will be able to find the inseparable connections and the profound differences between society's role in shaping our future and our utopia.[6] Previous scholars mentioned that the future will come regardless; it remains always ahead of us, no matter in which direction we are heading, no matter which path we choose to take.[7] Utopia is always the mirage, like a vision of what may be lying ahead at the end of one of these paths.[8] Considering this argument, it seems logical to refer

DOI: 10.4324/9781003243069-6

Strategies towards Utopian Urban Vision 63

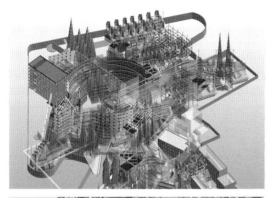

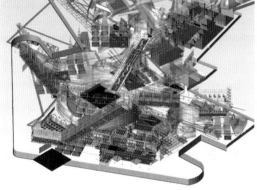

Figure 4.1 A perspective view of a utopian urban vision for Nicosia represents the multicultural interrelations between existing structures and new transgressive design strategies devised in 2110. Image credit: drawn by the author, 2022.

to both terms utopia and future in plural only, because there is actually no singular future but rather myriads which can co-exist in many different future scenarios.[9] Rather than forecasting futures by projecting traces of the past, it would be better to reflect upon our current understanding of global and social dynamics, intellectually grasping the utopian aspects of what we would like our futures to have attempted and to have achieved.[10]

Yet utopias are also created with the intention of changing current patterns of these hyper-complex realities, to indulge in a process of 'objectively' transforming current society from a stable standpoint.[11] Utopia cannot be understood in the restrictive manner of one single solution for all problems, but rather functions as the constant production of utopia; as a key to the door of otherwise unthinkable future scenarios.[12] As we have seen, utopias can only work as a commentary on current issues and on contemporary

64   *Bertug Ozarisoy*

design principles. Yet it lies in human beings to look endlessly for signs of what tomorrow might bring.[13] Utopia offers the possibility to dream, to visualise, to narrate, to imagine the impossible and can therefore develop the power, as a catalyst, to start a process of change.[14] On the contrary, in architectural discourse, where urban visionary strategies are carefully planned and contradictions eliminated, in fact, to achieve a utopian ideal of let us say, harmonic cohabitation in peace, freedom and justice, a set of mandatory rules and definite organizing principles is imperative.[15] Yet with respect to these rules and principles, the borderline force and control, rather than allowing collective happiness to emerge, is an alarming social paradox here; a perfectly beautiful utopia can also gradually degrade into repressive and controlled dystopia (Deluze, 1992, 3–7).[16]

Architectural discourse foresees the city differently in encapsulating an imaginary urban vision of a better place in the future.[17] It offers an insight on inherent demand for change and transformation in the future and past, caries a radical revolutionary impetus: utopia, perhaps as a fundamental change in power or organized structures; or utopia, as a withdrawal from short-term solutions in favour of a comprehensive solution that dramatically shakes the foundation of society.[18] In our study, we are animated by 'Dreams of a Unified Nicosia', and by utopian longings for fulfilment. This anticipatory element and unconscious dimension of the future is what we call the 'not yet conscious'. It illustrates emancipatory moments, which project visions of a better life, that question the organization and structure of life as we know it (Hejduk, 2007, 393–404).

This research strives to bring together today's architectural and urban visions of possible futures that rise above the disillusionment of the present and expand imaginative horizons of urban development potentials, whilst at the same time revealing the conflicts this architecture provokes, and outlines the potential implications for a unified Nicosia in Cyprus (Bowman, 2006, 119–127). In this study, transgressive strategies consider developing urban tactics for Nicosia, both as model as well as method, and can therefore be described as an optimistic process of possible realization in which the determination of the future carefully formulates itself, experimenting with the promise of remaking the city's architectural discourse (Bryant, 2002, 509–530). However, the out-of-reach diasporas featured in this research are, in creating strategies and visions of tomorrow for the city, becoming part of the actual creation of our future to come.

Transgression as a Way of Creating Urban Utopia

Today's cities are characterized by a climate of crisis, the urban community is of a divided and unjust nature and its geography is uneven in every sense.[19] This research predominantly focuses towards implementing transgression in between the contemporary global city, which appears to be increasingly divided and full of limitations; away from subversive acts, which have in themselves already been internalized by the border, conflict and tension and towards an architectural concept where the power lies in the processes of making the limitations visible for the communities, forces and structures of the principles of transgression, as shown in Figure 4.2 (Sassen, 2004, 67–69).[20] In this study, one of the main reasons of creating a new urban utopian vision and identity through the 'Architecture of Transgression' is because this research seeks to accommodate the changes in cultural practice and identity which have occurred in the last 45 years among the Cypriots (Psaltis et al., 2017). At the same time, this utopian urban scenario reveals the history, reclaiming the Green city as it was, to represent our own vision beyond the division (Ozarisoy & Altan, 2017a).

According to architects, urban planners and initiators, the best way of bringing together two communities is by re-reconstruction, revitalization

Figure 4.2 Walls, barricades, sandbags and wires are visible elements of the buffer zone in Nicosia, Cyprus. Image credit: photography by the author, 2022.

and restoration of the existing urban fabric by preserving the old cultural heritage values, bringing peace and harmony to the Cypriots (Ozarisoy & Altan, 2017b).[21] On the other hand, the theory of the 'Architecture of Transgression' looks at the other side of the image by taking into account the multidisciplinary role of changes in ethnic cultures and practices since the conflict.[22] At the same time 'transgression' follows the traces of cultural practices from before and adapts it into its new no-man's land character.[23]

Transgression is an action which involves the limit – that narrow zone of a line where it displays the flash of its passage – but perhaps also its entire trajectory, even its origin; it is likely that transgression has its entire space in the line it crosses.[24] Transgression happens in the infinitely narrow space defined by the limit that separates two worlds. The division line, though, must be traversable to be transgressed.[25] From violence to conflict, regardless of the power, the border between them has to be penetrable (Loizides, 2011, 391–401). If it were uncrossable, the unification as such would not exist.[26] The philosophical underpinning of the term of 'transgression' comes out of the possibility of crossing from one side to another, merging one substance with the other two opposite states (Miessen, 2007, 35–36).[27]

In his chapter 'De-, Dis-, Ex-', Bernard Tschumi acknowledges a parallel condition in architecture, arguing that the cities are the places of dispersion and disjunction of many often-invisible systems.[28] He refers to Foucault in relation to what Tschumi calls the 'essential disjunction' that exists in the process of architectural production. Tschumi's continuing strategy has been to turn these dispersions and complexities into advantages (Hadjipavlou, 2007, 53–73). He argues that the architect's ability to see the underlying dispersions as new regularities of an urban context can contribute towards finding a new creative solution for a particular problem in urban design.[29]

We were inspired by the ideas of Tschumi where he advises how problems and disadvantages caused by architects to the community can be transformed into an advantage by an architect (Lohtaja, 2021, 499–515). Drawing from the ideology of Tschumi, we went on to form our own idea of transforming the present chaotic urban planning and architecture of Nicosia City into our visionary utopian urban 'exchange', as shown in Figure 4.3. Foucault mentions that 'the role of the architect is restricted to large-scale movements in cities, public spaces and institutions rather than the private space of individuals' (Amini-Behbahani, 2016, 348–374). But what about the architects who choose to be transgressive? Drawing from Foucault's arguments, the position of an architecture as transgressive is undoubtedly complex, multilayered and, at times, a complete contradiction.[30]

Architecture, it seemed to us then and now, has become so obsessed with novel forms that the consideration of space as the real medium of architecture had sunk to envisage new urban visions.[31] How to redefine it in some abstract way? Clearly, it involves bringing together only the idea of the 'Architecture of Transgression' necessary to vividly define a desired space.[32] Making the task more difficult, the desired space, or set of spaces in the field

Strategies towards Utopian Urban Vision 67

Figure 4.3 The utopian urban vision of Nicosia sits on the grounds of collecting memories, narratives and cultural diasporas to disseminate storytelling of transgressive design strategies devised in 2110. The superstructure architectural elements represent the power and wealth of the city in conjunction with reclaiming its architectural discourse. Image credit: drawn by the author, 2022.

can be anything but reductive because it must embody spaces in the complex variants of continuous transformation.[33] From our point of view, architecture is also a technology depending on how it is used (Lending, 2018, 797–819). We are not demonising architecture but only want to stress that many times it is hardly innocent.[34] We are also strong believers that the boundaries and powers of architecture extend well beyond those physical spaces that have been designed and built by architects but also are embodied by spaces that end up more or less de facto (restrictions) in the urban environment; these would be seemingly inconsequential architectures, conflict spaces and default containers of power.[35]

In this research context, the abstract term of transgression addresses a world that, in a sense, is a prelude to the present one, a world in transition from the dialectical to the mesological order (Haddad, 2009). The dialectical world is a conflictual one, with different forces contending not for dominance so much as position (Lameira, 2021, 1163–1196). In the dialectical relationship, each side needs its opposite, which is the perquisite for choosing the architecture of transgression as a communication tool.[36] The aim of contention is not to destroy the opposition, but to find parity with it, to 'co-exist' (Mumford, 237–254). The methodology and its rationale seem from the present perspective to have been more than prophetic of global tendency.[37] In sharp contrast, the term of violence and conflict in this research still looks for the dialectic, for the possibility of creative dialogue between opposing forces and, most especially, between destruction and construction as equally vital elements of existence.

The City of Nicosia as Base Case Urban Scenario Development

Cyprus is positioned on the main route for travel and trade between the Middle East and Africa.[38] Due to its geopolitical position, Cyprus has been ruled by different civilizations – Lusignan, Venetians, Ottomans and the British Empire throughout the centuries (Cogaloglu & Turkan, 2019, 381–388). The present-day capital of Cyprus sits in the middle of the Mesoarial plain nestled between the Kyrenia mountain range and the Troodos Massif to the south.[39] It is a cosmopolitan and multicultural city. Nicosia has gained its identity of trade and agriculture going back centuries through the river Pedieos which runs across its centre (Lacher & Kaymak, 2005, 147–166).

Therefore, it had always been the first production destination of agriculture because of the water from the river Pedieos.[40] Beyond this rich historical character and cultural identity, Nicosia is the last divided capital in Europe today. This traumatic condition of the city brings us into focus with the current situation, where for 45 years they have been forced to live separate from each other (Turkish and Greek Cypriots) whereas before they always lived and mixed with each other throughout the island.[41] Hence it has remained the capital of Cyprus to this day where all the administration of culture, education, law and politics take place, as shown in Figure 4.4.

Strategies towards Utopian Urban Vision 69

Figure 4.4 The Buffer zone divides the urban historic core into two separate sectors – Turkish and Greek Cypriots. The route line demonstrates the highest flow of people in Southern Nicosia, which is due to become a vibrant point of many architectural and cultural discourses in the last decades. Image credit: drawn by the author, 2022.

70 *Bertug Ozarisoy*

It has a diverse architecture as it has preserved the old architectural aesthetic beauty belonging to different civilisations which has ruled it throughout history (Sertoglu & Ozturk, 2003, 54–70). It has been the main architectural epicentre with its architecture, trade and transportation of goods along the historic Silk Road.[42]

Nicosia is divided into two separate sectors (Turkish and Greek) using the traces of the river Pedieos which does not exist anymore.[43] Instead of the river, there is now a long street that has developed organically with its powerful architectural characteristic (Bryant, 2014, 681–697). This power considers the main commercial district of the city where the Cypriots and other nationalities use this district as the main centre of the walled city (Vural & Ozuyanik, 2008, 133–154). During the conflict in Cyprus, the United Nations Buffer Zone took over this part of the city, and it has since been in their control with no inhabitants living there (Anthias, 2009, 176–194).[44] This has turned into a no-man's land called the 'buffer zone' (Hughes-Wilson, 2011, 84–93). This space contains barricades, walls, wires, watchtowers and checkpoints. This forms the scene of military architecture, where the military is the main acting power (Heraclides, 2011, 117–139). But as the architecture has been left to itself, nature has been allowed to take its course with decayed buildings invaded by shrubs and trees, leftover spaces overgrown with different types of vegetation. This self-made, untouched nature reserve has provided unlimited resting and nesting space for different types of birds on their migration routes (Papadakis, 2004, 15–27). Hence, this has led to the bird's multiplication without disturbance by outside factors. This unique and architectural creation out of all the misery of conflict is beyond the natural beauty of the city (Deckers, 2005, 155–181). As Nicosia is a source of multi-diverse cultural identities, it develops in an organic form and allows us to see traces from all cultures in a peaceful environment until the division and creation of the United Nations Buffer Zone. Today the buffer zone (no-man's land) adds another natural diversity to the city.

A Representational Diaspora and Language of the Green Zone

The United Nations Buffer Zone today represents a space which is under military rule, an authorised separation both physically and politically of the Cypriot community (Turkish and Greek Cypriots), a space filled with military watchtowers that is out of bounds for the Cypriot people, as shown in Figure 4.5.[45] This military power has taken over the architectural identity of the city by replacing it with watchtowers, inside and outside and on top of existing buildings (Thompson et al., 2004, 282–299). At the same time, adding its own fabrications of walls with holes in front of these buildings, barrels and barbed wire outside the buildings (Given, 2002, 1–22). In the leftover space, the United Nations added their own watchtowers to enable them to observe the buffer zone 24 hours a day. This has led to the measurable impact of dramatic change in the architectural and cultural

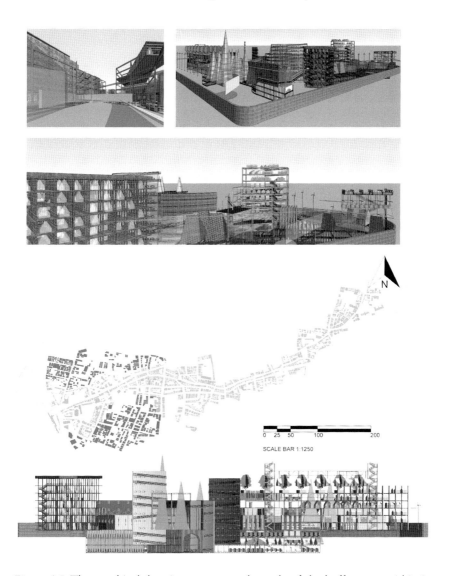

Figure 4.5 The graphical drawing represents the scale of the buffer zone within its buildings in Nicosia, Cyprus. Image credit: drawn by the author, 2022.

image of the city; hence, the Cypriot identity has been almost abolished in this space.

This physical change caused by the intervention of military power has left voids and abundant buildings just next to the Green Line, providing an opportunity for the creation of informal settlement areas along the Green Line by different ethnic migrant communities (Ghilardi et al., 2015,

72 *Bertug Ozarisoy*

184–201). This shows that in spite of the isolation of the Cypriot community, other cultures have been able to migrate and take over this abandoned area and give rise to different types of cultures hence replacing the original Cypriot culture of 45 years, changing the diaspora of the buffer zone (Loizides & Antoniades, 2010, 37–41).[46] This shows, that in spite of the forced isolation of the Cypriot community from the buffer zone and from each other, instead of having an isolated sterile area with no life of its own, these outside ethnic communities have been able to migrate and accommodate this abandoned area and create a different cultural practice and language replacing the original Cypriot culture hence causing a change in the diaspora of the buffer zone.[47]

We need a new word for the United Nations Buffer Zone. Its name is so laden with its past that when we try to postulate a present buffer zone that may extend into an unforeseen future, we are flung backwards. In fact, the more we try to project forward, the more others will remind us of what the United Nations Buffer Zone has been and ought to be (Faustmann, 2008, 453–458). The word 'United Nations Buffer Zone' possesses an inverse elasticity of meaning in relation to radical vision. Is there any future in the world of the United Nations Buffer Zone? The work presented in this research is thus an invitation to undertake a critical architectural and political thought experiment: let's think about the current conditions of the world from the perspective of Cypriots; let's think of today's struggles, not from the point of view of conflict, but from that of a continued struggle of 'Unification'.

Scoping the Field

This research is neither a single perspective of the idea of creative possibilities of conditions nor a unified narrative; it is made of architectural investigations on different scales, locations, with different intensities and speeds. By extracting a selection of theoretical research and spatial experience of the context, it attempts to elaborate on several key concepts informing the overall transgressive design strategies for Nicosia, Cyprus. The concepts in this research should be understood as a set of architectural fables speculating about the seemingly impossible, the actual transformation of the structures of domination.[48] It is thus also, and fundamentally so, an invitation to rethink the problem of political subjectivity not from the point of view of a 'Unify Nicosia' conception of a local citizen but rather from the point of view of 'Transgression' and 'Power'.[49]

Before discussing the theoretical framework of the research and narrating the development of transgressive design strategies, an exploratory introduction is needed to scope the field of this study by capturing a number of key indications about how critical design, architecture and creative ideas are likely to evolve in the future, through political cycles and in the wake of current policies and programs.[50] As 'critical design' is the primary reference adopted throughout the literature, studies were undertaken in urban utopia, architectural discourse and transgression at the level of theoretical underpinnings and creative direction (Sheil, 2005, 20–32). It seems to be that it is necessary to explore and envision how design itself might evolve in the future, towards different organisational models, towards an increasingly diverse and differentiating role in addressing visionary urban development ideas and towards its very own future scenarios.[51]

Additionally, the role of design intervention in the city is the object of close examination and deep analysis in countless academic and professional references; therefore, all desk research, archival studies, photographic documentation thorough field studies and computational visual techniques in this subject can offer a rich, textured image of the working mechanisms that regulate relationships across the field, taking into consideration the viewpoints of different layers of case study location. Available historical data range from studies of the conflict between two communities to qualitative action research for change among communities, with direct, co-creative participation of citizens. From this wealth of consolidated information, by cross-referencing visual diagrams based on research questions, it is possible to form a preliminary critical opinion regarding the term of 'The Architecture of Transgression' in the development of utopian urban vision for Nicosia.[52] This statement would be the ideal platform from which to elaborate insights to the future (Faustino, 2013, 120–123).

This research was conducted on the practice of a combination of architectural elements and a theoretical study on several key concepts on the 'United Nations Buffer Zone'. The mapping of both visible and invisible architectural elements aimed to use spatial practice as a form of visionary urban development strategy to implement transgressive design strategies for policy making decisions in urban planning. Notably, there are not many precedents for the idea of a transgression and power beyond 'Unification', but there were many young practitioners from the region and many internationals that were eager to take part. The key principle of utopian urban vision was established with the aim of engaging with a complex set of architectural problems centred on one of the most difficult dilemmas of conflict: how to act both propositionally and critically in an environment in which the political force fields, as complex as they may be, are so dramatically skewed. Are imaginary urban design interventions at all possible? How could spatial practice within the here and now of the conflict over the United Nations Buffer Zone negotiate the existence of institutions and their spatial realities? How can we define an architectural discourse that is both critical and transformative?

A Manifesto: Mapping Invisibility to Define a Utopian Urban Vision for Nicosia

The conceptual mapping of Nicosia has multiple entry points and demands negotiation for a way through a labyrinthine path to find a new terminology

74 *Bertug Ozarisoy*

for the United Nations Buffer Zone.[53] This research attempts a new reading and narration of mapped reality beyond invisibility (Stepnik, 2020, 127). It seeks to activate the space around and between the collective memories and to create, through a renegotiation of the memories, a new topography of perceptual possibilities. This renegotiation is particularly important today. The outcome of the research points out that historical time is again the essence, only that this historical time is not linear and undefined steady progress imagined by Cypriots, but a multitude of competing and overlapping memories.

The movement of Cypriots inscribes an assemblage of relations in their effective becoming and maps the passage of deterritorialisation as seen in this research process, as shown in Figure 4.6. This research shows how time has changed on the map of the city; its somewhat haphazard structure mirrors the puzzle that the city has become. This mapping methodology is evident for our utopian vision, an important survey in terms of the remapping of the city both architecturally and figuratively to represent the diaspora of the city beyond division. Maps which are central to the colonial and post-colonial projects are re-envisioned in this research which moves beyond the presentation of the city as being fixed, frozen in time and continually bleeding its timelessness.[54]

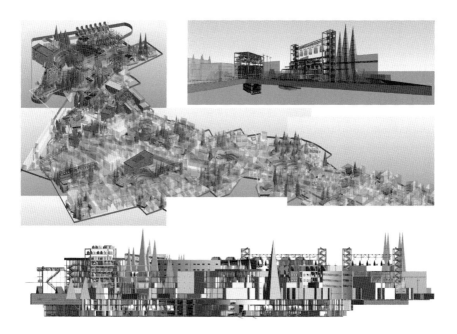

Figure 4.6 The map of utopian urban vision of the buffer zone, Nicosia. The map illustrates different transgressive design strategies devised to reunite local citizens in engaging with various social and commercial activities throughout the Green Line. Image credit: drawn by the author, 2022.

The mapping of invisibility looks from the perspective that there has been little attempt to think through the importance of the United Nations Buffer Zone as a trans-locational space: that is, one where interculturally, movement and flow have been important aspects of social reality. In particular, the urban utopian vision has represented the city in terms that look beyond a static nationalism or as a site of permanent wounding. The Green Zone hints instead at an underlying ambiguity of the space and presents an openness that addresses the shifts away from the cultural binaries that are implicit in traditional narratives of the capital.

Mapping the Notion of Transgression and Vice Versa

Mapping the invisibility of the city seeks to find how we attach ourselves to our historic and cultural norms to consider our own perception and illusions when reality is reflected in a thousand other ways. What has appeared in this world and the next will disappear, and that which has disappeared on one level will reappear on another in a different form. In conjunction with exploring interrelations between the transgressions and architectural discourse through mapping several layers of the city, we aimed to understand the invisible and what is visible that reflects where we are in time and space and consciousness.[55] Perhaps architecture is a means of identification with reality, of making the invisible visible, sounds taking form sound shaping consciousness, refracted light revealing our delirium and desire, our world shaped by the word.[56] Our journeys take us into the territory of the imagination of several materialised ideas mapping the invisible elements for utopian urban scenario developments.

The aim of these mappings was to carry out urban and scientific analysis of the case study location from past to future in order to understand its support of our theory of utopian vision for the city of Nicosia. Instead of using traditional urban design principles, artistic drawings have been used as tools to configure this theory of utopian vision. In our mapping's theory, we defined that the river Pedieos was reclaimed. The frame found on every map symbolises or incorporates the architectural character of the old city of Nicosia as it was before. This frame also acts as an urban catalyst to bring together all the diaspora passing through it to form the multicultural diversity beyond the division of the current state of the city.

From the research of our field trip to Cyprus, we have experienced first-hand how the city of Nicosia had changed dramatically since the division of the island. Beyond this change, we gathered data on its cultural process showing how every civilisation which ruled it left its traces in Nicosia City. In order to understand the chronology of the collected data, we devised a methodology for a mapping technique. This technique is not a traditional urban analysis but a conceptual representation of that particular part of Nicosia. This representation entails various issues and elements which creates the scene for critical thinking in developing our utopian urban vision.

In this cultural mapping, we created a frame which will be placed in all the maps and as we previously mentioned that it will act as an urban catalyst for all different cultural diasporas passing through it. The name of this frame is the catalyst in and around the peripheries of the case study location. In a layered form, it all fits into this frame and forms the theory for our utopian urban vision which materialises in the last layer.

To create our urban vision, we have chosen the United Nations Buffer Zone of the (divided) capital of Cyprus as a base case scenario for development. In the buffer zone, we selected certain spaces of importance to symbolise culture, military, nature, transition routes, nodes and edges of the city, medieval walls and bastions, historic and existing agricultural lands in order to trace all these variables onto our urban mapping strategies. The above-mentioned cultural diasporas were divided into grids (as in urban planning), and these grids can fit into the frame individually or all together. This grid system will act as a network for the design of the urban utopian vision across entailing different perimeters within the city. These grids are connected to each other with green routes which are used for transportation and networking of data. In these grids the agricultural fields are placed horizontally and vertically resulting in a form of agricultural tower. Also, there is a marketplace in each grid to represent unification of the city as a metaphor.

The Key Design Principles of Creating an Urban Utopia

The old preserved fortifications of Nicosia and the river Pedieos are now home to a rich and diverse set of functions. Some typical – neighborhood living, multicultural streets and historic urban quarters. The ambition is to transform and connect these varied spaces in such a way that one utopia of 'Green Zone': an invisible one unified city, as shown in Figure 4.7. The inhabitants of the city gradually evolve a new 'Green Religion', which fortifies them psychologically from the unpredictable forces of nature. Created from the wreckage of the old city, the new settlement is formed from a palimpsest of reorganised debris, rituals and the ordinary requirements of daily urban life. Through time, the use of the revealing multilayered traces of the city has changed from merely telling us to a more diverse urban function, which has now focused completely on 'Green Zone' – both for the residents of Nicosia and for visitors. The monumental value of the existing structures is dependent on beauty, uniqueness and the role they play in the narrative of the city.[57] Although everyone sees the buffer zone primarily as a green space, its monumental value is almost completely derived from its physical and storytelling of its historic character. In many cases, the green functions as a generic backdrop for these monuments. A more monumental approach to the re-bringing of urban agriculture fields and accommodating bird towers will lead to a more diverse mix of monuments.

Strategies towards Utopian Urban Vision 77

Figure 4.7 In 2110, new routes will represent the multicultural diversity of the city. All cultural norms will be transgressed between existing physical structures and newly devised superstructure architectural elements. Image credit: drawn by the author, 2022.

Once the urban agricultural fields along the mature vegetation of the buffer zone are connected, they transform into not only a linear system but a triangular one. The creation of this network will change presently isolated neighbourhood spaces into integral parts of the city. This 'Green Zone' will be a full circle connection that lets people and ecology circumnavigate the city. The methodology for this transformation follows four themes: maximum diversity, intuitive navigation, cosmopolitan nature and free space. The utopian 'Green Zone' is designed to stimulate diversity of life and variety of use in one continuous green loop – its layout is tailored for residents of various backgrounds. Seen from afar, the buffer zone will be a 'Green Zone' around the city centre, and a continuous ribbon form of the backbone of the old walled city, as shown in Figure 4.8. It is recognizable and always present, composed of the River Pedieos (water reservoir) and extensive vegetation of the city, with routes and trails the connecting elements. Next to this ribbon are the individual spaces with their differences enhanced – resulting in a 'multi-colored' Nicosia.[58]

The utopian 'Green Zone' holds a different ideology about how people move through the urban agricultural fields and how they can obtain, process and generate information. The 'Green Zone' with a route system

Figure 4.8 The longitudinal section of utopian urban vision demonstrates the hybrid elements of transgressive strategies devised to unite all Cypriots. The city of agriculture design principle brings a diverse environment to the city in 2110. Image credit: drawn by the author, 2022.

that is obvious and intuitive appeals to people's innate sense for direction. All the routes are accompanied by water or natural elements. The urban agricultural fields path system does not pass directly through the existing abandoned buildings but links them together with new routes. There is one route that is ideal for transportation and trade of products. This route is composed of broad walks, major production lines and places to create your own space for free. Another route is quieter, more natural. There is of course also the route over the water, as shown in Figure 4.9. As the time of day, the weather, or mood changes, people can meander along a path of their preference.

The location and shape of the buffer zone and the manner in which it connects to a network of other green structures allows nature to move deep within the city. The key is to relink the natural flow of flora and fauna and optimise movements between city and country. Additionally, these links can extend beyond the microclimate, and the flow of nature can become truly international. The renowned space acts as a botanical condenser, making sure species from all over the world find their way to the right agricultural fields and conditions in the 'Green Zone', as shown in Figure 4.10. A series of spectacular agriculture towers through the city of Nicosia 'echo' the special planting inside the agricultural lands. A new composition of agriculture and bird towers will redefine the skyline of Nicosia making the 'Green

Strategies towards Utopian Urban Vision 79

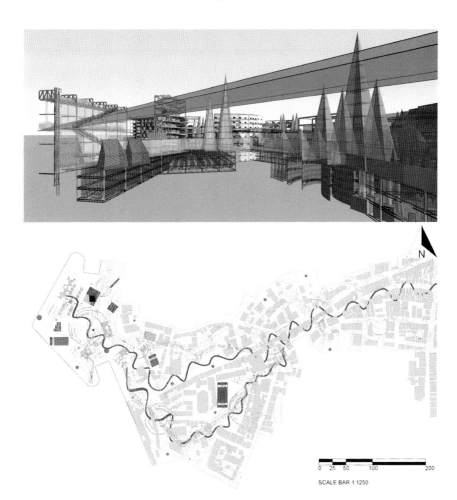

Figure 4.9 The institutional power of the diaspora is located through the life cycle of River Pedieos. The image represents the importance of the flow of existing natural elements into bringing diverse community engagements for the local citizens and international visitors. Image credit: drawn by the author, 2022.

Zone' visible from the Pentaklythos (mountains) in the heart of the city and from many of the tall buildings around the centre.[59]

The 'Green Zone' is not a regular project – it is a rather abstract ideal, shared by many citizens of Nicosia. The ideal can be seen as a comprehensive cloud of ideas and ambitions, a complex sequence of do's and don'ts (Foucault, 1977, 35).[60] The residents of Nicosia are enthusiastic about the utopian urban vision of the 'Green Zone' project and will aid in creating

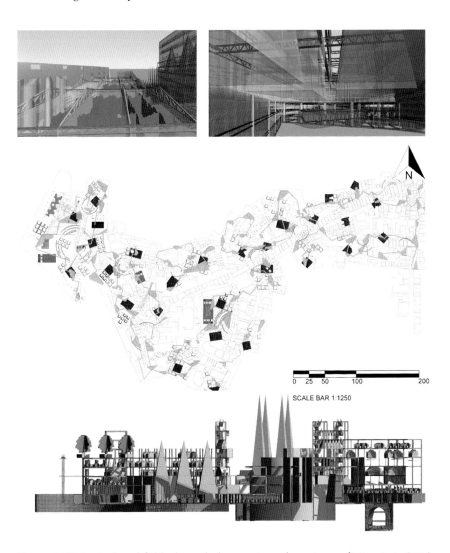

Figure 4.10 Agricultural fields through the utopian urban vision of Nicosia in 2110. Over time, the structural foundations will be grassed over, creating an embossed jade-green canvas. Image credit: drawn by the author, 2022.

a tailor-made green space for the larger community. To give the inner city breathing space, not everything should be planned and fixed in the buffer zone at one time. Each area within the boundaries of the 'Green Zone' has different users. They will be involved as much as possible by 'organising circles'. Each circle adopts a park area and selects the most viable programming functions and features for the space. Eventually a diverse, vibrant and unified Nicosia emerges.

Cultural Diasporas for Identifying Main Design Principles of an Urban Utopia

Revealing agriculture is an archetype; anecdotally, this is not a new cultural practice for the Cypriots – as said before, this is inbred in their culture.[61] The new design possibility offers grid-form agricultural lands which transgress to the organic form of the city, and these grid forms of lands are spread across the whole of the 'Green Zone' horizontally and vertically, as shown in Figure 4.11. At the same time, each grid zone is represented by aggressive line drawing. This shows us the intensity of cultivation and the hybridization of the Cypriot culture.[62] But each urban agriculture field is connected to each other by green routes which are used to transport and trade the produce of goods from one grid zone to the other. At the centre of the 'Green Zone' we design a goods yard.

This place is the centre of the showplace of all the goods produced and cultivated in other grid zones. This yard today is known as the 'Ledras Street Crossing Check-Point' where the movement of the Cypriot people is

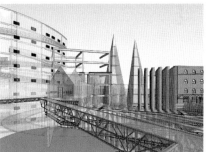

Figure 4.11 The combination of horizontal routes on the ground and vertical tower systems will accommodate future local citizens in the periphery of the buffer zone. The image represents the unification of the city that could be possible with effective transgressive strategies in 2110. Image credit: drawn by the author, 2022.

82 Bertug Ozarisoy

the highest. This is our new utopian urban vision of the city. These movements extend through other urban agricultural lands in the 'Green Zone'. On the same level of the agricultural grids there are 'Bird Towers' which are meant for birds to use as stopping ports on their migration route to nest and deposit seeds which will enable the agricultural lands to enrich and flourish with different types of flora continuously. We built 'Bird Towers' because urban agriculture is a long-term strategy for 'Unification', and 'Bird Towers' are used as a support for this creative possibility, as birds symbolize 'Peace'.

City of Agriculture: Cultivating Green Communities

Agriculture has played a defining role in the historical cause of much conflict and dispute over land ownership throughout the centuries.[63] Land reform programs designed to redistribute possession and the use of geographic land is one characteristic of the strategic role agricultural potential has on the development of our communities.[64] Agriculture in Cyprus went through a period of change to cater to an increased demand for food caused by a rapidly growing population in the 18th century.[65] The excessive flooding of the river Pedieos and unrest through Cyprus prevented all trade, consequently forcing Nicosia City to increase its food production or face the threat of starvation. The prices of food rose rapidly throughout the country, increasing profitability and encouraging an expansion of agricultural production.[66] Small villages that had previously been self-sufficient began to look at producing food for a wider market. Changes ensued, and a new capitalist business ethic encouraged farmers throughout Nicosia to grow new crops such as potatoes, red clover and turnips for the first time.[67] Food production encouraged farmers and communities to become more confident in self-sufficiency. Settlements and the hinterlands of local population areas were thus extended, allowing more farmers to produce the market.[68] The steel structure, topped with a working agricultural land, brings the farm back to the city by stretching it, concertina-like. The scheme concentrates on the notion of urban farming and attempts to make the unified city more sustainable by slashing the distances needed to transport produce to the store, as shown in Figure 4.12.

The utopian urban vision can cultivate social action, helping the community social enterprises to deliver public services. This can entail forming an agriculture cooperative where Cypriot people can all collaborate in the working of the agricultural fields from seed to the trading of the harvested produce. These agricultural fields will always need extra labour for activation. This labour force will be supplied by the ethnic immigrant workforce who will be coming into Nicosia seasonally. This collaboration between these communities of diverse culture practices can lead to their transgression of their own identity resulting in a homogenous and stronger identity. Beyond this, alteration of the Cypriot identity will lead to increase of the green spaces ratio of Nicosia City resulting in climate change of more humidity, more rainfall, clean atmospheric air with breeze and lower summer temperatures making

Strategies towards Utopian Urban Vision 83

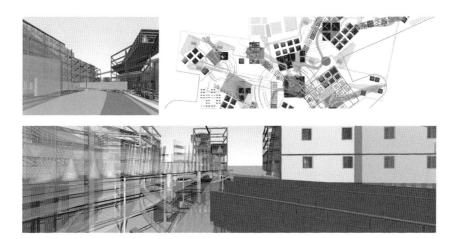

Figure 4.12 In the development of a utopian urban vision, megastructures will have enabled us to reclaim agricultural elements of the city just before the division of the island. The image demonstrates the food harvesting in and around the new physical structures in 2110. Image credit: drawn by the author, 2022.

Nicosia liveable as it was before (just like rebirth of the old green Nicosia City). At the same time Nicosia will be saved from being a dry and unproductive city being used just by the civil servants into a city of agriculture which is self-supporting as well as supplying the rest of the island.

City of Trees: Celebrating Annual Food Festival

In the design of the urban utopian vision for the Green Zone, there is space for fruit trees to grow, such as, oranges, grapefruits, lemons, figs, etc. The aim of growing these types of trees in these spaces is to counteract the force of the wild natural habitat in the Green Zone around these grids. In these grids, these trees are side by side with other diasporas and all interconnect to form a more diverse and colourful habitat, as shown in Figure 4.13. At the same time, the growing of these trees will add to the climate change which will lead to environmentally cleaner air, more rainfall and humidity and decrease in the temperature of the surrounding city during the summer.

From the harvesting of these different types of seasonal fruit trees – fruit festivals will be held on different dates according to the type of the harvest which will lead to having event days more than just once a year. On these event days, the harvested fruits are processed into jams, preserves, sweets, etc. by the women holding workshops to show the making of these traditional foods and help to continue the preservation of the Cypriot culture,[69]

84 Bertug Ozarisoy

Figure 4.13 Exploring vertical densities for agriculture and mixed-use programmes. The image illustrates that agricultural fields will have converted the city as a botanical condenser in 2110. Image credit: drawn by the author, 2022.

at the same time contributing to the local economy. This will also provide employment opportunities to the young local Cypriots. Hence people will be cooperating, participating and interchanging trade (cultural crossing) which will help in the formation of the hybridity among Cypriots. These types of inter-communal activities among the Cypriots will lead to the regeneration and reclamation of some of the lost Cypriot culture, which as mentioned before, had been eroded by globalisation.[70]

City of Birds: Echoes from the Green Zone

In the design of the urban utopian vision for the Green Zone, there are grids in which bird towers of different heights and dimensions are placed to provide extra space beside the existing spaces of natural habitat of the Green Zone for the birds on their migration routes to nest, breed and rest, as shown in Figure 4.14. These bird towers are designed like pyramids to symbolize power and placed together as a colony to represent the idea of a hybrid community living.[71] As it is already known, birds have been part of the Cypriot culture since medieval civilizations in using birds for communication and sending of peace messages to each other. At the same time, birds have been part of the domestic Cypriot culture where holes or wooden boxes were placed in the outside of the walls of houses to

Strategies towards Utopian Urban Vision 85

Figure 4.14 Existing military watchtowers will have brought a new way of life to the city in 2110. The image represents global citizens and local communities; global networks for social integration and ethnic diversity; inverted to accommodate more global citizens in the periphery of the buffer zone. Image credit: drawn by the author, 2022.

accommodate them and were used for their domestic consumption. The many diversities of birds in the utopian urban vision change the atmosphere due to their different exotic signings and create echoes from the Green Zone.

The bird towers symbolise the monumental representation of the city as they are visible objects and are seen from all angles.[72] The bird towers are placed at different angles to each other so that every bird song is reflected and echoed to produce different types of sounds. These sounds echo the traces of a multicultural city, conflict and division and create a feeling of yearning for peace among its inhabitants, the Cypriot people. These echoes also represent the storytelling of people, the voice of the muezzin (religious role) calling people to pray, the sounds of bells from the church and the first day of opening of the border.[73]

City of Watchtowers: Reinhabit Birds

In the design of the urban utopian vision for the Green Zone in the grids, we designed watchtowers for our utopian urban vision because we were inspired by the now existing abundant watchtowers which were originally meant to be used by the United Nations for military purposes but are now abandoned and are being used by the migrating birds on their migration routes for nesting and resting. The watchtowers which we have designed for our urban utopian vision are movable structures as their use is meant to be flexible. They could be used as bird watchtowers for the event of nature reserve bird watching during the time of birds stopping in the Green Zone on their migration route. For this event, visitors will be attending from all over the world. They would also be used as watchtowers during the food harvesting, for the efficient transportation of the harvested produce as the controllers of this transportation on the watchtowers will be directing the traffic of transportation from above.

During the food festivals they could be used as methods of transport to ease the intensity of traffic on the routes. This will be achieved by the watchtowers being attached to the main route acting as a connector between the routes through which people will be passing. As these watchtowers would be movable, they could be moved to any strategic point at any time and act as a control mechanism to check the condition of the natural habitat (birds, flora and trees). In the Green Zone these watchtowers represent the power of the supreme court of the city as they act as a catalyst by being able to be attached to any of the other diasporas in the grid and control these diasporas.[74] This control can be like legislative agencies which decide what the function of each grid is.

Utopia Versus a New Green Zone

The story of our manipulations and desires, however, is preeminently the Green Zone of the city. That story is also the best way to help Cypriots understand the value of nature and landscape because they reflect our society. The revealing history and multicultural traces of the city provide much insight into our culture's interaction with nature and landscape, the relationship that it maintains and the common future ahead of us.

Our time urgently requires a context that is more than just a visual experience.[75] Perception of landscape and nature is a complex cultural process of movement and well-being, sometimes even of uneasiness and the sense of being out of place.[76] The meaning of place is determined by one's memory, which is also triggered by subconscious sensations. After all, the definition of culture is complex and closely connected with the landscape of the 'Green Zone'. First, culture may be described as the paradoxical manner to treat the existing physical environment, deliberately trying to transform it.[77] The new vision imposes order upon wilderness, while ironically to the rebirth of the river Pedieos, it is within wildness and disorder that the re-reconstruction of the city is hidden. In addition, culture is the way in which Cypriot identity shapes itself as a product of that nature: handling its own body sometimes in extremes. Further to that, culture is the manner in which Cypriots deal with their rural way of living background and shared thought and norms. This environment is partly the result of their self-invented rules, practices and rituals regarding nature, wilderness, city and landscape.

From this point of view, culture is creating something: it is a production of multilayered history; but culture is also expressing thoughts: it is a memory of representation as well as the contribution of different meanings, and acts are always being considered.[78] The diaspora of the Green Zone is supposed to be a catalyst itself, a field of change, while always taking the landscape as the lens of ideas, acts, concepts and visions. Green Zone will continue to be an arena of social, political, personal and cultural battles with differences of opinion.[79] In this way, the diaspora of the architecture of transgression generates the production of culture: it commends acts by hybridised Cypriots that reshape the city, producing a peaceful environment for future generations. The Green Zone also seeks an understanding with nature that is at the same time an agony to deal with memories.[80] It is impossible to think about Cypriot culture and identity without considering the relationship we have with nature and the landscape surrounding us. Therefore, it is also unthinkable without hybridisation. This requires not only unification, but also direction for new movements.

All the above dimensions represent the different diaspora of the city (city of agriculture, city of trees, city of birds and city of watchtowers), and the connectors connecting them to each other represent political and military power, conflict and unification. Beyond this representation, these connectors also act as a catalyst to form a complete city which consists of plaques very close to each other reflecting the multicultural diversity of the city. At the same time, the lines which represent the connecting routes cross each other to form junctions where cultural practice among Cypriots takes place with the other ethnic subcultures around them interconnecting with them. This shows how multicultural Nicosia City has been transformed by implementing transgressive urban design strategies into the reconciliation processes in Cyprus.

Conclusions

This research combines ways of using practice to provoke architectural discourse to reveal itself and act upon it. Instead, through creative possibilities of conditions in architecture, we sought critical proximity. This research seeks to inhabit the subject of the 'transgression and power' to enter, so to speak, into the respective idea of 'Unification' to become part of the awakening of invisible forces that shapes our environment. Although the form of research and practice is collective, relational and active, it would be beneficial to think of it as 'catalyst'. It does not work in an ameliorative manner; it has never proposed the kind of radical reconstruction of architecture. It seeks to respond worldwide as a solution to alleviate conflict.

88 *Bertug Ozarisoy*

It does not use architecture to reveal the existing hierarchy of the city or rebuild it. Rather it has sought to establish a different balance between withdrawal and engagement, action in the world and research, fiction and proposal. This research should be interpreted as an attempt to articulate an architectural utopia as a hybrid policy making tool to devise future urban scenarios for Nicosia. This practice is not reactive to dominant forms of power; it has a different vision.

In a place like the United Nations Buffer Zone, there is a risk of it becoming dependent on the frenetic rush of mainstream reporting. This research envisions the practice instead as an attempt to produce a space from which it is possible to operate in the here and now but with critical long-term transformative urban visions. Architectural proposals are a form of fiction. Their effects could be the opening of imagination. This research aims to find a place for architecture to act in the world and not in the service of a preexisting agenda. The critical thinking of architecture has materialized in both built and political space, and in the cultural collective imagination of designing transgressive urban visions in conjunction with sociocultural paradox.

A quest for what is in between: between two worlds, future and past, social and marginal, private and public, unspeakable and expressed. Between the world of seeing, doing, standards and uses and dreams, fantasies and psyche.[81] Like the storytelling and never-ending route of the utopian urban vision of Nicosia. This space in between creates a hybrid environment as well as a desire beyond the division of the city. It is both a connecting space between the visible and the invisible, and a connection from established rules for 'unification'.[82] This notion of the space in between is being developed through diasporas in the utopian urban vision of Nicosia.

In creating the utopian urban vision, several series of design principles were used to form different layers of strategies (the existing urban layout, traces of the river Pedieos, conflict, the grid, public spaces, green route, new urban layout and diasporas). These strategies define the concept of invisibility behind visibility.[83] At the same time confronting our theory of how using the past and the present situation of Nicosia, enables one to visualise the future – the utopian urban vision. In the attempt of designing this scenario, we used the traces of the past and narratives from the mapping strategies developed throughout this study as a foundation to construct a utopia. This approach enabled us to transgress the philosophy of utopian terminology beyond the division of cities.

Transgression suggests operating beyond accepted norms and radically reinterpreting practice by pushing the boundaries of both what the architectural value of the context is, and what it could or even should be.[84] In this context, the current crisis and accompanying political/social unrest have exacerbated the difficulty into which architecture and urban strategy has long been disseminated in accordance with cultural norms and physical barriers. Challenged by a culture of practice, identity is in danger of losing its praised status as one of the prominent visions of the city. Transgression would open up new possibilities for reconstruction of the Cypriot society.[85]

Our key point here is to suggest that the spirit of transgression is required and arises in periods of processing diasporas of the city where the old ways need better solutions rather than radical practices and new potential future paths are chartered. The transgressive strategy needs to be supplemented by a utopia that is able to develop a new viable paradigm that might eventually mature to replace the prior mainstream practice, and to take on the responsibility of advancing global best practice in the Green Line with the new social demands and opportunities. The buffer zone design of a utopian urban vision for Nicosia did not embrace a realistic approach to revitalise the city for Cypriots use.[86] Two concluding counterpoints manifest, namely that transgressions are only productive during revolutionary periods at the beginning of a major cycle of innovation, and that in order to be productive, transgressions must remain within the discipline's bounds determined by the functional differentiation of the Cypriot society.

Utopian urban vision for Nicosia will be a powerful response for Cypriots' desires because of its ability to abstract and crystallise a problem into a concise and internally consistent solution. This proposed scenario unifies both communities that depict new kinds of architecture and radically innovative concepts of urbanity that might well become reality in years to come. This vision would merge and erase borders. The movement and behaviour of its inhabitants would reflect the dynamic motion in and around the city. The unique social characteristics of the real world would be dynamically merged and mixed into a new unpredictable synthesis. The scheme would provide a way to experience and populate a new environment, which would be built to reflect the 'Green Zone' laws of a manifold city in motion. The city would be simultaneously diurnal and nocturnal. Absorbing data from real and imagined diasporas, it would engage and extend our perception and experience via continuous narratives. Here, the transformative laws of nature would divulge new stories. Condensed into virtual space, the city would be tangible yet not tangible, visible yet invisible, physical yet ethereal, and yet, nevertheless, clearly representing utopian urban vision.

The concept of a utopia is developed for a society that is currently not responding effectively enough to the political crisis of Cyprus. A utopia, in this case, refers to a point in between our current conditions and the 'ultimate' possibilities when the philosophy of transgression has reached, or surpassed, that of visionary intelligence. The utopian city model explores the concept of a technological and scientific plurality where Cypriots may have evolved to transcend their enthusiasm, forming a hybrid system with the participation process, and in turn overcoming through their stories. The project highlights the impact of 'transgression' on society, the realisation of the tension between two communities, and the worrying lack of effective practices. It suggests the role of the city as a critical component in the

90   Bertug Ozarisoy

development of a unified future, the conception of the integrity of diasporas as a necessity in Cypriot's future evolution.

A utopia would be embedded within a greater future society, uniting humanity as well as preserving nature and cultural identity rather than suppressing, or ignoring, cultural ideology. The society of the future will hopefully have improved, especially with regard to the perception of unification beyond division. The evolution of the utopian urban vision of the Cypriot society is one of the key ameliorations that should become visible and influenced by the improvement of the built environment. The utopian city model would be a model for the future. A place of perpetual transformation and self-generation. A new way to reflect Cypriot desires and hopes. It represents a new blueprint of urbanism that would engage contemporary communication, density, lifestyle, cultural practice and globalisation, structured in an ideal urban and architectural space.

Notes

1 Manaugh, G., *On Utopia and Beyond: Utopia Generator* (Berlin: Gestalten Express, 2011).
2 Woods, L., *The Storm and The Fall* (New York: Princeton Architectural Press, 2004).
3 The Painter of Modern Life, 11. An interesting treatment of this essay, more sympathetic than mine, can be found in Paul De Man, 'Literary History and Literary Modernity', in *Blindness and Insight: Essays in the Rhetoric of Contemporary Criticism* (Oxford, 1971, especially pp. 157–161). See also Henri Lefebvre, *Introduction a la Modernite*, Chapter 7, for a critical perspective similar to the one here.
4 Van Schaik, M., 'Psychogeogram: An artist's utopia (Parts I, II and II)', in M. van Schaik and O. Mace (eds) *Exit Utopia: Architectural Provocations 1956–76* (Munich: Prestel Verlag, 2005, pp. 36–54, 104–124, 220–235).
5 Weizman, I., 'Interior exile and paper architecture: A spectrum for architectural dissidence', in F. Kossak, D. Petrescu, T. Schneider, R. Tyszczuk, and S. Walker (eds) *Agency: Working with Uncertain Architectures.* (London: Routledge, 2009, pp. 23–25).
6 See W.W. Rostow, *The Stages of Economic Growth: A Non-Communist Manifesto* (Cambridge, 1960). Alas, Rostow's account of Marx is garbled and shallow, even for the opponent. A more perceptive account of the relationship between Marx and recent studies of modernisation can be found in Robert C. Tucker, *The Marxian Revolutionary Idea* (Norton, 1969, Chapter 5). See also Shlomo Avineri, *The Social and Political Thought of Karl Marx* (Cambridge, 1968), and Anthony Giddens, *Capitalism and Modern Social Theory* (Cambridge, 1971, especially Parts 1 and 4).
7 Nieuwenhuys, Constant Anton, 'Unitary urbanism', trans. Robyn de Jong-Dalziel, in M. Wigley (ed.) *Constant's New Babylon: The Hyper Architecture of Desire* (Rotterdam: Witte de With, Center for Contemporary Art, 1998, pp. 131–135); 010 Publishers [originally delivered in Dutch as 'Unitar Urbanisme', a lecture at the Stedelijk Museum, Amsterdam, 20 December 1960].
8 Shepheard, P., *How to Like Everything: A Utopia* (London: Zero Books, 2013).
9 Feireiss, L., *On Utopia and Beyond: This Time Tomorrow* (Berlin: Gestalten Express, 2011).

Strategies towards Utopian Urban Vision   91

10 Chen, D., *On Utopia and Beyond: Productive Dystopia* (Berlin: Gestalten Express, 2011).
11 Cuff, D., 'Tabula futura imperfecta: The architecture of disaster, in Dana Cuff, Roger Sherman (eds.), *Fast Forward Urbanism: Rethinking Architecture's Engagement with the City* (Cambridge, MA: MIT Press, 2011, p. 76).
12 Michel Foucault, *The Order of Things: An Archeology of the Human Sciences*, translated by Alan Sheridan; Forward to the English edition, p. IX (Pantheon Books, 1970). Originally published as Les Mots et les Choses, Editions Gallimard, 1966.
13 See Philippe Mangeot, 'Velvet Agitators', in Feher M., Krikorian G., and McKee Y. (eds), *Nongovernmental Politics* (New York: Zone Books, 2007, pp. 592–603).
14 Jeremy W. Crampton, 'Thinking philosophically in cartography: Toward a critical politics of mapping', in *Cartographic Perspectives*, Number 41, Winter 2002, p.7.
15 Eyal Weizman, *Forensic Architecture and Speech of Things*, conversation with Rosemary Bechler. https://www.opendemocracy.net/en/forensic-architecture-and-speech-of-things-conversation/ (accessed 03-05-2019).
16 Gilles Deluze, 'Postscript on the societies of control', October, 59, Winter 1992. 3–7.
17 Tschumi, B., 'Architecture and Transgression', in *Architecture and Disjunction* (Cambridge, MA: MIT Press, 1996, p.78). Originally appeared in *Oppositions* 7, winter 1976.
18 Bataille, G., 'Architecture', in N. Leach (ed), *Rethinking Architecture* (London: Routledge, 1997 p. 21).
19 Sassen, S., 'Afterword', in J. Gugler (ed.), *World Cities Beyond the West* (Cambridge University Press, 2004, pp. 371–386).
20 Sassen, S., 'To Occupy', in *Beyond Zuccotti Park* (New York: Penguin Publishing, 2004, pp. 67–69).
21 For an analysis of some key postcolonial modernist urban visions for Cyprus, see for example: Panayiota Pyla and Petros Phokaides, 'Ambivalent politics and modernist debates in postcolonial Cyprus', in *Journal of Architecture* 16:6, 2011, pp. 885–913.
22 Bernard Tschumi, *The Manhattan Transcripts* (New York: St Martin's Press, 1981).
23 Foucault, M., 'A preface to transgression', in *Language, Counter-Memory, Practice: Selected Essays and Interviews*, Ed & Trans, 1963).
24 Foucault, M., 'Space, Knowledge, Power', (in N. Leach, 1976), p.371.
25 Balletto, L., *Ethnic Groups, Cross-social and Cross-cultural Contacts in Cyprus* (London: Cass Press, 1996).
26 Miessen, M., *Did Someone Say Participate? An Atlas of Spatial Practice* (Cambridge, MA: MIT Press, 2006).
27 Miessen, M., *The Violence of Participation* (Berlin: Architectural Association School of Architecture Bookshop Publishing, 2007, pp. 35–36).
28 Tschumi, B., 'Architecture and Transgression', in Architecture and Disjunction, Bernard Tschumi (Cambridge, MA: MIT PRESS, 1996) p.78. Originally appeared in Oppositions 7, winter 1976.
29 Tschumi, B., 'Architecture and Disjunction', (Cambridge, MA: MIT Press, 1996, p. 83).
30 '... which can be applied to medieval culture, or even classical culture, only by a retrospective hypothesis, and by an interplay of formal analogies or semantic resemblances; but neither literature, nor politics, nor philosophy and the sciences articulated the field of discourse in the seventeenth or eighteenth century as they did in the nineteenth century.' Michel Foucault, 'The Unities of Discourse', in *The Archeology of Knowledge* (p. 22).

31 'The Modernisation of Man', in Myron Weiner (ed), *Modernisation: The Dynamics of Growth* (Basic Books, 1966 p. 149). This collection gives a good picture of the mainstream American paradigm of modernization in its heyday. Seminal works in this tradition include Daniel Lerner, *The Passing of Traditional Society* (Free Press, 1958) and W. W. Rostow, *The Stages of Economic Growth: A Non-Communist Manifesto* (Cambridge, 1960). For an early radical critique of this literature, see Michael Walzer, 'The Only Revolution: Notes on the Theory of Modernisation', in *Dissent*, 11 (1964), 132–140. But this body of theory also evoked much criticism and controversy within the mainstream of Western social science.

32 Tschumi, B., *The Manhattan Transcripts* (New York: St. Martins' Press, 1981).

33 Benjamin, W., *Interpretations, Meanings and Environments* (Aldershot: Ashgate, 1999).

34 Lefebvre, H., *The Production of Space* (Oxford: Blackwell Publishing, 2003).

35 Tschumi, B., *Space and Events* (London: Architectural Association, 1983, p. 54). [Originally appeared in a different form in Themes III: The Discourse of Events.]

36 Tschumi, B., 'Architecture and Limits I, II and III' in *Art Forum* December 1980, March 1981 and September 1981, respectively; in *Violence of Architecture* September 1981.

37 Agamben, G., *Means Without End* (Minneapolis: University of Minnesota Press, 2000, p. 43).

38 Hunt, D., *Footprints in Cyprus. An Illustrated History* (London: Trigraph, 1982).

39 Balletto, L., *Ethnic Groups, Cross-social and Cross-cultural Contacts in Cyprus* (London: Cass Press, 1996).

40 Costantinou, G., *The Birth of an Island, in Monuments and Sites Cyprus* (ICOMOS, 1996).

41 Demetriou, O., *Displacement in Cyprus: Consequences of Civil and Military Conflict – Report 1* (Peace Research Institute Oslo (PRIO), 2012, p. 6).

42 Kyris, C., 'History of Cyprus, with an introduction to the geography of Cyprus', *Nicosia*, 1985., H., *Cyprus Under the Turks, 1571–1878* (London: Humphrey Milford, 1921).

43 Christophoros, C. & Craig, W., *Greek Cypriots, Turkish Cypriots and the Future: The Day After the Referendum*. A Development Associates Occasional Paper in Democracy and Governance, No. 16, 2004. https://www.cyprusreview.org

44 Anthias, F., 'Researching society and culture in Cyprus: Displacements, hybridities, and dialogical frameworks', in Y. Papadakis, N. Peristianis, & G. Wlez (eds), *Divided Cyprus: Modernity, History and an Island in Conflict* (Bloomington: Indiana UP, 2009, pp. 176–194.

45 PIO Cyprus Center, *International Displacement in Cyprus*, www.prio-cyprus-displacement.net (accessed 04/05/2019)

46 Loizides, N. & Antoniades, M., 'Settlers, Refugees, and Immigrants: Alternative Futures for Post-Settlement Cyprus,' *ISP Discussion Paper*, Discussion Paper 2004-03, (Belfer Center for Science and International Affairs, March, 2010, 37–41).

47 Loizides, N., 'Refugee and settler issues in negotiating the Cyprus problem: What is dead and what is living in the Annan Plan', *The Association for Cypriot, Greek and Turkish Affairs* (London School of Economics, May, 2007).

48 Miessen, M., *Did Someone Say Participate? An Atlas of Spatial Practice* (Cambridge, MA: MIT Press, 2006).

49 Mouffe, C., 'Deliberative democracy or agonistic pluralism?' *Social Research* 66, no.3, 1999, pp. 745–758.

50 Ibid. Agonistic pluralism provides a theoretical framework for multiplicity of actors collaborating without arriving at a consensus. Conflict and differentiation

Strategies towards Utopian Urban Vision 93

replace the deliberative method where essential identities cooperate to justify a singular and exclusive agreement.

51 Latour, B., *Politics of Nature: How to Bring the Sciences into Democracy* (Harvard University Press, 2009, p. 55).

52 Jakobsen, J., *The Future is Self-Organised* (London: Black Dog Publishing, 2006).

53 Hannula, M., 'Self-organisation: A short story of a family tree', in *Self-organisation/Counter-Economic Strategies* (Berlin: Sternberg Press, 2006, p. 207); Hill, G., *A History of Cyprus* (Cambridge: Cambridge University Press, 1948).

54 Sassen, S., 'Afterword', in J. Gugler (ed), *World Cities Beyond the West* (Cambridge: Cambridge University Press, 2004, pp. 371–386).

55 Bataille, G., 'Architecture', in N. Hirsch and S. Sarda (eds), *Cybermohalla Hub* (Berlin: Sternberg Press, 2012, p.140).

56 Cruz, T., *The Microscope as Hammer: Mapping Border Conditions* (Amsterdam: Architecture & Natura Press, 2010, p. 43).

57 Foucault, M., 'Preface to transgression', in D. Bouchard (ed.), *Language, Counter Memory, Practice* (Ithaca: Cornell University Press, 1977, p. 35).

58 Shepheard, P., *How to Like Everything: A Utopia* (London: Zero Books, 2013).

59 Hackauf, U., *On Utopia and Beyond: A Project on Visionary Cities* (Berlin: Gestalten Express, 2011).

60 Foucault, M., 'Space, knowledge, power', in N. Leach (ed), (Cornell University Press Publication, 1977, p. 35).

61 Hatay, M. & Bryant, R., 'The jasmine scent of Nicosia: Of returns, revolutions, and the longing for forbidden pasts', *Journal of Modern Greek Studies*, 26, 2008, pp. 423–449.

62 Bryant, R., *Imagining the Modern: The Cultures of Nationalism in Cyprus* (London: I. B. Tauris, 2004).

63 Gregoriou, G., *Cyprus, a View from the Diaspora* (New York: Smirna Press, 2000).

64 Kelling, G., *Countdown to Rebellion: British Policy in Cyprus, 1939–1955* (New York: Grenwood Press, 1990).

65 Tofallis, K., *A History of Cyprus: From the Ancient Times to the Present* (London: Greek Institute, 2002).

66 Maier, F., *Cyprus from Earliest Time to the Present Day* (London, Elek Books, 1968).

67 Hadjipaschalis, A. *Maps and Atlases* (The Bank of Cyprus Cultural Foundation, Nicosia, 1989).

68 Kyris, C., *History of Cyprus, with an Introduction to the Geography of Cyprus* (Nicosia, 1985); H., *Cyprus under the Turks, 1571–1878*, (London: Humphrey Milford, 1921).

69 Panteli, S., *Historical Dictionary of Cyprus* (London: Lanham, 1995).

70 Joseph, J., *Cyprus, Ethnic Conflict and International Politics: from Independence to the Threshold of the European Union* (London: Palgrave Macmillan, 1991).

71 Stefanidis, I., *Isle of Discord: Nationalism, Imperialism and the Making of the Cyprus Problem* (London: C. Hurst, 1999).

72 Chen, D., *On Utopia and Beyond: Productive Dystopia* (Berlin: Gestalten Express, 2011).

73 James, A., *Keeping the Peace in the Cyprus Crisis of 1963–64* (New York: Palgrave, 2002).

74 Hardt, M., *Multitude: War and Democracy in the Age of Empire* (London: Hamish Hamilton Publications, 2005).

75 Miessen, M., *East Coast Europe* (Berlin: Sternberg Press, 2008).

94 Bertug Ozarisoy

76 Foucault, M., 'A preface to transgression', in D. F. Bouchard (ed. and trans.), *Language, Counter-Memory, Practice: Selected Essays and Interviews* (Ithaca, New York: Cornell University Press, 1977, p. 30). [A Preface to Transgression was an essay in homage to his deceased friend Georges Bataille.]

77 Williams, R., *Keywords: A Vocabulary of Culture and Society* (London: Fontana Press, 1976, p. 90).

78 Bataille, G., 'Architecture', in N. Leach (ed.), *Rethinking Architecture* (London: Routledge, 1997, p. 21).

79 Tschumi, B., 'Architecture and transgression', in *Architecture and Disjunction* (Cambridge, MA: MIT Press, 1996, p.78). [Originally appeared in *Oppositions* 7, winter 1976.]

80 Ford, S., *The Situationist International: A User's Guide* (London: Black Dog Publishing, 2005).

81 Cuff, D., *Architecture: The Story of Practice* (Cambridge, MA: MIT Press, 1991, p. 4).

82 Latour, B. & Yaneva, A., 'Give me a gun and I will make all buildings move: An ant's view of architecture', in R. Geiser (ed.), *Explorations in Architecture: Teaching, Design, Research* (Basel: Birkhauser, 2008, pp. 80–89).

83 Awan, N., Schneider, T., & Till. J., *Spatial Agency: Other Ways of Doing Architecture* (London, Routledge, 2011, p. 29).

84 Shane, G., *Recombinant Urbanism, Conceptual Modeling in Architecture, Urban Design and City Theory* (London: John Wiley & Sons, 2005, pp. 14–15).

85 For more detailed reference see: Socrates Stratis, 'Architecture-as-urbanism in uncertain conditions', in *European 12 Results: Adaptable City* (Paris: European Editions, 2014, pp. 28–35).

86 For an analysis of the concept of thresholds see Stavros Stravrides, 'Towards the city of thresholds', *Professional Dreamers*, Vol.10, Italy, 2011.

References

Amini Behbahani, P., Ostwald, M. J., & Gu, N. (2016). A syntactical comparative analysis of the spatial properties of Prairie style and Victorian domestic architecture. *Journal of Architecture*, *21*(3), 348–374. https://doi.org/10.1080/13602365.2016.1179661

Anthias, F. (2009). Researching society and culture in cyprus: Displacements, hybridities, and dialogical frameworks. In Y. Papadakis, N. Peristianis, & G. Wlez (Eds.), *Divided cyprus: Modernity, history and an island in conflict* (pp. 176–194). Bloomington, IN: Indiana UP.

Bowman, J. (2006). Seeing what's missing in memories of Cyprus. *Peace Review*, *18*(1), 119–127. https://doi.org/10.1080/10402650500510776

Bryant, R. (2002). The purity of spirit and the power of blood: A comparative perspective on nation, gender and kinship in Cyprus. *Journal of the Royal Anthropological Institute*, *8*(3), 509–530. https://doi.org/10.1111/1467-9655.00120

Bryant, R. (2014). History's remainders: On time and objects after conflict in Cyprus. *American Ethnologist*, *41*(4), 681–697. https://doi.org/10.1111/amet.12105

Cogaloglu, M., & Turkan, Z. (2019). Plan organization in XX. Century housing architecture in North Cyprus. *Amazonia Investiga*, *8*(22), 381–388. Retrieved from https://www.amazoniainvestiga.info/index.php/amazonia/article/view/738

Deckers, K. (2005). Post-roman history of river systems in western Cyprus: Causes and archaeological implications. *Journal of Mediterranean Archaeology*, *18*(2), 155–181. https://doi.org/10.1558/jmea.2005.18.2.155

Deluze, G. (1992, October). Postscript on the societies of control. *The MIT Press*, 59(Winter), 3–7.

De Man. (1971). Literary history and literary modernity. In Steven E. Cole (ed.), *Blindness and Insight: Essays in the rhetoric of contemporary criticism* (pp. 157–161). Oxford: Wayne State University Press.

Faustino, D. (2013). In praise of transgression: The work of Didier faustino/bureau de mésarchitectures. *Architectural Design*, 83(6), 120–123. https://doi.org/10.1002/ad.1685

Faustmann, H. (2008). History in the making? A new drive for a solution to the Cyprus problem: Profile. *Mediterranean Politics*, 13(3), 453–458. https://doi.org/10.1080/13629390802387034

Foucault, M. (1977). Rethinking Architecture. Space, knowledge, power. In N. Leach (Ed.), (p. 35). Cornell University Press Publication.

Ghilardi, M., Cordier, S., Carozza, J. M., Psomiadis, D., Guilaine, J., Zomeni, Z., … Morhange, C. (2015). The Holocene fluvial history of the tremithos river (South central Cyprus) and its linkage to archaeological records. *Environmental Archaeology*, 20(2), 184–201. https://doi.org/10.1179/1749631414Y.0000000057

Given, M. (2002). Maps, fields, and boundary cairns: Demarcation and resistance in colonial Cyprus. *International Journal of Historical Archeology*, 6(1), 1–22. https://doi.org/10.1023/A:1014862125523

Haddad, E. (2009). Charles Jencks and the historiography of post-modernism. *Journal of Architecture*. https://doi.org/10.1080/13602360902867434

Hadjipavlou, M. (2007). Multiple stories: The "crossings" as part of citizens' reconciliation efforts in Cyprus? *Innovation: The European Journal of Social Science Research*, 20(1), 53–73. https://doi.org/10.1080/13511610701197866

Hejduk, R. (2007). Death becomes her: Transgression, decay, and eROTicism in Bernard Tschumi's early writings and projects. *Journal of Architecture*, 12, 393–404. https://doi.org/10.1080/13602360701614672

Heraclides, A. (2011). The Cyprus Gordian knot: An intractable ethnic conflict. *Nationalism and Ethnic Politics*, 17(2), 117–139. https://doi.org/10.1080/13537113.2011.575309

Hughes-Wilson, J. (2011). The forgotten war a brief history of the battle for Cyprus, 1974. *RUSI Journal*, 156(5), 84–93. https://doi.org/10.1080/03071847.2011.626281

Kraftl, P., & Adey, P. (2008). Architecture/affect/inhabitation: Geographies of being-in buildings. *Annals of the Association of American Geographers*, 98(1), 213–231. https://doi.org/10.1080/00045600701734687

Lacher, H., & Kaymak, E. (2005). Transforming identities: Beyond the politics of non-settlement in North Cyprus. *Mediterranean Politics*, 10(2), 147–166. https://doi.org/10.1080/13629390500124341

Lameira, G. (2021). Readings on multifamily housing: Models, discourses, and aesthetics in A Arquitectura Portuguesa (1908–1958). *Journal of Architecture*, 26(8), 1163–1196. https://doi.org/10.1080/13602365.2021.2001558

Lending, M. (2018). Negotiating absence: Bernard Tschumi's new acropolis museum in Athens. *Journal of Architecture*, 23(5), 797–819. https://doi.org/10.1080/13602365.2018.1495909

Lohtaja, A. (2021). Henri Lefebvre's lessons from the Bauhaus. *Journal of Architecture*, 26(4), 499–515. https://doi.org/10.1080/13602365.2021.1923551

Loizides, N. (2011). Contested migration and settler politics in Cyprus. *Political Geography*, *30*(7), 391–401. https://doi.org/10.1016/j.polgeo.2011.08.004

Loizides, N., & Antoniades, M. (2010). 'Settlers, Refugees, and Immigrants: Alternative Futures for Post-Settlement Cyprus,' *ISP Discussion Paper*, Discussion Paper 2004-03, (Belfer Center for Science and International Affairs, March, 2010, 37–41).

Miessen, M. (2007). *The violence of participation* (pp. 35–36). Berlin: Architectural Association School of Architecture Bookshop Publishing.

Mumford, E. (2009). CIAM and the communist bloc, 1928–59. *Journal of Architecture*, *14*(2), 237–254. https://doi.org/10.1080/13602360802704810

Ozarisoy, B., & Altan, H. (2017a). Adoption of energy design strategies for retrofitting mass housing estates in Northern Cyprus. *Sustainability (Switzerland)*, *9*(8), 1477. https://doi.org/10.3390/su9081477

Ozarisoy, B., & Altan, H. (2017b). Energy performance development of non-regulated retrofit mass housing estates in Northern Cyprus. *Design Journal*, *20*(Suppl. 1), S1765–S1781. https://doi.org/10.1080/14606925.2017.1352697

Papadakis, Y. (2004). Discourses of "the Balkans" in Cyprus: Tactics, strategies and constructions of "others". *History and Anthropology*, *15*(1), 15–27. https://doi.org/10.1080/027572004200191064

Psaltis, C., Carretero, M., & Čehajić-Clancy, S. (2017). *History education and conflict transformation: Social psychological theories, history teaching and reconciliation* (pp. 1–384). Springer International Publishing. https://doi.org/10.1007/978-3-319-54681-0

Roberts-Hughes, R. (2017). Transgression and conservation: Rereading Georges Bataille. *Journal for Cultural Research*, *21*(2), 157–168. https://doi.org/10.1080/14797585.2016.1239608

Sassen, S. (2004). To occupy. In Shiffman et al., (Eds.) *Beyond zuccotti park* (pp. 67–69). New York: New Village Press.

Sertoglu, K., & Ozturk, I. (2003). Application of Cyprus to the European Union and the Cyprus problem. *Emerging Markets Finance and Trade*, *39*(6), 54–70. https://doi.org/10.1080/1540496x.2003.11052557

Sheil, B. (2005). Transgression from drawing to making. *Architectural Research Quarterly*, *9*(1), 20–32. https://doi.org/10.1017/S1359135505000059

Stępnik, M. (2020). The house that lars built: The architecture of transgression. *Arts*, *9*(4), 127. https://doi.org/10.3390/arts9040127

Thompson, S., St. Karayanni, S., & Vassiliadou, M. (2004). Cyprus after history. *Interventions*, *6*(2), 282–299. https://doi.org/10.1080/1369801042000238373

Vural, Y., & Ozuyanik, E. (2008). Redefining identity in the Turkish-Cypriot school history textbooks: A step towards a united federal Cyprus. *South European Society and Politics*, *13*(2), 133–154. https://doi.org/10.1080/13608740802156521

Weizman, I. (2009). Interior exile and paper architecture: A spectrum for architectural dissidence. In F. Kossak, D. Petrescu, T. Schneider, R. Tyszczuk, & S. Walker (Eds.), *Agency: Working with uncertain architectures* (pp. 36–45). London: Routledge.

5 A Utopia

Bertug Ozarisoy

Introduction

'Utopia' is a word invented 500 years ago at the start of the modern age as a description of the ideal society by Tomes More (Coleman, 2013, 135–166). It is composed of Latin parts that, taken together, mean 'no place' or 'nowhere'. We now use the word 'utopia' to mean an impossible dream of perfection. The New Green Zone of Nicosia recasts the actual world, the changing world we already live in, as utopia – to make the impossible possible.

What began as a cooperative community inspired by utopian ideals, is relentlessly put to an end by the powers of nature (McKeown et al., 2016, 3–17). Neither utopian ideals nor higher visions can withstand the inevitable reality of existence. Our general understanding of the notion of utopia today is a token for a concept of complete political and social ideals on cities (Garcia-Vergara & Pizza, 2021, 1117–1145).

In the field of architecture and urbanism, utopias have always been confronted with the same complexities and paradoxes inherent in the search for the perfect city model (Dovey, 2013, 82–89). Of the arts, it may well be architecture that provides the most sustainable vehicle to imagine possible futures due to the inherent notion of progress in the discipline, which is naturally linked to the discourse on utopia (Sara & Littlefield, 2014, 295–304). In fact, the entire discipline is consequently focused on the future world, from basic process all the way to the inevitable configurations of social and political space (Kliot & Mansfield, 1997, 495–521). This research strives to bring together today's architectural and urban visions of possible features that rise above the disillusionment of the present and expand the imaginative horizons of human potential, whilst at the same time, reveal the conflicts this architecture provokes and outlines the potential implications for a unified Nicosia.

In diasporas (City of Hybridity, City of Agriculture, City of Trees, City of Birds and City of Watchtowers), strategies are carefully planned, contradictions eliminated and outside intrusions minimised (Altay, 2013, 102–109). In fact, to achieve a utopian ideal of, let us say, harmonic cohabitation in

DOI: 10.4324/9781003243069-7

98 *Bertug Ozarisoy*

peace, freedom and justice, a set of mandatory rules and definite organising principles is imperative (Denison & Ren, 2013, 38–43). Yet with respect to these rules and principles, the borderline force and control, rather than allowing collective happiness to emerge, is alarmingly thin here; a perfectly beautiful utopia can also gradually degrade into a repressive and controlled dystopia (Littlefield, 2013, 124–129).

Moreover, as diasporas tend to see the city differently in their vision of a better place in the future, their inherent demand for change and transformation in the here and now, carries a radical revolutionary impetus; utopia, perhaps, as a fundamental change in power or organised structures or utopia as a withdrawal from short-term solutions in favour of a comprehensive solution that dramatically shakes the foundations of society (Mosley & Sara, 2013, 14–19).

In this research, we are animated by 'Dreams of a Unified Nicosia', and by utopian longings for fulfilment. This anticipatory element and unconscious dimension of the future is what we call the 'not yet conscious' (Cunningham, 2001). It contains emancipatory moments which project visions of a better life that question the organisation and structure of life as we know it.

All issues consider the utopian vision of Nicosia, both as a model as well as method and can therefore be described as an optimistic process of possible realisation in which the determination of the future carefully formulates itself, experimenting with the promise of the researcher horizon. However, the out of reach diasporas featured in this research have, in creating images and visions of tomorrow for the city, become part of the actual creation of our future to come.

Of Futures and Utopias

The future will arrive no matter what happens to us (Sharp, 2022). Utopia, on the other hand, is a concept we have created in order to instigate innovation and change; to 'make things happen'. Within this logical twist, we will be able to find the inseparable connections and the profound differences between society's role in shaping our future and our utopia. Hejduk (2007) mentions that the future will come regardless; it remains always ahead of us, no matter in which direction we are heading, no matter which path we choose to take. Utopia is always the mirage-like vision of what may be lying ahead at the end of one of these paths.

Considering this argument, it seems logical to refer to both terms utopia and future in plural only, because there is no singular future but rather myriads which can co-exist in many different future scenarios (Mumford, 2009, 237–254). Rather than forecasting futures by projecting traces of the past, it would be better to reflect upon our current understanding of global and social dynamics, intellectually grasping the utopian aspects of what we would like our futures to have attempted and to have achieved, as shown in Figure 5.1.

A Utopia 99

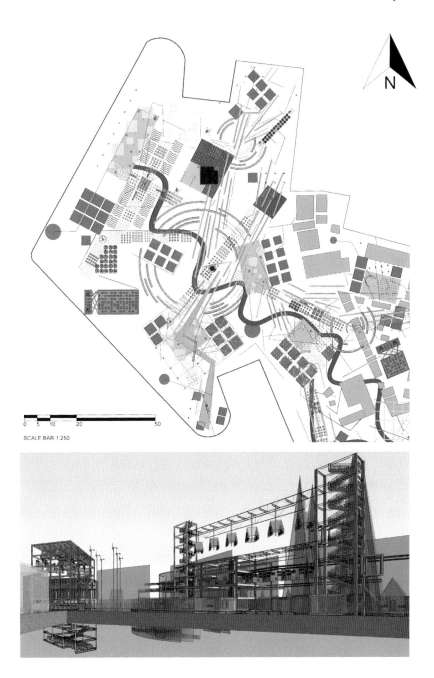

Figure 5.1 A visionary view of Nicosia, 2110. Image credit: drawn by the author, 2022.

100 *Bertug Ozarisoy*

Let us turn now to the function of utopias: this subjective perspective provides a means of escape to a place of hope, a purposefully vague ideal to counterbalance reality's hyper-complexity (Pullan, 2011). Yet utopias are also created with the intention of changing current patterns of these hyper-complex realities, to indulge in a process of 'objectively' transforming current society from a stable standpoint.

Utopia cannot be understood in the restrictive manner of a single solution for all problems but rather functions as the constant production of utopia: as a key to the door of otherwise unthinkable future scenarios (Jung & Cinn, 2020, 736–758). As we have seen, utopias can only work as a commentary on current issues and on contemporary hopes. Yet it lies in human beings to look endlessly for signs of what tomorrow might bring (Grubbauer, 2019, 469–486). Utopia offers the possibility to dream, to visualise, to narrate, to imagine the impossible and can therefore develop the power, as a catalyst, to start a process of change.

The shaping of the future by political decisions and individual initiatives cannot be left to projecting past or less than ideal paths into the future, but to create alternatives, options and futures to look forward to. It seems that in particularly dire situations, dreams and hopes are even more important. To consider the future means to come up with more utopias – again and again, never to give up.

Visionary Utopian Urban Design Scenarios

The utopian vision of the city of Nicosia is a speculative architectural and urban project. It has tried to explore what architecture could possibly generate when faced with extreme cultural and political scenarios like the current crisis in Cyprus. Under the political, economic and social conditions, modern Nicosia is simply unsustainable. The conflict causes a no-man's land at the heart of the city core. The project, a utopian vision of Nicosia, suggests that we can no longer afford any further growth on the periphery of Nicosia. Therefore, in order to facilitate the population growth, there is a need to maximise our resources and unite – not remain apart.

The proposed utopian vision assumes that by the year 2110, new planning initiatives in Nicosia will have incubated a self-sustaining city of 'hyper density' through the Buffer Zone. Growth will be germinated from the heart of the old medieval walled city. Nicosia has not yet grown further out into a suburban sprawl, but rather upwards and downwards. This project proposes densification through layering along the Buffer Zone as potential new spaces which accommodate diasporas to construct a utopian urban city. The main driving force behind the utopian vision of Nicosia is to consistently explore the ambiguities that surround our current lives through the design process, not only as producers of space, but also as global spectators.

Utopian Urban Vision of Nicosia

Cities tell stories. In the future Nicosia, 'Unified Cypriots', will also have their multiple stories, narratives and possibilities to tell, as shown in Figure 5.2. A recurring theme in this scenario is the idea of the existence of parallel worlds of utopia and the old. Utopia proposes a new parallel city above the old and poses the question of how the two might co-exist. Will they be populated similarly? How will the two meet? Will the new city supersede the old?

Based on the principles of peace, power and liberty, the idea of the utopia is – in contrast to conventional approaches to typical architectural concepts – described with a brief and naive story reminiscent of a storytelling (Doron, 2000, 247–263). This approach is taken in order to activate the inhabitants' known patterns of experience and to provide a unified city for their ideas to flourish between the architectural intervention and the narration of their stories (Roberts-Hughes, 2017, 157–168). On the one hand, A utopia reintroduces the recurrent ideas of the layered city, and on the other hand it creates a paradox, as shown in Figure 5.3. Of all things, it is huge, (allegedly) soulless machines that will transport natural artefacts back into the city on their backs, in order to make a point, and to challenge, once more, the parameters of human action.

The story of our manipulation and desires rather than reconstruction of the 'Green Zone' is aiming at creating a unique possibility of conditions for the future urban vision of Nicosia (Given, 2005, 207–213). The fundamental approach for this project is to create an evolution rather than a revolution. The key concept to this approach is not to create new structures by replacing existing buildings but rather to respect the context by inserting a secondary layer of architecture which would be overlaid onto the existing structures of any dense urban fabric. The proposed architectural system aims to contribute towards creating a hybrid cross-cultural

Figure 5.2 Storytelling of the city. Image credit: drawn by the author, 2022.

102 Bertug Ozarisoy

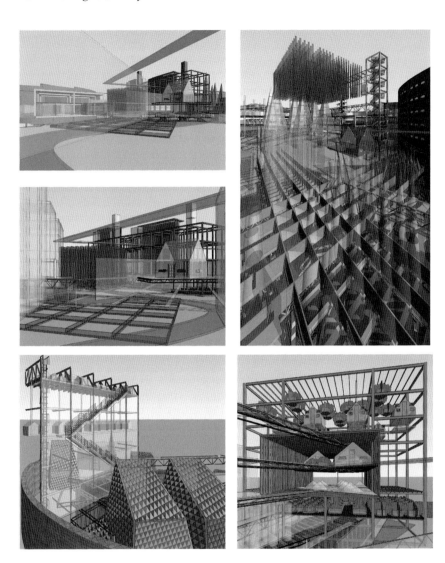

Figure 5.3 This vision represents the power and liberty of the city. Image credit: drawn by the author, 2022.

community model particularly the historic central core (Walsh, 2007, 81–86). Along with many aspects, creating more public spaces (agricultural lands, bird towers, etc.) in this dense environment was both important as well as challenging for the inhabitants (Briel, 2013, 27–43). The strategy that the researcher has taken in this project is to expand both horizontally and vertically, by utilising existing urban fabric and the voids between them.

Utopia versus a New Green Zone

The key principle of this project is to create an architectural system that would create a symbiotic relationship with the existing fabric of the city, as shown in Figure 5.4. The existing buildings would become the primary structure for the system to be attached to; the scheme would provide a network of connections, public spaces and green spaces between the buildings (Ozarisoy & Altan, 2021a). Energy would also be exchanged in a symbiotic way by wind turbines, which would generate electricity in order to be self-sustainable (Ozarisoy & Altan, 2021b). Any excess energy could be sent to other buildings or to the city grid (Ozarisoy & Altan, 2022).

The story of our manipulations and desires, however, is pre-eminently the Green Zone of the city. That story is also the best way to help Cypriots understand the value of nature and landscape because they reflect our society (Barnaba, 2006, 14–18). The revealing history and multicultural traces of the city provide much insight into our culture's interaction with nature and landscape, the relationship that it maintains and the common future ahead of us (Bryant, 2014, 681–697).

Our time urgently requires a context that is more than just a visual experience (Bryant, 2002, 509–530). Perception of landscape and nature is a complex cultural process of movement and well-being, sometimes even of uneasiness and the sense of being out of place, as shown in Figure 5.5. The meaning of place is determined by one's memory, which is also triggered by

Figure 5.4 A unified harmony between diasporas. Image credit: drawn by the author, 2022.

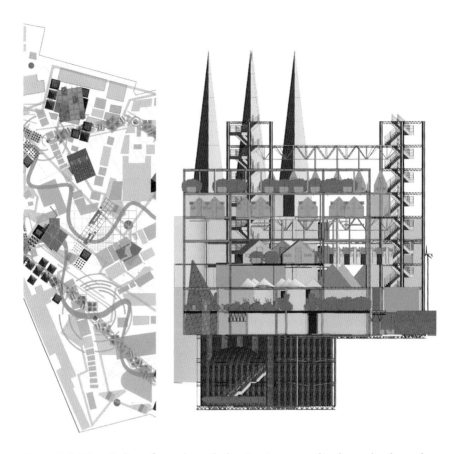

Figure 5.5 River Pedieos flows through the city. Image credit: drawn by the author, 2022.

subconscious sensations (Psaltis, 2016, 19–27). After all, the definition of culture is complex and closely connected with the landscape of the 'Green Zone'. First, culture may be described as the paradoxical manner to treat the existing physical environment, deliberately trying to transform it. The new vision imposes order upon wilderness, while ironically to the rebirth of the river Pedieos, it is within wildness and disorder that the re-reconstruction of the city is hidden (Hadjipavlou, 2007, 53–73). In addition, culture is the way in which Cypriot identity shapes itself as a product of that nature: handling its own body sometimes in extreme cases (Manning, 1998, 39–58). Further to that, culture is the manner in which Cypriots deal with their rural way of living background and shared thought and norms (Bragina, 2012, 343–348). This environment is partly the result of their self-invented rules, practices and rituals regarding nature, wilderness, city and landscape.

A Utopia   105

From this point of view, culture is creating something: it is a production of multilayered history; but culture is also expressing thoughts: it is a memory of representation as well the contribution of different meanings and acts that are always being considered (Papadakis, 2003, 253–270). The diaspora of the Green Zone is supposed to be a catalyst itself, a field of change, while always taking the landscape as the lens of ideas, acts, concepts and visions (Papadakis, 2004, 15–27).

Green Zone will continue to be an arena of social, political, personal and cultural battles with differences of opinion. In this way, the diaspora of the architecture of transgression generates the production of culture: it commends acts by hybridised Cypriots that reshape the city, producing a peaceful environment for future generations. The Green Zone also seeks an understanding with nature that is at the same time an agony to deal with memories. It is impossible to think about Cypriot culture and identity without considering the relationship we have with nature and the landscape surrounding us. Therefore, it is also unthinkable without hybridisation (Deckers, 2005, 155–181). This requires not only unification but also direction for new movements.

The new utopian vision of the 'Green Zone' positioned itself in intentional opposition to the dominant political and architectural conditions of its time in a provocative bid to reclaim and reimagine not only the city but both communities themselves. The New Green Zone concept is a poetic vision of a borderless world that resonates with the cultural identity of both communities.

Symbolic Representation of a New Green Zone

All the above dimensions represent the different diaspora of the city (city of hybridity, city of agriculture, city of trees, city of birds and city of watchtowers), and the connectors connecting them to each other represent political and military power, conflict and unification. Beyond this representation, these connectors also act as a catalyst to form a complete city which consists of plaques very close to each other reflecting the multicultural diversity of the city, as shown in Figure 5.6. At the same time, the lines which represent the connecting routes cross each other to form junctions where cultural practice among Cypriots takes place with the other ethnic subcultures around them interconnecting with them. This shows how multicultural Nicosia City has become.

In the utopian urban vision of the city, the city is divided into grids. All the diaspora (city of hybridity, city of agriculture, city of trees, city of birds and city of watchtowers) are placed in every grid in order to form a hierarchy and network to create an opposition and augment the organic development of the city. This representational drawing when placed on a grid shows the network of the 'past–future matrix' of the city.

The conceptual mapping of Nicosia has multiple entry points and demands negotiation for a way through a labyrinthine path to find a zone

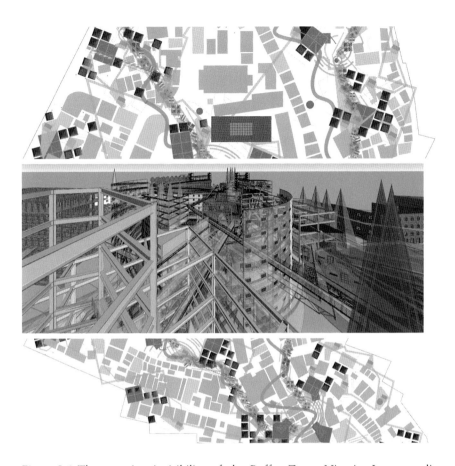

Figure 5.6 The mapping invisibility of the Buffer Zone, Nicosia. Image credit: drawn by the author, 2022.

of green. This research attempts a new reading and narration of mapped reality beyond invisibility. It seeks to activate the space around and between the collective memories and to create, through a renegotiation of the memories, 'a new topography of perception possibilities'. This renegotiation is particularly important today. The outcome of the research points out that historical time is again of the essence, only that this historical time is not a linear and undefined steady progress imagined by Cypriots but a multitude of competing and overlapping memories.

The movement of Cypriots inscribes an assemblage of relations in their effective becoming and maps the passage of deterritorialization as seen in this research process. This research shows how time has changed the map of the city; its somewhat haphazard structure mirrors the puzzle that the city has become. This mapping methodology is evident for my utopian vision,

A Utopia 107

an important survey in terms of the remapping of the city both architecturally and figuratively to represent the diaspora of the city beyond division, as shown in Figure 5.7. Maps which are central to the colonial and postcolonial projects, are re-envisioned in this research which moves beyond the presentation of the city as being fixed, frozen in time, continually bleeding its timelessness.

Figure 5.7 The map of utopian urban vision of the Buffer Zone, Nicosia. Image credit: drawn by the author, 2022.

108   *Bertug Ozarisoy*

The mapping of invisibility looks at the perspective that there has been little attempt to think through the importance of Cyprus as a trans-locational space: that is, one where intercultural movement and flow have been important aspects of social reality (Thompson et al., 2004, 282–299). The urban utopian vision has represented the city in terms that look beyond a static nationalism or as a site of permanent wounding. The Green Zone hints instead at an underlying ambiguity of the space and presents an openness that addresses the shifts away from the cultural binaries that are implicit in traditional narratives of the capital. From the research of my field trip to Cyprus, I have experienced first-hand how the city of Nicosia had changed dramatically since the division. Beyond this change, I gathered data on its cultural process showing how every civilisation which ruled it left its traces in Nicosia City.

To understand the chronology of the collected data, I devised a methodology for a mapping technique. This technique is not a traditional urban analysis but a conceptual representation of that part of Nicosia. This representation entails various issues and elements which creates the scene for critical thinking in developing my urban utopia vision.

In this mapping I created a frame which will be placed in all the maps, and as I said it will act as a catalyst for all the diaspora passing through it. The name of this frame is the catalyst in it. In a layered form, it all fits into this frame and forms the theory for my utopian urban vision which materialises in the last layer. To create my urban vision, I have chosen the Buffer Zone of Nicosia City. In the Buffer Zone I selected certain spaces of importance to symbolise religion, military, commercial district, routes, nodes and edges of the city, medieval walls and bastions, historic and existing agricultural lands and political points. Among this layout of these spaces there is a sense of conflict in the air which is waiting to be resolved.

The above diaspora was divided into grids (as in urban planning), and these grids can fit into the frame individually or all together. This grid system will act as a network for the design of the urban utopian vision. These grids are connected to each other with green routes which are used for transportation and networking of data. In these grids, the agricultural fields are placed horizontally and vertically resulting in an agricultural tower. Also, there is a marketplace in each grid.

Lifelines

The old fortifications of Nicosia have been preserved, and the river Pedieos is now home to a rich and diverse set of functions (Ghilardi et al., 2015, 184–201). Some typical neighbourhood living, multicultural streets and historic urban quarters are accepted cultural transitional points of the city. The ambition is to transform and connect these varied spaces in such a way that one utopia of 'Green Zone' is realised: an invisible unified city, as shown in Figure 5.8. The inhabitants of the city gradually evolve a new 'Green Religion', which fortifies them psychologically from the unpredictable forces

A Utopia 109

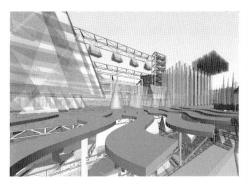

Figure 5.8 Diasporas find their own way through the river Pedieos. Image credit: drawn by the author, 2022.

of nature. Created from the wreckage of the old city, the new settlement is formed from a palimpsest of reorganised debris, rituals and the ordinary requirements of daily urban life (Given, 2002, 1–22).

This map represents the past and present urban quarters of Nicosia City. It will be used as a reference for my utopian vision of the city. In this map, the horizontal countered lines represent the visionary river Pedieos. In the background, the frame symbolises Nicosia City and acts as a catalyst for all the diaspora passing through it.

- The rectangular quarter represents Ataturk Square.
- The octagonal quarter represents Sarai Square.
- The curve shaped quarter represents Eleftheria Square.

The above three squares in this map represent the historic culture and heritage values of the city. To this day, traces of past civilisations are still visible, and today, as in the past, these squares are used by Cypriots to gather and show their unity and the force of the Cypriot identity. The horizontal space represents the Buffer Zone. The vertical line pierces through these spaces and unifies and ties them together. The triangular spaces represent the moments of the Cypriots through history. The small curve shape spaces represent the different code of cultural practices interchanging with each other and giving rise to the diversity and diaspora of the Cypriots.

110 Bertug Ozarisoy

Monumental Representation

Through time, the use of revealing the multilayered traces of the city has changed from merely telling to a more diverse urban function, which has now focused completely on the 'Green Zone' – both for the residents of Nicosia and for visitors (Loizides, 2011, 391–401). The monumental value of the existing structures is dependent on beauty, uniqueness and the role they play in the narrative of the city, as shown in Figure 5.9. Although everyone sees the Buffer Zone primarily as a green space, its monumental value is almost completely derived from its physical and storytelling of its historic character (Lacher & Kaymak, 2005, 147–166). In many cases, the green functions as a generic backdrop for these monuments. A more monumental approach to the re-bringing urban agriculture fields and accommodating bird towers will lead to a more diverse mix of monuments.

This map represents the urban planning process of Nicosia City from the past to the present. Before going on to explain the map itself the history which shaped Cyprus must be mentioned in order to enable us to understand the present state of the city. The Lusignans, Venetians and the Ottomans were influenced by each other and at the same time adapted their

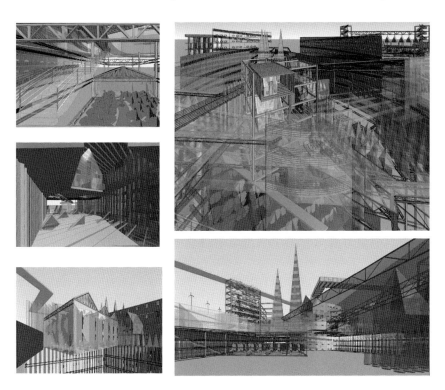

Figure 5.9 The institutional power of the diaspora is located through the life cycle of the river Pedieos. Image credit: drawn by the author, 2022.

own architectural culture to the existing culture hence the city was allowed to develop in an organic way where this type of development resulted in buildings close to very each other with narrow streets and cul-de-sacs between them leaving space for small courtyards between these buildings and streets (Leonard, 2014, 66–76). This type of urban planning was the root of moulding the Cypriot identity as a close community despite originally coming from different cultures.

In this conceptual map, the horizontal countered lines represent the visionary river Pedieos. In the background, the multinominal lines symbolise hybridity between culture and everyday practise. This intervention in urban planning of the city was organised, and it divided the city into grids where the public services building was built as a monument to the organised power of the British Empire. These monuments which still exist today in Nicosia transgressed the past organic urban development of the city by creating its own urban identity.

The rectangular spaces represent the narrow streets which still exist today, and the practice of close neighbourhood Cypriot culture continues today in every 'mahalle'. The other spaces in curved horizontal lines represent the rest of the British architecture posed by the organic developments, hence resulting in hybridisation of the architecture of the city.

Full Circle

Once the urban agricultural fields along the mature vegetation of the Buffer Zone are connected, they transform into not only a linear system but a triangular one. The creation of this network will change presently isolated neighbourhood spaces into integral parts of the city. This 'Green Zone' will be a full circle connection that lets people and ecology circumnavigate the city, as shown in Figure 5.10. The methodology for this transformation

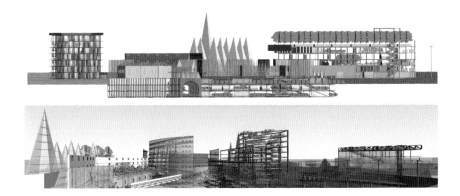

Figure 5.10 Agricultural fields through the utopian urban vision of Nicosia, 2110. Image credit: drawn by the author, 2022.

112 *Bertug Ozarisoy*

follows four themes: maximum diversity, intuitive navigation, cosmopolitan nature and free space.

This conceptual map represents how the Green Line divides the city at this present time. In this conceptual map, the horizontal countered lines represent the visionary river Pedieos.

The green triangular space represents the Green Line and the Buffer Zone. This Green Line divides the city and at the same time causes juxtaposition to the urban planning development of the city, because this no-man's land (the Buffer Zone) has been allowed to develop at its own pace undisturbed by outside interference. This uncontrolled development resulted in the rebirth depicted as a curviliniear line passing through the Buffer Zone of the river Pedieos decaying, overtaken by the indigenous natural flora and trees and creating the right environment for this flora and birds to grow and breed. This caused a massive diversity to the Buffer Zone. The red spaces represent peoples' movements through Ledras Street. The violet colour represents military and political powers trying to pierce through these lines, creating a field of tension.

Maximum Diversity

The utopian 'Green Zone' is designed to stimulate diversity of life and variety of use in one continuous green loop – its layout is tailored for residents of various backgrounds. Seen from afar, the Buffer Zone will be a 'Green Zone' around the city centre, and a continuous ribbon will form the backbone of the old walled city. It is recognisable and always present, composed of the river Pedieos (water reservoir) and extensive vegetation of the city, with routes and trails as the connecting elements. Next to this ribbon are the individual spaces with their differences enhanced – resulting in a 'multicoloured' Nicosia, as shown in Figure 5.11.

This conceptual map represents the changes taking place in the Green Line from past to present. In this conceptual map, the horizontal countered lines represent the visionary river Pedieos. The horizontal green space represents the Green Line before the division and the diversity of the different communities thereof than living and working together because this was the main commercial district of Nicosia. Just to add further going back to recent history of this area, most of the tradesmen were Armenians and the most Jews, Greeks, and Turks. The vertical lines represent the military forces of the United Nation, Greek and Turkish armies who at this present time are in total control of the Buffer Zone, the division.

The circular, oval and long rectangular spaces depicted in orange and red colours represent the aggregation of settlements of the Cypriot communities going back to ancient civilisations because of the presence of the river Pedieos (water reservoir) and the fertile line surrounding it. Even at these times visibly Cypriots lived in harmony but to some extent they were in conflict with each other because of the diversity of the cultures.

A Utopia 113

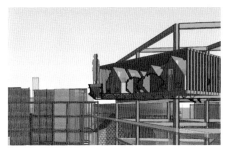

Figure 5.11 A vision of diversity and cultural variety. Image credit: drawn by the author, 2022.

Intuitive Navigation

The utopian 'Green Zone' holds a different ideology about how people move through the urban agricultural fields and how they can obtain, process and generate information. The 'Green Zone' with a route system that is obvious and intuitive appeals to people's innate sense for direction, as shown in Figure 5.12. All the routes are accompanied by water or natural elements. The urban agricultural fields path system does not pass directly through the existing abandoned buildings, but links them together with new routes. There is one route that is ideal for transportation and trade of products. This route is composed of broad walks, major production lines and places to create your own space for free. Another route is quieter, more natural. There is of course also the route over the water. As the time of day, the weather, or mood changes, people can meander along a path of their preference.

This map represents how entertainment was introduced into the Cypriot culture by the British and its aftereffects. In this conceptual map the horizontal countered lines represent the visionary river Pedieos.

- The horizontal straight lines represent Ermou Street.
- The vertical straight lines represent Ledras Street.

The grid nodes situated in the frame represents the open-air activities such as open-air cinemas, theatres, musical concerts and fairs (panayiri) introduced

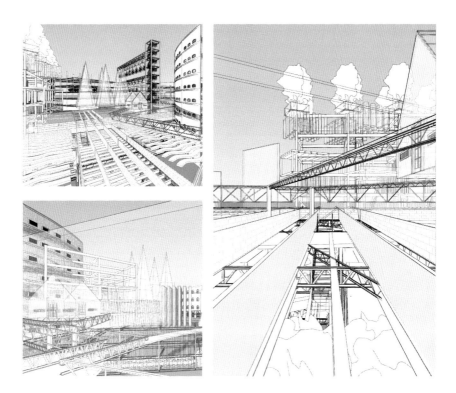

Figure 5.12 The existing river Pedieos flows through the city, 2110. Image credit: drawn by the author, 2022.

into the Cypriot culture by the British. These activities were held in open spaces (meydan) all over the city where all the Cypriots gathered as well as (men and women). This idea of leisure practice led to the gradual change (in loops) in the social behaviour of the Cypriot culture. This change was more obvious in some communities than others which led to conflict in cultural practice and identity among some Cypriot communities. Some welcomed this alteration in social behaviour while others wanted to hold on to the old Nicosia of the past and hoped that it will one day resurface.

Cosmopolitan Nature

The location and shape of the Buffer Zone and the way it connects to a network of other green structures allows nature to move deep within the city (Given, 2000, 209–230). The key is to re-link the natural flow of flora and fauna and optimise movements between city and country. Additionally, these links can extend beyond the microclimate and the flow of nature can become truly international. The renowned space acts as a botanical condenser, making sure species from all over the world find their way to the right agricultural fields and conditions in the 'Green Zone', as shown in Figure 5.13. A series of spectacular agriculture towers through the city of Nicosia 'echo' the special planting inside the agricultural lands. A new composition of agriculture and bird towers will redefine the skyline of Nicosia making the 'Green Zone' visible from the Pentaklythos (mountains) in the heart of the city and from many of the tall buildings around the centre.

This conceptual map represents collective memories of the Cypriots. The horizontal countered line represents the river Pedieos passing through the Green Line. The frame placed in the background symbolises the old Nicosia and acts as a catalyst to bring to the surface the theory of urban vision

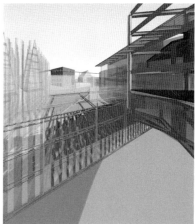

Figure 5.13 Agricultural fields convert the city into a 'botanical condenser'. Image credit: drawn by the author, 2022.

116 *Bertug Ozarisoy*

of the city by bringing together all the elements passing through it (Scott, 2002, 217–230). The vertical knotted and red lines represent the division of the city and reflects the chaos resulting from this conflict and division passing through the frame. The vertical thin sharp lines represent changes in the nature of the space of the Buffer Zone and Nicosia, which are both represented horizontally inside the frame. The angled and straight horizontally placed lines which cross the frame represent the movements and flow of the Cypriots from North to South and South to North at the present time. The different coloured squares in the frame represent the topography of the city as it is now. These different shaped squares reflect on different types of memories of the people. This map depicts Nicosia City as a central marketplace before the division and its present situation. The horizontal line represents the division and my vision of the reclaimed river Pedieos passing through Ermou Street.

The vertical line represents Ermou Street as the central point of the city at that time. The horizontal lines represent the main routes which gave access into the city and the outside main routes which gave access. The shapes in different forms and colours on Ermou Street represent the different lively communities in Nicosia City during the time before division.

The horizontal rectilinear on the right line represents Ledras Street as it goes into Ermou Street and stops there. This depicts the present situation in this region where it is proceeding as normal on this side of the city but there is no life on the other side of the Buffer Zone. This also represents Ermou Street as the main supplier of fresh fruit and vegetables to many places outside the city via the many routes.

Public Spaces

The 'Green Zone' is not a regular project – it is a rather abstract ideal, shared by many citizens of Nicosia (Bowman, 2006, 119–127). The ideal can be seen as a comprehensive cloud of ideas and ambitions, a complex sequence of dos and don'ts. The residents of Nicosia have enthusiastically supported the utopian vision of the 'Green Zone' project and will aid in creating a tailor-made green space for the larger community, as shown in Figure 5.14. To give the inner-city breathing space, not everything should be planned and fixed in the Buffer Zone at one time. Each individual area within the boundaries of the 'Green Zone' has different users. They will be involved as much as possible by organising 'circles'. Each circle adopts a park area and selects the most viable programming functions and features for the space. Eventually a diverse, vibrant and unified Nicosia emerges.

This map represents Nicosia City from past to future. The horizontal countered line represents my visionary river Pedieos. The frame situated in the background symbolises the old walled city of Nicosia and acts as a catalyst to bring to the surface the theory of utopian urban vision of the city by bringing to the surface all the diaspora passing through it. The curved

A Utopia 117

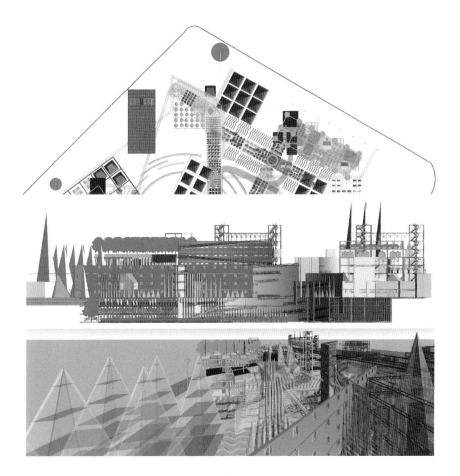

Figure 5.14 Public spaces represent the diversity of the city. Image credit: drawn by the author, 2022.

horizontal orange line represents Turkish Cypriots as the majority. The thin turquoise colour spaces represent Turkish Cypriots as the minority, and these two communities used to live mixed side-by-side before the division (Faustmann, 2008, 453–458). The curved horizontal light orange space represents the movement and interaction of the two communities within each other and how this shaped the Cypriot identity before the division. At the same time the other small spaces (green, pink and yellow) in the frame represent how the other small sub-culture communities lived nearby and they also interacted with both communities and contributed to the unique shaping of the Cypriot identity before the division.

The black coloured multi-curved line represents the massive migration which took place after the division and resulted in the collapse of the

118   *Bertug Ozarisoy*

multicultural community settlement. The triangular light and dark green spaces represent the Turkish and Greek Cypriots living completely separately from each other after the division.

After the division the other small minorities (Armenians, Jews) appeared from this area. The white coloured oval space represents the Buffer Zone today. After all this migration and resettlement, one can see the informal settlement of other ethnic recent migrant communities around the Buffer Zone today. This after effect of the resettlements has created major diversity which has reshaped the Cypriot culture and identity. This map represents Nicosia City at the present time. The horizontal countered white line on top symbolises my visionary river Pedieos. The light orange horizontal space represents the Buffer Zone.

The pink shaped rectangular space represents the Turkish military controlling the Buffer Zone from the Turkish sector of the city. The black rectangular space represents the Greek military controlling the Buffer Zone from the Greek sector of the city. The other pink and black spaces represent the distribution of the United Nations military controlling the Buffer Zone on both sides; hence the United Nations is in total control.

The continuous lines up and down the Buffer Zone represent the invisible power of the military. The dotted looped lines represent the movements of the Cypriot people among this invisible power. All the above is taking place in the frame symbolising Nicosia.

Green Religion

In the design of my utopian urban vision, the connection of all the mentioned diasporas in the grid brings together the form of a self-sustainable city which is in interaction with the surrounding natural environment to create this Green Zone, bringing forward the idea of a new Green Zone and consequently the idea of a new green religion, as shown in Figure 5.15. The Green Religion is more than just agriculture and birds for the Green Zone, it provides ecological and social wealth for the city by expanding the commonly received notion of wealth to include fresh air, water, natural daylight and green spaces (Stepnik, 2020). Beyond these natural advantages to the environment, it also helps to bring the communities together to form one diverse community and single Cypriot identity that lives in peace.

The concrete blocks of urban sprawl, which is present now outside the walls of Nicosia City, is synonymous with climate change, air pollution, increased traffic and energy over-consumption resulting in negative health for its inhabitants. The regions of the green belt and the urban concrete block belt are located next to each other, and the self-sustainable environment of the green belt acts as a catalyst to reduce temperatures in the summer and its aftereffects (Hawkes & Lawrence, 2021, 861–892). The Green Zone ensures its inhabitants the freedom to exercise their new green

A Utopia 119

Figure 5.15 Agricultural fields through the city. Image credit: drawn by the author, 2022.

120 *Bertug Ozarisoy*

religion, cultivating a green notion of wealth – hence the city is made ready for the future.

In the event of 'Creative Possibilities: Birds, Narratives and Artefacts' as I was describing my utopian urban vision to the participants, they informed me that as this urban vision is open to discussion, they wanted to create their own free spaces there, as shown in Figure 5.16. The idea of these free spaces to the participants of my event came from their experiences of seeing and meeting the ethnic migrant workers from Asia of different cultures all coming together on their free days and creating their own free spaces in the city where they socialise, entertain themselves and set up markets for food, etc., hence creating a new type of cultural practice in Nicosia City.

Figure 5.16 New spaces bring cultural practice between the two communities. Image credit: drawn by the author, 2022.

In the design of my utopian urban vision, I allocated rectangular forms which depict these free spaces, and they are placed at various points as part of the network of the Green Zone without interfering with its function. This is a historical tradition of the Cypriots which was held about twice a year in every region of Cyprus. In these panayiris (fun-fairs) people of all trades brought their goods to sell including handmade clothes, furniture and homemade produce of cheese (halloumi) or sweets. There were also live animals (chickens, oxen, cows, goats, donkeys) brought there to be sold or exchanged. There were also cooked kebabs and lokmades (sweets) to eat. The exchange of these goods was either with cash or with other goods. This event went on for about a week.

In the public spaces of the Green Zone, we aim to capture this traditional culture of the panayiri at the same time benefiting the local community economically and socially by enabling them to sell their own hand made produce (rather than imported goods) and bringing the whole Cypriot community together hence reclaiming the traces and the air of traditional Cyprus.

This tradition of open-air entertainment was introduced into the Cypriot culture by the British. This enabled the Cypriots (men and women) to come out of their houses and gather side by side in these places. This event was one of the main factors in breaking the chains of the Cypriots from the Ottoman culture, replacing it with another culture (more Western civilization). In the public spaces of the Green Zone, we aim to recapture this type of gathering of the Cypriots to watch their own cinemas, theatres, shows and concerts all depicting the Cypriot culture and bringing back the old feeling of the Cypriots as a chosen community at leisure.

Conclusions

Mapping the invisibility of the city seeks to find how attached we are to our own perceptions and illusions when reality is reflected in a thousand other ways. What has appeared in this world and the next will disappear, and that which has disappeared on one level will reappear on another in a different form.

Embracing paradox, we approach the invisible, and what is visible reflects where we are in time and space and consciousness. Perhaps architecture is a means of identification with reality of making the invisible visible, sounds taking form sound shaping consciousness, refracted light revealing our delirium and desire, our world shaped by the word. Our journeys take us into the territory of the imagination of a thousand materialised ideas mapping the invisible. The aim of these mappings is to carry out urban and scientific analysis of the Nicosia City from past to future to understand its support of my own theory of utopian vision for the city of Nicosia. Instead of using traditional urban designs, artistic drawings have been used as a tool to configure this theory of utopian vision.

122 *Bertug Ozarisoy*

In my mapping theory, I define that the river Pedieos is reclaimed. The frame found on every map symbolises or incorporates the old Nicosia as it was before. This frame also acts as a catalyst to bring together all the diaspora passing through it to form the multicultural diversity beyond the division for the city of Nicosia.

A quest for what is in between: between two worlds, future and past, social and marginal, private and public, unspeakable and expressed; between the world of seeing, doing, standards and uses, and dreams, fantasies and psyche. Like the storytelling and never-ending route of the utopian urban vision of Nicosia. This space in between creates a hybrid environment as well as a desire beyond the division of the city. It is both a connecting space between the visible and the invisible and a connection from established rules of 'unification'. This notion of the space in between is being developed through diasporas in the utopian urban vision of Nicosia.

In creating the utopian urban vision, several series of design principles were used to form different layers of strategies (the existing urban layout, traces of river Pedieos, conflict, the grid, public spaces, green route, utopian urban vision route, new urban layout and diasporas). These strategies define the concept of invisibility behind visibility at the same time confirming my theory of how using the past and the present situation of Nicosia enables one to visualise the future – the utopian urban vision. In the attempt of designing this scenario, I used the traces of the past and narratives from the event of 'Creative Possibilities' as a foundation to construct a utopia. This approach enabled me to transgress the philosophy of utopian terminology.

Transgression suggests operating beyond accepted norms and radically reinterpreting practice by pushing at the boundaries of both what the architectural value of the context is and what it could or even should be. In this context, the current crisis and accompanying political/social unrest have exacerbated the difficulty into which architecture and urban strategy has long been sliding. Challenged by a culture of practice, identity is in danger of losing its prized status as one of the prominent visions of the city. Transgression would open new possibilities for reconstruction for the Cypriot society.

My key point here is to suggest that the spirit of transgression is required and arises in periods of processing diasporas of the city, where the old ways need better solutions rather than radical practices, and new potential future paths are chartered. The transgressive strategy needs to be supplemented by a utopia that can develop a new viable paradigm that might eventually mature to replace the prior mainstream practice and to take on the responsibility of advancing global best practice in the Green Line with the new social demands and opportunities. The Buffer Zone design of a utopian urban vision for Nicosia did not embrace a realistic approach to revitalising the city for Cypriot use. Two concluding counterpoints manifest, namely that transgressions are only productive during revolutionary periods at the beginning of a major cycle of innovation, and that in order to be productive, transgressions must remain within the discipline's bounds determined by the functional differentiation of the Cypriot society.

Utopian urban vision for Nicosia will be a powerful response to Cypriots' desires because of its ability to abstract and crystallise a problem into a concise and internally consistent solution. This proposed scenario unifies both communities that depict new kinds of architecture and radically innovative concepts of urbanity that might well become reality in years to come. This vision would merge and erase borders. The movement and behaviour of its inhabitants would reflect the dynamic motion in and around the city. The unique social and characteristics of the real world would be dynamically merged and mixed into a new unpredictable synthesis. The scheme would provide a way to experience and populate a new environment, which would be built to reflect the 'Green Zone' laws of a manifold city in motion. The city would be simultaneously diurnal and nocturnal. Absorbing data from real and imagined diasporas, it would engage and extend our perception and experience via continuous narratives. Here, the transformative laws of nature would divulge new stories. Condensed into virtual space, the city would be tangible yet not tangible, visible yet invisible, physical yet ethereal, and yet, nevertheless, clearly representing utopian urban vision.

The concept of a utopia is developed for a society that is currently not responding effectively enough to the crisis of Cyprus. A utopia, in this case, refers to a point in between our current conditions and the 'ultimate' possibilities when the philosophy of transgression has reached, or surpassed, that of visionary intelligence. The utopian city model explores the concept of a technological and scientific plurality where Cypriots may have evolved to transcend their enthusiasm, forming a hybrid system with the participation process, and in turn overcoming through their stories. The project highlights the impact of 'transgression' on society, the realisation of the tension between two communities, and the worrying lack of effective practices. It suggests the role of the city as a critical component in the development of a unified future, the conception of the integrity of diasporas as a necessity in Cypriot's future evolution.

A utopia would be embedded within a greater future society, uniting humanity as well as preserving nature and cultural identity rather than suppressing, or ignoring, cultural ideology. The society of the future will hopefully have improved, especially about the perception of unification beyond division. The evolution of the utopian urban vision of the Cypriot society is one of the key ameliorations that should become visible and influenced by the improvement of the built environment.

The city would be a model for the future. A place of perpetual transformation and self-generation – a new way to reflect Cypriot desires and hopes. It represents a new blueprint of urbanism that would engage contemporary communication, density, lifestyle, cultural practice and globalisation, structured in an ideal urban and architectural space.

References

Altay, C. (2013). Transgression in and of the city. *Architectural Design*, 83(6), 102–109. https://doi.org/10.1002/ad.1682

Barnaba, S. (2006). *Cyprus from the eighth century to the beginning of British rule* (pp. 14–18). Nicosia: Mouflon Bookshop Publishing.

Bowman, J. (2006). Seeing what's missing in memories of Cyprus. *Peace Review*, 18(1), 119–127. https://doi.org/10.1080/10402650500510776

Bragina, L. G. (2012). Radiolarian biostratigraphy of the perapedhi formation (Cyprus): Implications for the geological evolution of the troodos ophiolite. In *Bulletin de la Societe Geologique de France* (Vol. 183, pp. 343–348). https://doi.org/10.2113/gssgfbull.183.4.343

Briel, H. (2013). The uses of oral history in Cyprus: Ethics, memory and identity. *Language and Intercultural Communication*, 13(1), 27–43. https://doi.org/10.1080/14708477.2012.748788

Bryant, R. (2002). The purity of spirit and the power of blood: A comparative perspective on nation, gender and kinship in Cyprus. *Journal of the Royal Anthropological Institute*, 8(3), 509–530. https://doi.org/10.1111/1467-9655.00120

Bryant, R. (2014). History's remainders: On time and objects after conflict in Cyprus. *American Ethnologist*, 41(4), 681–697. https://doi.org/10.1111/amet.12105

Coleman, N. (2013). Building in empty spaces: Is architecture a degenerate Utopia? *Journal of Architecture*, 18(2), 135–166. https://doi.org/10.1080/13602365.2013.783225

Cunningham, D. (2001). Architecture, Utopia and the futures of the avant-garde. *Journal of Architecture*. https://doi.org/10.1080/13602360110048195

Deckers, K. (2005). Post-roman history of river systems in western Cyprus: Causes and archaeological implications. *Journal of Mediterranean Archaeology*, 18(2), 155–181. https://doi.org/10.1558/jmea.2005.18.2.155

Denison, E., & Ren, G. (2013). Transgression and progress in China: Wang Shu and the literati mindset. *Architectural Design*, 83(6), 38–43. https://doi.org/10.1002/ad.1672

Doron, G. M. (2000). The dead zone and the architecture of transgression. *City*, 4(2), 247–263. https://doi.org/10.1080/13604810050147857

Dovey, K. (2013). Architecture the challenge of informal. *Architectural Design*, 83(6), 82–89.

Faustmann, H. (2008). History in the making? A new drive for a solution to the Cyprus problem: Profile. *Mediterranean Politics*, 13(3), 453–458. https://doi.org/10.1080/13629390802387034

García Vergara, M., & Pizza, A. (2021). The Mediterranean and modern architecture: The dissemination of a myth in architectural media. *Journal of Architecture*, 26(8), 1117–1145. https://doi.org/10.1080/13602365.2021.1980419

Ghilardi, M., Cordier, S., Carozza, J. M., Psomiadis, D., Guilaine, J., Zomeni, Z., ... Morhange, C. (2015). The Holocene fluvial history of the tremithos river (South central Cyprus) and its linkage to archaeological records. *Environmental Archaeology*, 20(2), 184–201. https://doi.org/10.1179/1749631414Y.0000000057

Given, M. (2000). Agriculture, settlement and landscape in Ottoman Cyprus. *International Journal of Phytoremediation*, 21(1), 209–230. https://doi.org/10.1179/lev.2000.32.1.209

Given, M. (2002). Maps, fields, and boundary cairns: Demarcation and resistance in colonial Cyprus. *International Journal of Historical Archeology*, 6(1), 1–22. https://doi.org/10.1023/A:1014862125523

Given, M. (2005). Architectural styles and ethnic identity in medieval to modern Cyprus. In J. Clarke (Ed.), *Archaeological perspectives on the transmission and assimilation of culture in the eastern Mediterranean* (Vol. 2, pp. 207–213). Famagusta: Council for British Research in the Levant.

Grubbauer, M. (2019). Postcolonial urbanism across disciplinary boundaries: Modes of (dis)engagement between urban theory and professional practice. *Journal of Architecture*, 24(4), 469–486. https://doi.org/10.1080/13602365.2019.1643390

Hadjipavlou, M. (2007). Multiple stories: The "crossings" as part of citizens' reconciliation efforts in Cyprus? *Innovation: The European Journal of Social Science Research*, 20(1), 53–73. https://doi.org/10.1080/13511610701197866

Hawkes, D., & Lawrence, R. (2021). Climate, comfort, and architecture in Elizabethan England: An environmental study of Hardwick Hall. *Journal of Architecture*, 26(6), 861–892. https://doi.org/10.1080/13602365.2021.1962389

Hejduk, R. (2007). Death becomes her: Transgression, decay, and eROTicism in Bernard Tschumi's early writings and projects. *Journal of Architecture*, 12, 393–404. https://doi.org/10.1080/13602360701614672

Jung, Y., & Cinn, E. (2020). Conflicting ideals and realities: The architecture of South Korea's first high-rise housing complex. *Journal of Architecture*, 25(6), 736–758. https://doi.org/10.1080/13602365.2020.1802613

Kliot, N., & Mansfield, Y. (1997). The political landscape of partition: The case of Cyprus. *Political Geography*, 16(6), 495–521. https://doi.org/10.1016/s0962-6298(96)00020-0

Lacher, H., & Kaymak, E. (2005). Transforming identities: Beyond the politics of non-settlement in North Cyprus. *Mediterranean Politics*, 10(2), 147–166. https://doi.org/10.1080/13629390500124341

Leonard, M. (2014). Echoes from the past: Intergenerational memories in Cyprus. *Children and Society*, 28(1), 66–76. https://doi.org/10.1111/j.1099-0860.2012.00445.x

Littlefield, D. (2013). Ashes thrown to the wind: The elusive nature of transgression. *Architectural Design*, 83(6), 124–129. https://doi.org/10.1002/ad.1686

Loizides, N. (2011). Contested migration and settler politics in Cyprus. *Political Geography*, 30(7), 391–401. https://doi.org/10.1016/j.polgeo.2011.08.004

Manning, S. W. (1998). Changing pasts and socio-political cognition in late Bronze Age Cyprus. *World Archaeology*, 30(1), 39–58. https://doi.org/10.1080/00438243.1998.9980396

McKeown, S., Haji, R., & Ferguson, N. (2016). *Understanding peace and conflict through social identity theory* (pp. 3–17). https://doi.org/10.1007/978-3-319-29869-6

Mosley, J., & Sara, R. (2013). The architecture of transgression: Towards a destabilising architecture. *Architectural Design*, 83(6), 14–19. https://doi.org/10.1002/ad.1668

Mumford, E. (2009). CIAM and the communist bloc, 1928–59. *Journal of Architecture*, 14(2), 237–254. https://doi.org/10.1080/13602360802704810

Ozarisoy, B., & Altan, H. (2021a). Developing an evidence-based energy-policy framework to assess robust energy-performance evaluation and certification schemes in the South-Eastern Mediterranean countries. *Energy for Sustainable Development*, *64*, 65–102. https://doi.org/10.1016/j.esd.2021.08.001

Ozarisoy, B., & Altan, H. (2021b). A novel methodological framework for the optimisation of post-war social housing developments in the South-Eastern Mediterranean climate: Policy design and life-cycle cost impact analysis of retrofitting strategies. *Solar Energy*, *225*, 517–560. https://doi.org/10.1016/j.solener.2021.07.008

Ozarisoy, B., & Altan, H. (2022). Significance of occupancy patterns and habitual household adaptive behaviour on home-energy performance of post-war social-housing estate in the South-Eastern Mediterranean climate: Energy policy design. *Energy*, *244*. https://doi.org/10.1016/j.energy.2021.122904

Papadakis, Y. (2003). Nation, narrative and commemoration: Political ritual in divided Cyprus. *History and Anthropology*, *14*(3), 253–270. https://doi.org/10.1080/0275720032000136642

Papadakis, Y. (2004). Discourses of "the Balkans" in Cyprus: Tactics, strategies and constructions of "others". *History and Anthropology*, *15*(1), 15–27. https://doi.org/10.1080/027572004200191064

Psaltis, C. (2016). Collective memory, social representations of intercommunal relations, and conflict transformation in divided Cyprus. *Peace and Conflict*, *22*(1), 19–27. https://doi.org/10.1037/pac0000145

Pullan, W. (2011). Frontier urbanism: The periphery at the centre of contested cities. *Journal of Architecture*. https://doi.org/10.1080/13602365.2011.546999

Roberts-Hughes, R. (2017). Transgression and conservation: Rereading Georges Bataille. *Journal for Cultural Research*, *21*(2), 157–168. https://doi.org/10.1080/14797585.2016.1239608

Sara, R., & Littlefield, D. (2014). Transgression: Body and space. *Architecture and Culture*, *2*(3), 295–304. https://doi.org/10.2752/205078214X14107818390513

Scott, J. (2002). Mapping the past: Turkish Cypriot narratives of time and place in the Canbulat Museum, Northern Cyprus. *History and Anthropology*, *13*(3), 217–230. https://doi.org/10.1080/0275720022000025529

Sharp, D. (2022). Concretising conflict. *Journal of Architecture*. https://doi.org/10.1080/13602365.2022.2029026

Stępnik, M. (2020). The house that lars built: The architecture of transgression. *Arts*, *9*(4), 127. https://doi.org/10.3390/arts9040127

Thompson, S., St. Karayanni, S., & Vassiliadou, M. (2004). Cyprus after history. *Interventions*, *6*(2), 282–299. https://doi.org/10.1080/1369801042000238373

Walsh, M. (2007). The re-emergence of the forty martyrs of Sebaste in the church of Saint Peter and Paul, Famagusta, Northern Cyprus. *Journal of Cultural Heritage*, *8*(1), 81–86. https://doi.org/10.1016/j.culher.2006.04.008

6 Representations of Diaspora, Cultural Identity and Difference

Bertug Ozarisoy

Introduction

The domestic space plays a crucial role in the everyday living of a Turkish Cypriot family. Because of their close-knit relationship with each other and their extended families, the inside of the house is used for their cultural codes and rituals and for family meetings of all kinds.[1] Hegglund (1997) points out 'Home is where one starts from'. In contrast, Foucault (1979) describes the term of 'domestic space' as that of 'A whole history remains to be written of spaces – which would at the same time be the history of powers from the great strategies of geopolitics to the little tactics of the habitat'. In the past decade, far from being taken for granted, houses have been the subject of growing and interesting multidisciplinary inquiry. The immensity in reach and influence of global and transnational economies have provoked a contrary desire for the local and domestic, which has in turn promoted an increased scrutiny of the home. This scrutiny inevitably generates a multitude of questions, which the following sections of this research seek to address: how does one configure and interpret the home in relation to the nation, political ideologies, daily routines, domestic rituals and social relationships? How is the construction of self and subjectivity connected to one's domestic space? What does it mean to belong? And by what means is a distinction made between the domestic interior and architectural metaphors as representational or analogical and the architectural and domestic as epistemological and ontological, as ways of thinking, knowing, experiencing? Because the Cypriot culture is so strong and family-dominated, they use whatever space they are living in at any given time to their full advantage by using all the means from their living space culture in Cyprus.

The house, quite obviously, is a privileged entity for a phenomenological study of the intimate values of inside space, provided, of course, that we take it in both its unity and its complexity and endeavour to integrate all the values of Turkish Cypriots in one fundamental value. For the house furnishes us with dispersed images and a body of images at the same time. In both cases, we shall prove that imagination augments the values of reality. A sort of attraction for images concentrates them on the house. Foucault

DOI: 10.4324/9781003243069-8

128　*Bertug Ozarisoy*

(1986) contended that our era seems to be that of space. We are in the age of the simultaneous, of juxtaposition, the near and the far, the side by side and scattered (Beeckmans, 2014, 849–871). According to Foucault's ideology, the main reason to look at the Turkish Cypriot community living through domestic space reading as an increasingly pertinent subject of inquiry is obviously linked to the mid-20th century 'spatial turn' in critical thinking.[2] The selection of four Turkish Cypriot families across London in this research sketches the changes, influences and varieties of domestic interiors from traditional rural Turkish Cypriot houses to modern British houses and across different cultural practices (Jacoby et al., 2022, 1–33). As underscored by these selections, the significant role of the interior is a way of mapping and crossing the boundaries in terms of education, marriage and interaction with other cultures.[3]

This research demonstrates how discussions on domestic space not only led us to a deeper understanding of the Turkish Cypriot community living in London, but also to question traditional perceptions of memories from Cyprus, their degree of adaptation while living among other cultures in the society and also how these interactions with other cultures changed or eroded their original Cypriot culture and identity. The aim is to examine the major issues relevant to each of these four Turkish Cypriot family groups, as well as to assess the reasons for their migration from Cyprus to London.

Narrative Memories of Turkish Cypriots' Living and Their Domestic Space Use

In this exploratory research study, Turkish Cypriot families were chosen because they migrated to London from rural villages in Cyprus in the 1950s, and they mainly settled in East London and worked in the textile and catering industries. These families today live in different boroughs of London; Kingsbury, Lewisham, Barking and Highgate. We were interested in their migration histories, memories and lifestyles, as well as their own experiences through generations living in London. This research therefore aims to provide a greater understanding of the complex and contradictory factors of how these four Turkish Cypriot families adapted and practiced their own cultural identity in order to live inside a British house.

Data for the research was collected by using a combination of participant observations and semi-structured interviews. During the period of our fieldwork, we visited these four Turkish Cypriot families three times, and we divided the structure of interviews into three phases. Firstly, we collected information through conversations and photographic documentation from the past. Secondly, we asked them to write their own memories of their first arrival to London and to draw the plans of their previous houses. Finally, we looked at the interior of their houses and asked them if they had got any traces from Cyprus, such as furniture, paintings, or artefacts. In the conclusion part of this research, we attempt to analyse how our personal

Diaspora, Cultural Identity and Difference   129

experiences from the research process itself compares to our life and culture as a Turkish Cypriot born and growing in Cyprus.

History and Reasons for Immigration

Turkish Cypriots started immigrating to Britain in the late 1940s and early 1950s, in large measure in the 1950s when EOKA (a Greek nationalist paramilitary group whose fundamental goals were 'the liberation of Cyprus from the British yoke' and unification with motherland Greece) began attacking Turkish Cypriot communities on the island.[4] Trapped then between the Greeks and the British troops, the Turkish Cypriots became poorer and poorer, with no appropriate infrastructure, little education and less and less money.[5] They then decided to escape all of these difficulties and earn money quickly in London. Because Cyprus was a colony at the time, and Britain needed a labour force, they chose to immigrate to London and work in its factories – a decision made easier by the fact that Cypriots were familiar with the British way of administration, culture and the English language.[6]

Legal immigration to England was restricted after the 1960 declaration of independence of Cyprus, but it nevertheless continued unabated between 1960 and 1974 because of the 'cold civil war' where the Greek Cypriots had autonomy of the island, and the Turkish Cypriots were kept in enclaves with restricted movement and lack of employment.[7] This type of immigration continued after 1974 until the early 1980s because of a broken economy and infrastructure after the 1974 Turkish military intervention due to the internal conflict. The type of immigration between the 1960s and early 1980s was by way of single young men and women going to London on 'tourist' visas and staying in London illegally until they married someone with a UK passport and were able to stay legally (Calotychos, 1998, 45–47).[8] This contrasts with the type of immigration common in the 1950s, where it was men with young families immigrating to London, as shown in Figure 6.1.

Notably, immigrating to London was always the first choice as, by the time of the second wave of immigration, almost everyone had a relative whom they could stay with, and work was easy to find as many Cypriots had started their own businesses. It is interesting to note that the other country of choice to immigrate for many Turkish Cypriots was Australia. Immigration there started in the 1950s, but it was very slow compared to immigration to London. The reason that Australia became a popular destination for immigrating Turkish Cypriots was because of its language, easy visa access and job opportunities.[9]

Migration and Cultural Practices of Turkish Cypriots from Cyprus to London: Narrative Memories

The importance of domestic space and its interrelations between the way of living space and cultural interactions to the Cypriot community's social norms in everyday living in Cyprus just before immigrating to London in

130 Bertug Ozarisoy

Figure 6.1 First-generation family in London with children; one son was born in Cyprus; the other son and daughter were born in London just after their immigration in 1956. The image was taken at a weekend retreat to the Greenwich Market in London in 1964. Image credit: the author, 2022.

the 1950s is described the context.[10] At the same time, the family lives in the village, their own private house and land.[11] As shown in Figure 6.2, the whole family cooked, ate, rested and slept in two rooms inside the house. They had no electricity or water. They used a paraffin lamp at night for light. The water was drawn from a well in their garden. They washed clothes by hand in a stone sink outside the house using soap made from olive oil which they produced themselves. They made their own bread from the flour which they milled from wheat they harvested. Every house had a stone and mud oven outside the house fuelled by wood collected from the bushes outside the village. Outside the house, they always had a vegetable plot where they grew their own vegetables throughout the year. They lived by a strict community code which was not religiously dominated. The neighbourhood relationships were very close, and they always helped each other with all their work.[12] Although Cyprus was under British rule for nearly 80 years, these families living in these rural villages were isolated from town centres, not exposed to any kind of modernism or interference in their cultural practices.[13]

As a result of this, plus the civil war conflicts over many years, they were left poor and deprived.[14] These factors forced many men to leave rural village life and seek employment abroad. London was the first choice because they were given work visas, and then they invited their families to join them.[15] They all travelled by boat from Limassol, and the whole village used to gather in the family home for several days, giving out long poetic cries before the departure. Most of the village people used to get into the old village bus and go to Limassol for the sendoff. The boat trip took ten

Diaspora, Cultural Identity and Difference 131

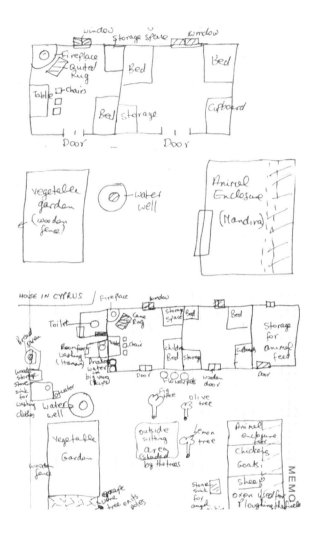

Figure 6.2 The conditions of domestic space and internal floor layout of typical Turkish Cypriots' residences in the 1950s. Image credit: drawn by the subject respondent at the time of undertaking semi-structured interviews, 2018.

days, and then there was a train journey from Dover to Waterloo station in London, where they were met by their relatives. Their domestic space was generally just one or two rooms in basements or derelict houses where they had to share cooking and washing spaces with other Cypriots or others of different nationalities.[16] After a few years, most families who worked and saved money, with children contributing to the family budget, bought their own terraced house with a small garden near other Cypriots. Gardens were

132   *Bertug Ozarisoy*

planted with vegetables, herbs (such as mint and basil) and vine trees for leaves to use in traditional Cypriot cooking; olive trees provided leaves for ceremonial burning.[17]

In the Cypriot culture, it is the tradition to provide a home for their sons when getting married; hence they would convert one or two rooms of their terraced houses into flats and settle their sons there until they could afford to buy their own homes.[18] Their sons or daughters would buy a semi-detached or detached home further away from other Cypriots. As they became more affluent, they would buy more luxury furnishings and decorations for their houses.[19] With the first comers, there was a very strict code of conduct, even more so than in the village in Cyprus, because there was fear of the unknown outside.[20] This strict code of conduct got hybridised over generations; this reflected on the domestic space and the inside decoration of these spaces concurrently.

Representational Space and Cultural Identity

As far as space is concerned, decisive changes occurred at this juncture which are effectively obscured by invariant, surviving or stagnant elements, especially on the plane of representational space (Kimmel, 2020, 659–678). Space presents obstacles on every side to the kind of history that we have been discussing – the history of space/the space of history; representations of space/representational space. It pushes us back towards a purely descriptive understanding, for it stands opposed to any analytic approach and even more to any global account of the generative process when we are looking at the four Turkish Cypriot communities in London.[21] In some cases, such as Turkish Cypriot migrants, for example, migrants seek to slow down communication within other communities so as to preserve their cultural norms, customs and representational spaces from their newly adapted environment.[22] Rapoport (1969) mentions that this kind of preservation makes the anthropology of the home 'so interesting'. The traditional Turkish Cypriot house is indeed just as worthy of study as those anthropological connections within culture and representations of space.

In order to fully understand the importance and symbolic value attached to the traditional Turkish Cypriot house in the representation of space, one must appreciate that it functions as a magical frontier, a place of a logical inversion and the obligatory place of passage and meeting between two contexts, which are defined in relation to the socially qualified movements between Cyprus and London (Hughes-Wilson, 2011, 84–93). To understand the way Turkish Cypriots use their living space in London, one must examine and understand their way of using and living in any given space while they were living in Cyprus before moving to London.

The raw material of the production of space is not, as in the case of objects, a particular material (straw, brick and mud): it is rather nature itself, nature transformed into a product, rudely manipulated, now threatened in

Diaspora, Cultural Identity and Difference   133

its very existence, probably ruined and certainly and most paradoxically localized (Heraclides, 2011, 117–139). The interior of the Turkish Cypriot house is rectangular in shape and is divided into two parts at a point one-third of the way along its length by a timber framed lattice work wall half as high as the house. Of these two parts, the larger is covered by a layer of brick and clay; this part is reserved for human use. The smaller part is paved with flagstones and is used for the purpose of service and storage facilities.

We should therefore have to say how we inhabit our vital space, in accordance with all the dialectics of life, how we take root, in any given 'corner of the world' (Benjamin, 1999, 23–25). The first-generation Cyprus migrants said that 'We bring our lures with us' because, in their culture of conservatism, there is an attachment to any kind of object or material which they owned and used in their life in Cyprus. In taking these with them, it allowed them to continue practicing their cultural values in London, as they felt they would feel more at home if they have these objects around them in their new, unfamiliar space. In this remote region, memory and imagination remain associated, each one working for their mutual deepening. In the order of values, they both constitute a community of memory and image. Now my aim is clear: I must show that the house is one of the greatest powers of integration for the thought and memories of mankind. The binding principle in this integration is the experiences of Turkish Cypriots.

Concerning space in a broad sense, there are some differences between houses, as a physical artefact, and homes, places of identity and social construct (Lohtaja, 2021, 499–515). Many social units (are communities) whose behaviour gives identity to a home and to which a home gives identity (Shadar & Maslowski, 2021, 516–540). Because individual and social behaviours are also related to value systems, houses form and materially express values of identity as well (Gitler, 2021, 316–339). To bridge universality and particularity of behaviour, three concepts of global interest play a crucial role: family (Turkish Cypriots), social hierarchy (interaction within cultures) and mode of activity (education or marriage). This leads us to look at the broader issues concerning the relation between identity, home and society (Dawes & Ostwald, 2014). The main fact is the identity of space. This reflects a sedentary, agrarian set of values, and a particular concept of 'rootedness'. It is the fact that one's abilities to maintain an identity between culture and space, that is actually to dwell in the place one regards as home, are strongly related to the social and individual behaviour of the community.

Context of Change and Displacement

Focus of this research is an assessment of the extent to which contemporary patterns of change and mobility are affecting representations and meanings of space. A hybrid, mobile subject is the iconic figure of an increasingly distant geography that connects the past and the future. Urry (2000)

134   *Bertug Ozarisoy*

mentions that social structure is defined by mobility rather than presence/ place. While the concept of home is an idea that unites a range of spatial scales from homeland – the nation – to the home – the house or the earth. A first-generation migrant describes 'The Turkish Cypriot's residence in Cyprus' comprising two rooms: in one room, there was a fireplace around which family gatherings and living took place. There was a small, enclosed space just outside the house reserved for growing their own vegetables and next to it an enclosed space for their domestic animals.

Foucault (1986) observes that

> Perhaps our life is still governed by a certain number of oppositions that remain inviolable in everyday lives of Cypriots. To this extent, our institutions and practices have not yet dared to break down. These are the oppositions that we regard as simple givens to describe urban manifestos. For example, between private space and public space were articulated transitional spaces.

This reference is used to enable us to understand how their use of their living space in Cyprus is transferred or adapted to their new living space in London. Foucault's 'simple givens' have not gone unchallenged. The idea of home as a fixed place, capable of connecting past and future, and separate from public space, has been queried by scholars who have pointed out how such an idea, absent from many premodern or non-Western societies, is predicated on settled and unitary communities and has been remapped by migration. Thus, this cultural practice is future-oriented research of constructing a sense of belonging in a context of change and displacement.[23]

Cultural Practice of Turkish Cypriot Communities

The main objective of this study highlights the complexity of the issues surrounding the generations and the writing of narrative transcripts in which individuals have different experiences in their lives. In addition, the review of the existing literature in culture and anthropology highlights the importance of examining the cultural practice of Turkish Cypriots in terms of how they interact with other communities, their educational upbringing and marriage preferences in the past decades.[24] Therefore, this theoretical underpinning examines the identity of domestic living and other factors and their influence on the creation, maintenance and transformation of culture and identity among Turkish Cypriots in London (Lameira, 2021, 1163–1196). In doing so, it demonstrates the importance of kinship and ethnic ties for sustaining and enhancing collective solidarity for the Turkish Cypriots in Britain.[25]

Oakley (1979) mentions that 'Cypriots can be seen as far more "family centered" than any other large ethnic minority in Britain and certainly more so than the population "at large"'. In one of our interviews, we asked a

Diaspora, Cultural Identity and Difference 135

second-generation London adult migrant, 'What kind of communities did you mix with when you first came to London?' And the respondent replied:

> We met and worked together with other Cypriots (both Turks and Greeks) in the early 1950s. Additionally, we always visited each other's houses at weekends for social gathering. We also had big weddings where many people, sometimes up to 1,000 people came.[26] We generally rent in Hackney, Shoreditch or Islington town halls for weddings or other celebrations.

We also asked the respondent, 'Are you still mixing with the Turkish Cypriot community?' 'Not as much as before' he said, 'as their houses have moved further away from each other, the children are grown up and work away from home'.[27] From our point of view, the second- and third-generation migrants are within the stream of the society and have become part of the hybridisation process (Bhabha, 1993, 67–71).

According to Ballard (1994), the third-generation participants are more fully in the wider social order and are therefore subject to different moral and cultural conventions. As a result, they are skilled cultural navigators. For Ballard, the problem with the notion of 'culture conflict' stemmed from the mistaken notion that culture is the comprehensive determinant of the code of discipline. Instead, Ballard conceives of culture as codes and individuals possessing the ability to switch from one code to another.

During our interviews, we asked four Turkish Cypriot families, 'What about the education of children in London?' The reply from one first-generation migrant was,

> Like many Cypriots, when we first moved to London and then brought our families for providing them wealthier life and proper education. This is the reason that we were expecting our children to go to the university and become doctors and lawyers. Hence, we never expected the difficulties like language barrier. To this extent we had been experiencing cultural differences with other ethnic groups. As a result they would have in adapting to a new language environment and the culture shock that the first generation lost to the English education system.[28]

Almost 99% of the second generation of immigrants went into the service sector and became good at business but the third generation went to the university. From our point of view, the children of the second generation did better because of better housing and more educated parents. This is the reason that they were encouraged to study and developed their knowledge in various academic positions in the UK. The girls were given more freedom to go to university anywhere (they chose) and live away from home. Hence with the third generation, both boys and girls were able to go to university.

136 *Bertug Ozarisoy*

These findings demonstrate that they crossed the education threshold that facilitates assimilation into the outside communities.[29]

Notably, the marriages of the Turkish Cypriots at that time were arranged by someone looking for a bride for their sons (or in some instances for daughters looking for a husband). According to the findings of our interviews with the subject respondents, regarding the common practice for marriage across second generation Turkish Cypriots, the answer from four families indicated clearly that second-generation Turkish Cypriot daughters were encouraged to marry within the community because it was felt that they would be socially restricted within the marriage and not allowed to mix outside. However, the second-generation boys married English girls because they were allowed to go out. It is also important to note that their marriages were not approved by their parents.[30]

On the other hand, third-generation girls' marriage preferences have changed significantly from those of their second-generation counterparts. Their parents mostly allowed them to marry other nationalities. We asked one third-generation London-born woman 'You are a third-generation girl married to a Sri Lankan instead of a Turkish Cypriot. Why?'. She explained, 'Well, I don't exactly know, it has just happened. I liked him as a person, and I felt he was the right person for me. I never felt that I was obliged to marry a Turkish Cypriot like my parents did, although I feel that my parents preferred me to marry a Turkish Cypriot, as we would have more in common 'culture wise'.[31] In our view, these results show this third generation have crossed the marriage border as more girls are marrying outside the Cypriot culture.

To sum up, this cultural practice of Turkish Cypriots shows that most of the children did well even though the number of children going to the university from this generation was rather low. They did well within the system to adapt and incorporate or abandon specific elements. For example, in their educational achievements and in crossing marriage boundaries in their search for an appropriate individual strategy. Turkish Cypriots are shown to be actively defining and redefining themselves because of the multifarious cultural and structural factors that they experience both on an individual and community level. Their way of life, education and marriage preferences are crucial to this process of cultural redefinition as first-generation parents' beliefs necessarily reflect and still reflect the structural forces that affect their own lives. The intersection of lifestyle, education and marriage preferences locates Turkish Cypriots in their social positions and subsequently elicits considerations of beliefs and identities.

Space Becomes a Way of Cultural Practice

The settlement patterns of migrants are highly significant in accounting for the concentration of services in any one area (Agarez, 2019, 950–981). Oakley (1970) points out that although Cypriots have tended to move gradually

Diaspora, Cultural Identity and Difference   137

further away from the central area of settlement, the degree of residential concentration has remained high, as ethnic services and employment have moved accordingly. Thus, Oakley argues, Cypriots have displayed a 'moving concentration' rather than a dispersal process. Kucukcan (1999) also stated that the establishment of a neighbourhood through 'clustering' around a particular area constitutes one of the first stages of the institutionalization and reproduction of values for migrants. In another interview, we asked a second-generation migrant, 'Where did you live when you first came to London?' She replied, 'Both in Angel and Islington. The housing was very bad, but it's cheap. Many Cypriots lived there, so we all socialized (Turks or Greeks), and it decreased the feeling of homesickness'.[32]

Concerning the domestic space of the Turkish Cypriots before and after they immigrated to London, it must be known that, although these people were rural village dwellers, they always had their own private family domestic space, which was passed down from generation to generation with wide spaces around them. After immigrating to London, the family first had to live in a bedsit rented accommodation. Next, they moved into two rented rooms, then they bought their own small terrace house with a tiny garden, then they bought a detached or semi-detached house with a big garden further out into the suburbs. The motive for moving into increasingly bigger living spaces was their desire to experience the same code of domestic culture in London which they had in Cyprus.[33]

Subject Participants' Interview Transcripts

This section predominantly examines memories of the earliest experiences of Turkish-Cypriots living in a house in London. At the time of conducting semi-structured interviews with subject respondents, we asked them to write their own memories of domestic living inside their British house and sketch their houses, as shown in Figure 6.3. The aim of this research was to look like a critical reader of the domestic space of the house, understand the physical and cultural forms of their earlier houses and develop a perspective of the way of life of the Turkish Cypriots.

Respondent A – a second-generation migrant recounted, 'We rented a basement flat in Westbourne Park. It was a five-storey terraced house. We lived in this house between 1957 and 1968.' He also describes the interior of the house.

> Under the stairs there was a large room called the coal cellar. We used to store coal for heating in the earlier times. The house also had fireplaces and chimneys. The bath was covered with wood planks and a plastic cover [and] acted as a table.

Respondent B – a second-generation migrant remembers, 'We rented a flat in Woodlands Park Road, Greenwich', and she described the interior of the house:

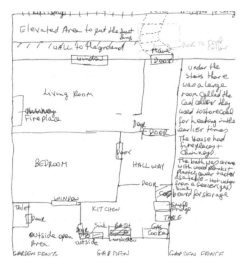

Figure 6.3 Cultural practice and adaptation of Turkish Cypriots in a terraced Victorian house in the late 1970s. Image credit: the author, 2022.

'The inside of the flat was carpeted and very clean. The windows had linen curtains and were thick. In the living room there was a bed set where my two sons and I slept together. There was a TV (of course at that time black and white). The TV set was on a small cupboard which was used to store my sons' clothes. The walls had flowery wallpaper and the ceilings were painted white.

Respondent C – a second-generation migrant relates,

We rented a flat privately on the third floor in Aldgate. It was a four-storey house, old with dark bricks. The interior of the flat had dark stone stairs and dark unpainted walls. There was no bathroom, so a large metal basin was used in the middle of the kitchen where the water was heated or taken from the gas geezer.

Respondent D – a second-generation migrant describes her accommodations,

We rented a flat in Highgate Road. This flat was a new building. It was located on the sixth floor. It had its own lift and intercom system. It was very clean and immaculate and very nicely furnished. The living room had a sofa and armchairs, TV, video, radio, etc. It was decorated with laces because my first-generation grandmother was an expert lace maker and it had memorabilia from Cyprus, such as old and new photographs.

The Poetics of Space

The diversity of ideas of the home is indicated in this research with four Turkish Cypriot communities in London, which range across their movements/historical periods (Cyprus to London and through London), geographical locations and cultures. Ideas of rereading the space of the home are contingent on place and time, reflect religious and cultural practices and are modulated by social factors (Hershenzon, 2021, 116–146). They shape and are themselves shaped by kinship structures (interaction with other communities). Bachelard (1958) evokes the phenomenological significance of the image of the house – its attics, cellars, doors, windows, hearths, drawers, corners and nooks and crannies – and the 'primitive hut' – for our intimate being and imaginative life. Through our observations from Cyprus and in-depth interviews with first-generation Turkish-Cypriot migrants in London, we describe their Cypriot way of living in these words:

> The house in Cyprus for that period consisted of two rooms as a living space, on its left it had a room for storing animal feed, on its right had a small room as a toilet. In its spatial layout organisation, the rooms were arranged in a row in order to provide natural ventilation into indoor occupied spaces. Generally, one-storey buildings were made of mud and local stones. In its construction materials, the floors were earthen. This was followed by the doors and windows which were made of wood.
>
> To describe the poetic of space, the first room had a fireplace which was used for cooking and heating in winter. The purpose of this was the main living space for all the family. In our memory, it should be noted that there was a table and chairs, a cane rug for sitting on the floor in front of the fire, water storage, kiln vases for drinking and cooking, storage space for all the harvested food and a child's bed. Following to the narratives, the other living space had beds and storage cupboards. On the contrary, the toilet was outside and had a hole in its floor. With regard the sanitary purposes, there was a small room for washing by warming water in pots. Outside there was an earth oven for cooking the bread and, next to it, a storage area for wood. This is not limited with habitation of animals; hence, next to this there was a stone sink for washing clothes by hand with water storage and heating purposes. Photographic documentation demonstrates that right next to all these there was a well, which got water from it using a rope and bucket. To follow up, after this next to the well there was an enclosed vegetable garden. With regard the vegetable harvesting, water for the garden was used from the well. On the other side there was an enclosure made of stone and mud walls for keeping animals for domestic use. In between there were trees – fig, olive and lemon trees people used to sit outside under their shades.[34]

140 *Bertug Ozarisoy*

From a sociological and structuralist perspective, the rereading of domestic space details the binary spatial organization of a Turkish Cypriot living inside/outside, nocturnal/daylight, nature/culture, while Turkish Cypriot's investigation of the sociality of religion, in this case Islam in modern Britain, demonstrates how the idea of home is connected to the ways in which religious symbols and practices are domesticated.[35] From the perspective of traditional rural (vernacular) Turkish Cypriot houses in Cyprus and modern British houses in London, it demonstrates how the idea of home is connected to the ways in which religious symbols and practices are domesticated and used through the generations (Lawrence, 2020, 419–443). From the perspective of traditional rural houses in Cyprus and modern British houses it shows how the house is not necessarily a high priority in four Turkish Cypriot families, how homes replicate their entire social systems and how families strive to maintain cultural continuity in the face of social change – a newly adapted environment in London.

Hybridity as a Role of Cultural Practice

The notion of hybridity is a useful abstract thinking (tool) to study the particularities of sociocultural interaction between different groups in circumstances of colonialism and contemporary globalisation.[36] We asked a third-generation London-born and adult participant, 'What do you feel about yourself being a British, Cypriot or Hybrid?' and she stated that

We don't feel exactly British since we are not of English origin. We don't feel exactly Cypriot because the real Cypriots (Greeks or Turks) live in Cyprus and have a different way of life. We think we have become 'hybrids', somewhere in-between as we had to merge two cultures in order to evolve our own personal culture and in order to live in this country.[37]

As Sonyel (1988) points out:

> As it was impossible for them to maintain their Turkish Cypriot identity in a foreign country owing to cultural differences in language, morals and religion, they developed a dynamism of their own and gradually ceased to be an exact replica of the home society. As a result, they have adapted and developed a new version of their Turkish culture and Turkish Cypriot sub-culture in the UK. The culture they now identify with is a re-cycled one; it resembles the homeland culture or subculture in many ways, but it is not quite the same thing. Hybridity has multiple connotations. It refers to the site of cultural practice that emerges on the margins of culture, between cultures. As such, it is a space where cultural elements are continually rearticulated and reconstituted.

Lefebvre (2003) mentions that hybridity also expresses the process of rearticulation of culture, hybridisation, a process in which cultural elements change in relation to themselves and to one another; they continue to hybridise.

For Bhabha, 'hybridisation is the most powerful sign of cultural productivity'. He resorts to the theories of cultural practice to prove that cultures and identities are fragmented, heterogenous and ambivalent (Roberts-Hughes, 2017, 157–168). For that reason, the perpetuation of cultures depends on their interaction with one another. Cultural hybridisation, then, represents the constant, never-ending process of cultural interaction through which cultures continue to exist. Representation of culture as partiality is a key issue in Bhabha's understanding of the term 'hybridity' (Sara & Littlefield, 2014, 295–304). According to literature reviews, which are discussed in this research, and in understanding the cultural practice of the Turkish Cypriot community in London, hybridity is an important concept in addressing questions about how Turkish Cypriots adapted to the new environment in London. Because they do not aim to reduce but rather to maintain difference as an inherent characteristic of all cultures, it permits the theorisation of space and identity as active participants in the continued production of culture.[38]

Critics on Cultural Practice and Space of the Turkish Cypriot Communities

This section of the research takes us inside the domestic space to investigate specific objects, rooms and arrangements. This research also looks at those spaces within the interior elements of the house that negotiate the relationship between traces from traditional Turkish Cypriot homes and modern British homes. 'To live is to leave traces' (Walter Benjamin, 1999, 35–36). He discusses the birth of the interior. In the interior, these traces are emphasised in the way that they are imprinted on the objects of everyday use. The traces of the community also leave their impression (interpretation) on the interior (Sanchez-Verdejo Perez, 2021, 67–89). This reference draws attention to emphasising the role that such spatial images (furniture, artefacts, paintings from Cyprus) play in the collective memory of the Turkish Cypriot house in London.

First, these old houses can be drawn – we can make a representation that has all the characteristics of a 'modern living'. An objective drawing of this kind, experiences of a Turkish Cypriot way of life, is a forceful, reliable document that leaves its mark on a cultural practice. But let this exteriorized representation manifest as an art of drawing or a talent for representation, and it becomes insistent, inviting. Merely to judge it as a good, well executed likeness leads to contemplation and contradictions in understanding how the Turkish Cypriots bring culture to their newly adapted environment. To explore the new adaptations into the domestic space in four different Turkish Cypriots' houses in London, we asked the subject respondents to express their way of living in their properties at the time of conducting semi-structured interviews. The aim is to understand cultural transitions and their impact on adaptive living at home in accordance with collecting narrative stories concurrently.

142 *Bertug Ozarisoy*

Respondent A – A sunroom, as the name implies, is a room built to admit as much sun as possible. An easy way to get the greatest amount of light and sun is to enclose a steam-heated porch with glass which may be removed at will (Wilde, 1982). The sunroom is the new experience of the Turkish Cypriot family. Sometimes part of a conservatory is turned into a sunroom with rugs, chairs, tables and couches, making it a fascinating lounge or breakfast room; useful, too, as a place to drink tea at the tea hour. Often when building a house, a room on the sunny side is given one, two, or three glass sides. To trick the senses, ferns and flowering plants, birds and vases are used as decor.

We assume that the colour scheme of the sunroom is dictated by the owner and is therefore sympathetic to them. If this be true, we can go further and assume that the delicate tones of the sunroom will harmonise the character of the space. In this space, walls, woodwork and furniture have been kept very light in tone, relying on the cushions and dark foliage of plants to give the character.[39]

Respondent B – The most convenient way of defining the real object of art is to describe it as any modern art object which adequately expresses an artistic conception. Any work of art, regardless of its intrinsic merit, must justify its presence in a room by being more valuable than the space it occupies, that is, to the general scheme of decoration (Harrison, 1965). The cultural practice of Turkish Cypriots is given a broader horizon in their receptivity to a certain number of simultaneous impressions, and the habit of displaying only one or two objects of art at a time shows a more delicate sense of these experiences than the Western passion for multiplying effects.

Respondent C – Among the most important occasions involved in the transformation of an ordinary architectural space into the culture of a Turkish Cypriot house are inauguration ceremonies when celebrating the family members who come for a short-term visit from Cyprus. It is also for celebrating children's birthdays and for engagement ceremonies. Through these celebrations, the house becomes a 'space of appearance'. There is a tendency to accumulate, to fill and close off the space. The emphasis is on universal functionality, immovability, imposing presence and hierarchical labelling. Each element has a strictly defined role corresponding to one or another of various functions of the family unit, and each ultimately refers to a view which conceives of the individual as a balanced assemblage of character. The pieces of furniture confront one another and implicate one another in a unity that is not so much spatial as moral in character.

Respondent D – The rage for glitter – because its idea has become one with that of magnificence in the abstract. It has led us, also, to the exaggerated illusion of mirrors (Benedict, 1996). It lines their dwelling with great British plates and then imagines the adaptation of Cypriot culture. Apart from its reflection, the mirror presents a continuous, flat, colourless, unrelieved surface, a thing always and obviously unpleasant. Considered as a reflector, it is potent in producing a monstrous and odious uniformity and determines the character of the space. Using the mirror as a decorative element is a new experience for Turkish Cypriots. Through my photographic documentation and observation, the entry porches of houses have their well-ornamented mirror. This shows that the mirror is a symbolic object which not only reflects the characteristics of the individual but also echoes in its historical expansion of individual consciousness. It thus carries the stamp of approval of an entire social order of Turkish Cypriots inside the British home.

This research found firstly, and drawing on previous studies in the area under discussion, that there is a vast diversity evident in terms of identity and the way of life for Turkish Cypriots in London. How they choose to adapt, their local identity, plays a vital and significant role in its impact on the newly adopted norms across the generations in London. Secondly, the findings of the research revealed the complex and changing nature of social identities as well as the cultural values in terms of lifestyle, education and marriage that actively select and interpret competing cultural practice within the space of their homes in London. It was found that most homes in London bear no relation to a traditional Turkish Cypriot house. However, traditional rural Turkish Cypriot homes and modern British homes are connected through the values and behaviours of the people who dwell in them (Tostoes & Ferreira, 2021, 1082–1106). Social structures, like all systems (norms, values and cultural codes) are inherently conservative, they endeavour to maintain themselves in the face of change. It is this self-maintaining characteristic that bridges the contradictions represented by the tradition and the newly adapted environment in British homes (Malone, 2020, 679–696). So, while striving to adjust to social change, people also play a determinant factor on social cohesion, they also strive to maintain cultural continuity. From my point of view, over generations furniture is less distinctly Cypriot. This is the result of a consumer culture and indicative of new modes of inhabitation. It is a part of the global marketplace and evidenced in a particular kind of taste.

Conclusions

From our point of view, understanding the structural and cultural aspects of the Turkish Cypriot community, has become an important part of our life. These four family groups predominantly give us an overall understanding of the cultural transition between Cyprus to London throughout the decades. Through the semi-structured interviews that were undertaken by these subject respondent groups, we heard their stories and the way of both adopting and transforming their cultural norms with changing cultural practice in London. Additionally, we have been observing their interactions or counter interactions with other ethnic groups at the time of conducting semi-structured interviews and writing the narrative transcripts. The diversity and range of material in this research suggests that the seemingly every day practical space of the investigation of Turkish Cypriot communities

144 *Bertug Ozarisoy*

in London offers a surprisingly rich resource to us for the understanding of their cultures (interaction with other communities), peoples (individual lifestyles) and histories (traces from Cyprus). This research draws attention not only to the cultural aspects of Turkish Cypriot communities in terms of education and marriage but also on how domestic space represents their identity and how potently and poetically they influence other cultures such as in ways of being, thinking and discourse.[40] It is interesting to note that rereading the domestic space of Turkish Cypriots has shown that rather than being opposed to the outside, it has become a kind of 'mediating skin' through which they have been influenced by the external world (food, clothes, furniture, language or behaviour) which passes and enters the inner private domain of the home, and thus continually transforms it.

The analysis of the interview data supports the claim that Turkish Cypriots display diversity in terms of their experiences and identities. They are also actively shaping their own identities and destinies in response to these diverse experiences, showing new behaviours of action. Yet they are inherently influenced and affected by the structural process operating in British society today (Foucault, 1977).[41] This research finds the importance of interaction with others of both similar and different ethnicities for the creation, maintenance and transformation of Cypriot culture. Cultural practice and the adaptation of domestic space through generations are all significant factors but they are experienced in different ways producing diverse and multiple outcomes. The greater interaction and participation of the second generation provide them with a more comfortable environment through education and space for managing ethnic disadvantages. Nevertheless, they must operate within the confines of multiple social, economic and historical processes that locate them within different fields of social differentiation producing contradictory social outcomes.

The exploration of the experiences of Turkish Cypriots highlighted the significance of cultural practice within other communities for the maintenance and transformation of identity. The second-generation Turkish Cypriot migrant believes they have been experiencing specific difficulties arising from traditional patriarchal norms and values that seek to control their identities. The views of our interviewees on the issues of 'identity' indicate a general acceptance that Cyprus was still an important influence on individuals, and the majority considered their Turkish Cypriot identity to be the most important to them. The idea of the hybridised identities is that individuals display different and often competing cultural symbols, values and patterns of behaviour that can be appropriated at different times and within different contexts.[42] Crucial to this process is an understanding of the way in which individuals use the various cultural resources at their disposal to maintain and transform their identities. In this way, the reading of the domestic space of Turkish Cypriots in London can be seen to represent 'diaspora spaces' where the diverse and heterogeneous experiences of Turkish Cypriots meet and collide. It is within these cultural practices that

Diaspora, Cultural Identity and Difference 145

the Cypriot identity is contested, transformed and resisted and where their relations and hierarchies are negotiated. These ways of cultural practices represent elements of the domestic space in terms of traditional values and norms adapted to the British way of living.

Notes

1 For more details on the recent history of Cyprus, see the following ethnographies: Loizos (1975: 13–23) and Argyrou (1996: 14–57), who provide us with an excellent political, economic and historical background of Cyprus. Sant-Cassia (2005: 18–22) gives a brief history of the inter-ethnic relations on Cyprus.
2 In this sentence I am using the term 'spatial turn' to denote repetitive behaviour.
3 See the collecting Hearing Cultures (Erlmann 2004) for detailed analyses of auditory perceptions in a range of contexts.
4 For an early courageous attempt by a Greek Cypriot author to move beyond one-sided views of the Cyprus Problem, see Zenon Stavrinides, *The Cyprus Conflict* (Nicosia, 1975). An excellent collection of articles from various disciplines and viewpoints is Vangelis Calotyschos (ed.), *Cyprus and Its People: Nation, Identity and Experience in an Unimaginable Community* (Colorado: Westview Press, 1998).
5 A fascinating account of the opposing views on the history of Cyprus presented by the British and the Greek Cypriots is provided by Michael Given in the first chapter of *Symbols, Power and the Construction of Identity in the City Kingdoms of Ancient Cyprus* (Unpublished Ph.D. Thesis, Cambridge University, 1991). A recent interdisciplinary overview of the Cyprus Problem inclusive of all the views of those involved is Alexis Heraclides, *Kypriako: Sigkrousi Epilisi* (Athens: Sideris, 2002). The most exhaustive and balanced internet source of academic writings on the Cyprus Problem is http://www .cyprus-conflict.net/.
6 For a general discussion on the histography of Cyprus, see Yiannis Papadakis, *Perceptions of History and Collective Identity: A Study of Contemporary Greek Cypriot and Turkish Cypriot Nationalism* (PhD Thesis, University of Cambridge, 1993).
7 On memory, forgetting and commemorations, see 'The politics of memory and forgetting in Cyprus', *Journal of Mediterranean Studies*, 3:1 (1993); and 'Nation, narrative and commemoration: Political ritual in divided Cyprus', *History and Anthropology*, 14:3 (2003).
8 On how Turkish Cypriots employ the notion of 'Enosis' and Greek Cypriots that of 'Turkish Expansionism', see Yiannis Papadakis, 'Enosis and Turkish expansionism: Real myths or mythical realities?', in V. Calotychos et al. (ed.), *Cyprus and its People* (Colorado: Westview Press, 1998, pp. 45–47).
9 'The social mapping of the unknown: Managing uncertainty in a mixed borderline Cypriot village', *Anthropological Journal of European Cultures*, 9:2 (2000); and 'Discourses of "the Balkans" in Cyprus: Tactics, strategies and constructions of "others"', *History and Anthropology*, 15:1 (2004).
10 As I will show later, this is not totally true. Many Turkish Cypriots actually fled their houses in the same way Greek Cypriots did.
11 In UN jargon, Cypriot immigrants are defined as 'internally displaced people', having been uprooted from their place of origin and forced to move out from their country of origin. Both Greek and Turkish Cypriots refer to themselves as immigrants, and for that reason I employ this term here. Although this paper focuses only on Turkish Cypriot immigrants, they are not the only ones on the island.

146 *Bertug Ozarisoy*

12 See Ladbury and King (1988) and Navaro-Yashin (2010) on the renaming of localities in North Cyprus. It is important to note also that Turkish-Cypriot village names were 'changed and assigned names more akin to places and connotations of Turkey'. Navaro-Yashin (2003: 122) coins this process 'Turkeyfication', which is different from 'Turkification'.

13 Turkish Cypriots older than 35 generally speak some level of the Greek Cypriot dialect given that they lived in an area before 1974, where they had daily contact with Greek Cypriots.

14 See the collecting *Hearing Cultures* (Erlmann, 2004) for detailed analyses of auditory perceptions in a range of contexts.

15 See Fosshagen (1999: 72–85) for an analysis of the notions of dirt and impurity (*pis*) among Turkish Cypriots.

16 It has been quoted from the collective memories of subjects' respondents at the time of conducting semi-structured interviews with four Turkish Cypriot families who immigrated to London.

17 Ibid.

18 *Echoes from the Past: The Turkish Cypriot Community of Limassol and Its Heritage* (Akif 2008) is an excellent collection of stories, photographs and background information on the Limassolian Turkish Cypriots. This book is in three languages (Turkish, Greek and English), which makes it accessible to a wide audience.

19 Personal communication with the subject respondents at the time of undertaking semi-structured interviews.

20 In what follows, I will highlight some issues regarding 'culture and complexity' in the Turkish Cypriot community living in London, but I will use different conceptual tools from the 'honour and shame' complex (for a similar approach, see Dubisch 1995: 280 n.7).

21 See Fosshagen (1999: 67–74) for an outline of Turkish Cypriot houses.

22 See Killoran (1988) for an exploration of cultural barriers in an urban Turkish Cypriot community.

23 On social memory, the work of Paul Connerton, *How Societies Remember* (Cambridge: Cambridge University Press, 1989) provides a good discussion. On the use and abuse of history, David Lowenthall, *The Past is a Foreign Country* (Cambridge: Cambridge University Press, 1985) provides a magisterial survey.

24 On the prevalence of the saint's everyday life of Turkish Cypriots, see Hart (1992: 193–223).

25 Names and dates have been changed to protect my subject respondents' privacy.

26 See Argyrou (1996) for a detailed analysis of Cypriot weddings in London.

27 From the collective memories of subject respondents at the time of conducting semi-structured interviews with four Turkish Cypriot families who immigrated to London.

28 Ibid.

29 Personal communication with the subject respondents at the time of undertaking semi-structured interviews.

30 It has been quoted from the collective memories of subject respondents at the time of conducting semi-structured interviews with four Turkish Cypriot families who immigrated to London.

31 Ibid.

32 Ibid.

33 It has been quoted from the collective memories of subject respondents at the time of conducting semi-structured interviews with four Turkish Cypriot families who immigrated to London.

34 D. Alastos, *Cyprus in History – A Survey of 5,000 Years* (London 1955); Sir David Hunt (ed.), *Footprints in Cyprus – An Illustrated History* (London, 1982); G. Hill, *A History of Cyprus* (Cambridge 1952).

Diaspora, Cultural Identity and Difference 147

35 G. Hill, *A History of Cyprus* (Cambridge, 1952, vol. II, p.37).
36 For an analysis of some key postcolonial modernist urban visions for Cyprus, see for example: Panayiota Pyla and Petros Phokaides, 'Ambivalent politics and modernist debates in postcolonial cyprus', *Journal of Architecture* 16:6, 2011, pp. 885–913.
37 It has been quoted from the collective memories of subject respondents at the time of conducting semi-structured interviews with four Turkish Cypriot families who immigrated to London.
38 Hybridity provides a theoretical framework for multiplicity of actors collaborating without arriving at a consensus. Conflict and differentiation replace the deliberative method where essential identities cooperate to justify a singular and exclusive agreement.
39 Personal communication with the subject respondents at the time of undertaking semi-structured interviews.
40 See Just (2000: 55) and Hart (1992: 172), who observed identical phrases during their fieldwork in Greece.
41 '… which can be applied to medieval culture, or even classical culture, only by a retrospective hypothesis, and by an interplay of formal analogies or semantic resemblances; but neither literature, not politics, nor philosophy and the sciences articulated the field of discourse in the seventeenth or eighteenth century as they did in the nineteenth century'. Michel Foucault, 'The unities of discourse', in *The Archeology of Knowledge* (New York: Penguin Publishing, 1977, p.22).
42 Anthias, F., 'Researching society and culture in Cyprus: Displacements, hybridities, and dialogical frameworks', in Yiannis Papadakis, Nicos Peristianis & Gisela Wlez (eds), *Divided Cyprus: Modernity, History and an Island in Conflict* (Bloomington: Indiana UP, pp. 176–194).

References

Agarez, R. C. (2019). Philanthropy, diplomacy and built environment expertise at the Calouste Gulbenkian Foundation in the 1960s and 1970s. *Journal of Architecture*, *24*(7), 950–981. https://doi.org/10.1080/13602365.2019.1698637

Bachelard, G. (1958). *Ethnic groups and boundaries: The social organisation of cultural difference*. London: Allen and Unwin.

Ballard, R. (1994). Family organisation among the Sikhs in Britain. *Journal of Ethnic and Migration Studies*, 2(1), 12–24.

Beeckmans, L. (2014). The adventures of the French architect Michel Ecochard in post-independence Dakar: A transnational development expert drifting between commitment and expediency. *Journal of Architecture*, *19*(6), 849–871. https://doi.org/10.1080/13602365.2014.982146

Benedict, J. (1996). *In the system of objects*. London: Verso, pp. 15–29.

Benjamin, W. (1999). 'Expose of 1935', the arcades project, translated by H. Eiland & K. McLaughlin; prepared on the basis of the German volume edited by Rolf Tiedemann. Cambridge, MA: Belknap Press.

Bhabha, H. (1993). *The location of culture*. London and New York: Routledge Classics.

Calotychos, V. (Ed.). (1998). *Cyprus and its people* (pp. 45–47). Colorado: Westview Press.

Dawes, M. J., & Ostwald, M. J. (2014). Testing the wright space: Using isovists to analyse prospect-refuge characteristics in Usonian architecture. *Journal of Architecture*. Routledge. https://doi.org/10.1080/13602365.2014.965722

Foucault, M. (1977). The unities of discourse. In Smith, S. (Ed.) *The archeology of knowledge* (p. 22). New York: Pantheon Books.

Foucault, M. (1979). *Discipline and punishment: The birth of the prison*. New York: Vintage.

Foucault, M., & Miskowiec, J. (1986). *Of other spaces*, translated by Jay Miscowiec. Diacritics 16/1 (pp. 75–78). London: Architectural Association School of Architecture Bookshop Publishing.

Gitler, I. B. A. (2021). New Brutalism, new nation: Ram Karmi's assimilation of Brutalism in Israel's arid region architecture. *Journal of Architecture*, 26(3), 316–339. https://doi.org/10.1080/13602365.2021.1896566

Harrison, J. (1965). *In the complete works of Edgar Allan Poe: Essay and miscellanies* (Vol. 14). New York: AMS Press.

Hegglund, J. (1997). Defending the realm: Domestic space and mass cultural contamination in Howards end and an Englishman's home. *English Literature in Transition*, 40(4), 400.

Heraclides, A. (2011). The Cyprus Gordian knot: An intractable ethnic conflict. *Nationalism and Ethnic Politics*, 17(2), 117–139. https://doi.org/10.1080/13537113.2011.575309

Hershenzon, M. (2021). The architect as civil servant: Aviah Hashimshoni's architecture education and historiography in 1960s Israel. *Journal of Architecture*, 26(2), 116–146. https://doi.org/10.1080/13602365.2021.1893789

Hughes-Wilson, J. (2011). The forgotten war: A brief history of the battle for Cyprus, 1974. *RUSI Journal*, 156(5), 84–93. https://doi.org/10.1080/03071847.2011.626281

Jacoby, S., Arancibia, A., & Alonso, L. (2022). Space standards and housing design: Typological experimentation in England and Chile. *Journal of Architecture*, 1–33. https://doi.org/10.1080/13602365.2022.2045340

Kimmel, L. (2020). Walter Benjamin's topology of envelopes and perspectives. *Journal of Architecture*, 25(6), 659–678. https://doi.org/10.1080/13602365.2020.1800791

Kucukcan, T. (1999). *Politics of ethnicity, identity and religion: Turkish Muslims in Britain*. Aldershot: Ashgate.

Lameira, G. (2021). Readings on multifamily housing: Models, discourses, and aesthetics in A Arquitectura Portuguesa (1908–1958). *Journal of Architecture*, 26(8), 1163–1196. https://doi.org/10.1080/13602365.2021.2001558

Lawrence, R. (2020). Halls, lobbies, and porches: Transition spaces in Victorian architecture. *Journal of Architecture*, 25(4), 419–443. https://doi.org/10.1080/13602365.2020.1767176

Lefebvre, H. (2003). *The production of space*. Oxford: Blackwell Publishing.

Lohtaja, A. (2021). Henri Lefebvre's lessons from the Bauhaus. *Journal of Architecture*, 26(4), 499–515. https://doi.org/10.1080/13602365.2021.1923551

Malone, P. (2020). Bourdieu in London. *Journal of Architecture*, 25(6), 679–696. https://doi.org/10.1080/13602365.2020.1800792

Oakley, R. (1970). The Cypriots in Britain. *Race Today*, 2(4), 99–102.

Oakley, R. (1979). Family, kinship and patronage: The Cypriot migration to Britain. In V. Saiful Lah-Khan (Ed.), *Minority families in Britain: Support and stress* (pp. 12–34). London: Macmillan.

Rapoport, A. (1969). *House form and culture*. Englewood Cliffs, NJ: Prentice-Hall.

Roberts-Hughes, R. (2017). Transgression and conservation: Rereading Georges Bataille. *Journal for Cultural Research*, *21*(2), 157–168. https://doi.org/10.1080/14797585.2016.1239608

Sánchez-Verdejo Pérez, F. J. (2021). 'It [the castle] is old, and has many memories': Transgression and cultural, literary idiosyncrasy of space in gothic tradition. *Revista Thélos*, *1*(13), 67–89. Retrieved from https://thelos.utem.cl/articulos/essay-it-the-castle-is-old-and-has-many-memories-transgression-and-cultural-literary-idiosyncrasy-of-space-in-gothic-tradition/

Sara, R., & Littlefield, D. (2014). Transgression: Body and space. *Architecture and Culture*, *2*(3), 295–304. https://doi.org/10.2752/205078214X14107818390513

Shadar, H., & Maslovski, E. (2021). Pre-war design, post-war sovereignty: Four plans for one city in Israel/Palestine. *Journal of Architecture*, *26*(4), 516–540. https://doi.org/10.1080/13602365.2021.1925946

Sonyel, S. (1988). *The silent minority: Turkish Muslim children in British schools*. Cambridge: The Islamic Academy.

Tostões, A., & Ferreira, Z. (2021). Social endurance at the Barbican Estate (1968–2020). *Journal of Architecture*, *26*(7), 1082–1106. https://doi.org/10.1080/13602365.2021.1978523

Urry, J. (2000). *Sociology beyond societies*. London: Routledge.

Wilde, O. (1982). The house beautiful. In K. O'Brien & O. Wilde (Eds.), *Canada: An apostle for the arts*. Toronto: Personal Library Publishers.

7 Housing and Policies in the United Kingdom

Young Ki Kim and Hasim Altan

Introduction

In most countries in the world, buildings are responsible for at least 40% of energy use (Ozarisoy, 2022). This figure is rising fast, as construction booms in countries such as China, India and the Gulf Cooperation Council (GCC). In the UK, the buildings and construction sectors combined are responsible for over 40% of energy consumption. The energy used in homes alone is responsible for more than a quarter of CO_2 emissions (Ozarisoy & Altan, 2021a). CO_2 is the main greenhouse gas and the most significant cause of climate change and carbon emissions, and its implications on the energy use policy are the superscripts of this chapter.

Most of the energy used in homes is produced using processes that release carbon dioxide (CO_2) into the atmosphere. Challenging targets for emission reductions have been set by the UK government with a recent commitment to a minimum of 80% reductions in greenhouse gas (GHG) emissions by 2050 compared to 1990 levels (Beizaee et al., 2013).

Energy is used in homes to provide useful services for households such as heat, hot water and power for appliances (Guerra-Santin et al., 2013). As a result of the use of fossil fuels to provide this energy either directly such as gas for central heating or indirectly such as coal for power stations to generate electricity, this energy use resulted in CO_2 emissions (Gupta & Gregg, 2012a). The need to reduce these emissions in housing is a key part of the UK's efforts to combat climate change (Gupta & Gregg, 2013). Energy use in homes is strongly affected by the population, the number of households, type of homes, level of insulation with heating systems, the age of a dwelling, household income and the temperature difference between inside and outside (Gupta & Gregg, 2016). In terms of heating energy consumption, it usually correlates more strongly to the size of dwellings and the type of dwellings; heating energy is related to external wall area and window area, and the household size makes little difference to heating (Ozarisoy & Altan, 2022a). The two most important determinants of heating energy use are insulation and the efficiency of heating systems. The age of a dwelling also affects its energy efficiency, and older homes typically have poorer

DOI: 10.4324/9781003243069-9

insulation than modern homes (Gupta & Gregg, 2012b). The difference in temperature between outside and inside homes in winter is the single most important factor shaping heating energy use at home as well. Hot water uses and the use of appliances increase in proportion to household size.

Energy Consumption and CO_2 Emissions

Energy use in homes is just under one-third of total energy use in the UK, up from a quarter in 1970 (Gupta & Gregg, 2018). Figure 7.1(a) shows

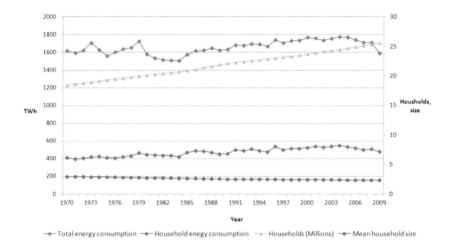

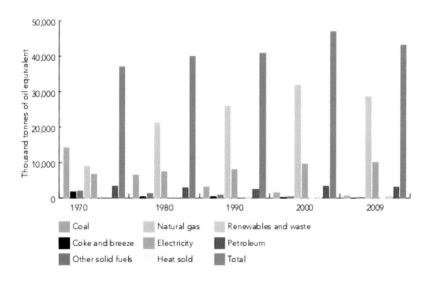

Figure 7.1 (a) Energy use for housing and total in UK; (b) Domestic energy consumption by fuel, 1970 to 2009. Source: DECC (2011).

that housing energy rose gradually until 2004 but has fallen by one-tenth since then. The total energy consumption shows all energy used: Transport, Industry, Public Sector and Housing. Total energy consumption in the UK rose and fell during the past 40 years. However, it finished the period a little below the level of use in 1970: 1,600 terawatt hours (TWh). Energy use in housing rose by 1.6% from 1970 to 2009, with an average increase of 0.4% per year. However, the number of homes also increased by two-fifths, and the average household size has fallen, as shown in Figure 7.1(b). This means that the average energy use per home has fallen from 22,235 to 18,639 kWh (DECC, 2008).

As shown in Figure 7.1(a), the Department of Energy and Climate Change (DECC, 2011) also provides a breakdown of domestic energy consumption, which has risen from 36,884,000 tonnes of oil equivalent in 1970 to 43,590,000 tonnes of oil equivalent in 2009. Breaking this down into types of fuel, between 1970 and 2009, total domestic electricity consumption increased by 59%, use of solid fuels decreased by 96% and natural gas consumption increased by more than 300%. Additionally, space heating is responsible for most of the domestic energy consumption, followed by lighting, appliances and water heating. Out of a total of over 43 million tonnes of oil equivalent in 2009, space heating was responsible for 61%, lighting and appliances for 18%, and water heating for 18%, as shown in Figure 7.2(a).

Figure 7.2(b) shows the energy consumption by end use in UK homes between 1970 and 2008. The energy consumed for space heating, lighting and appliances has increased while for cooking and water heating consumption has decreased. Reducing the energy used for space heating, lighting and appliances is important to achieve the government's carbon reduction target, which is 80% reduction by 2050 from 1990 levels.

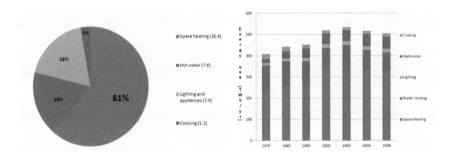

Figure 7.2 (a) Proportion of domestic energy consumption by end use in 2009 (million tonnes of oil); (b) Domestic final energy consumption by end use between 1970 and 2008 (TWh/year). Source: DECC (2011).

Energy Efficiency of Housing Stock

There were around 22.2 million dwellings in 2008. England has a relatively old housing stock with some 8.4 million homes built before 1945, of which 4.8 million were built before 1919. One-fifth of homes have been built since 1980. About 60% of homes in the UK were built before the introduction of the modern building regulations, which were introduced in 1965 with U-value limits for walls and roof, as shown in Figures 7.3(a) and (b).

Around 19% of the dwelling stock was flats; most of these were purpose-built low-rise flats. The most common types of dwellings were terraced houses, which was 29% in stock and semi-detached houses followed as 26%, as shown in Figure 7.3(c). The energy efficiency (SAP)[1] rating for the housing stock increased steadily from 42 points in 1996 to 53 in 2009. Based on the SAP methodology, assumptions regarding occupancy and heating of the stock, and mean carbon dioxide emissions per dwelling

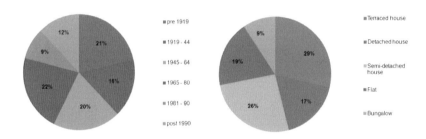

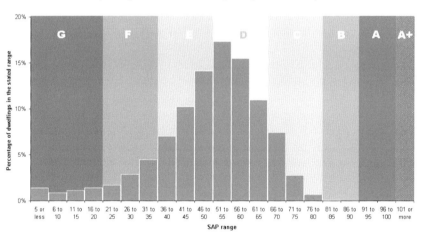

Figure 7.3 (a) Dwelling age in the UK in 2008; (b) Dwelling type in the UK in 2008; (c) Distribution of the housing stock and EPC bands, UK. Source: (a)–(b) English Housing Survey (DCLG, 2011); (c) BRE (2007).

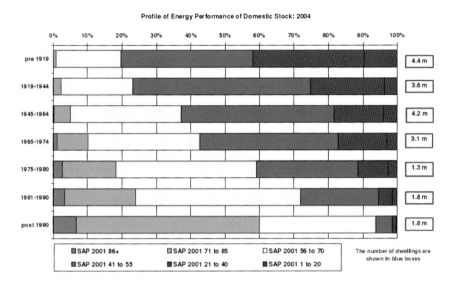

Figure 7.4 Profile of energy performance of domestic stock by age in 2004. Source: EHCS (2004).

were 6 tonnes/yr. Some 15% of all dwellings were in the lowest Energy Performance Certificate (EPC),[2] Energy Efficiency Rating Bands F and G (SAP less than 39). Figure 7.4 shows the current housing stock's SAP score within the EPC bands and more details about the SAP and other assessment tools to generate EPCs.

Over 40% of properties built before 1919 have an SAP rating of less than 41. Two-thirds of all properties have an SAP rating of 41 to 70, irrespective of age, whereas 60% of properties built since 1990 have an SAP rating greater than 70. Hard-to-treat homes generally have features such as solid walls, no gas supply, or no loft space, or are high-rise blocks, as shown in Figure 7.4.

Space Heating

Figures 7.5(a) and (b) show that even with the improvements in energy efficiency of UK dwellings, heating's share of total energy use in homes has grown from 58% in 1970 to 66% in 2008. In the UK, the main types of insulation are loft insulation, cavity wall insulation, double glazing and hot water tank insulation. Improving building fabric efficiency by government's policies, almost one-third of the UK's dwelling heat loss from building fabric has been reduced. Figure 7.5(a) shows how improved insulation for building fabrics and improved heating systems' efficiency has reduced energy consumption for space heating in the UK housing sector.

Housing and Policies in the United Kingdom 155

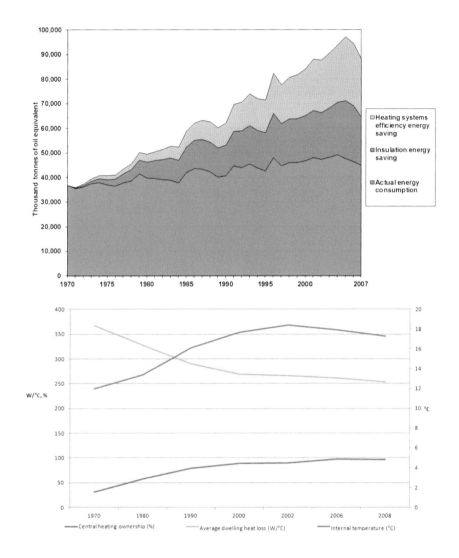

Figure 7.5 (a) Savings due to better insulation and heating efficiency, 1970 to 2007; (b) Relationship between internal temperature and energy efficiency of home. Source: (a)–(b) English Housing Survey (DCLG, 2011).

The combined savings from insulation and heating efficiency improvements reduced domestic space heating by an estimated 41.2 million tonnes of oil equivalent. Without these improvements, it is estimated that energy consumption would have been doubled. Heating and hot water account for around 84% of energy use in a typical home in the UK (DECC, 2011a). Improving the energy efficiency of heating systems, or reducing demand, by even a small amount, can have a far bigger effect on energy use than making changes to, for example, lighting. Studies from BEER (CIPHE, 2008) shows that turning a room's thermostat down by just 1°C can reduce heating bills by 10%.

People increasingly want to be comfortable in buildings. The average temperatures inside domestic dwellings are estimated by Building Research Establishment (BRE) to have increased from 12°C in 1970 to 17.3°C in 2008 (DECC, 2011b). The rise in temperatures has been helped by the increased energy efficiency of homes such as use of central heating systems and improved fabrics' heat loss. The central heating ownership increased from 79% of households in 1990 to 96% in 2008, as shown in Figure 7.5(b).

Temperature in a domestic dwelling is an important factor in energy consumption. According to Shorrock and Utley (2003), a comfortable living room temperature during occupancy hours is 21°C, but in other parts of the house it is 2°C lower. The thermostat setting and length of time heating influences a dwelling's space heating energy use (Shipworth et al, 2009). A 1% increase in heating temperature is estimated to cause a 1.55% increase in CO_2 emissions. The same percentage increase in heating duration is likely to result in a 0.62% increase in CO_2 emissions. Therefore, increasing the temperature in the home results in more CO_2 emissions than having the heating on for a longer time.

The temperature that occupants set their thermostat to is affected by many varied factors, such as social grade, type of dwelling, tenure and number of persons in the household. From the Department for Environment, Food and Rural Affairs (DEFRA), (DEFRA, 2009) shows higher social grades reported setting their thermostat to around 21°C. People in lower social grades reported setting their thermostat at least 3°C higher. DEFRA found the two important factors which are as follow: (i) people living in flats set their thermostat to as high as 28°C, 8°C higher than people living in detached houses and (ii) private renters set their thermostat to 27°C on average, which is higher than other tenure groups.

Further findings on internal temperature suggest that people living on their own tend to live in colder homes (Yohanis and Mondol, 2010). Meier and Rehadanz (2008) investigated the residential space heating behaviour of British households and accordingly, heating energy demand increases with households' size, average household age and number of children. Owners have higher consumption than renters. The reasons for this may include housing type, with renters mainly living in flats and most owners living in detached or semi-detached houses. In general, flats are more energy efficient than houses.

Background on UK Policies

In its Energy White Paper of 2003, the government announced a long-term target of reducing the UK's emissions of greenhouse gases 60% by 2050 compared with the levels in 1997 (after that, it was increased to 80% by

2050). Reducing energy use in housing is critical to the achievement of this target. Moreover, 27% of the UK emissions of CO_2 are attributable to energy use in the domestic sector, and the White Paper emphasised the need for action in both new and existing housing, including the introduction of low- and zero-carbon technologies and the greater use of renewable energy sources.

In December 2006, the Department for Communities and Local Government (DCLG) published its strategy for moving towards zero-carbon development including progressive improvements in the energy standards required by building regulations to achieve zero-carbon housing by 2016, as shown in Figure 7.6. Through changes to the building regulations, standards of thermal efficiency in new housing have been radically improved over the past three decades. Nonetheless, the average dwelling constructed to the Part L 2006 Building Regulations standard would consume around 3,600 kWh each year. Clearly, higher levels of thermal performance are required to meet the future targets, and therefore the Code for Sustainable Homes (CfSH) standard was introduced.

The measures required to achieve a 60~80% reduction in emissions from the housing sector were assessed in detail in a Tyndall Centre report published in 2005 (Tyndall Centre, 2005). This concluded that there would need to be significant investment to improve energy performance in the existing housing stock (two-thirds of which would still be in existence in 2050) together with a higher rate of demolition and new-build, and much greater use of low-carbon and renewable energy technologies on the supply side. Specifically, the report stated that new dwellings constructed after

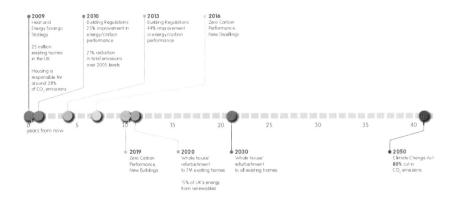

Figure 7.6 Major policies. Source: Getting warmer, 2010. HEES: Home Energy Efficiency Scheme, EESoP: Energy Efficiency Standard of Performance, HECA: Home Energy Conservation Act, EEC: Energy Efficiency Commitment, CERT: Carbon Emissions Reduction Target, CESP: Community Energy Saving Programme, LCBP: Low Carbon Buildings Programme, FIT: Feed-in-Tariff, RHI: Renewable Heat Incentive, Green Deal.

158 *Young Ki Kim and Hasim Altan*

Table 7.1 Domestic energy efficiency measures: costs and savings.

Measures	Costs (£)	Bill Savings (£/yr)	Carbon Savings (kgC/yr)	Payback (yrs)
Cavity wall insulation	342	133	242	2.6
Solid wall insulation	3150	380	694	7.5
Loft insulation	284	104	190	2.7
A-rated boiler	1500	168	177	8.9
Hot water cylinder insulation	14	29	53	0.5
Improved heating controls	147	43	77	3.4
Draught proofing	100	23	43	4.3
Double glazing	4000	41	26	97.6

2020 should consume on average no more than 2,000 kWh a year for space heating, in contrast to the 6,800 kWh that existing housing, on average, would consume even after the necessary improvements.

In addition, there are large challenges in bringing the existing stock up to a suitable level of performance without excessive cost, reduction in internal space or unacceptable changes to external appearance. New materials and insulation technologies may offer improved performance and the incorporation of renewable sources of energy in refurbishment projects will be an essential component of an overall strategy for reducing emissions from existing housing. The UK government has announced many different policies to improve the UK homes' energy efficiency especially for fuel poverty. The measures promoted through policies and supported by grants with a simple payback of less than seven years, which is determined 'energy efficiency measurements' and these are considered as cavity wall insulation, loft insulation, efficient central heating systems and controls, hot water tank jackets, draught-proofing and low-energy light bulbs. Table 7.1 shows some examples of domestic energy efficiency measures for installation costs and savings, which are based on a typical three-bed semi-detached property.

Scenarios for Carbon Emission Cuts from UK Housing

In the last two decades, several studies have examined methods of reducing the carbon emissions from the UK housing sector based on the technical feasibility of UK dwelling in order to achieve the UK government's target. The most notable work undertaken in earliest studies are that of Evans (1997), Letherman and Samo (2000) and Shorrock et al. (2001). These studies have attempted to predict the future energy use and CO_2 emissions attributable to the UK housing sector. The study by Evans (1997) considered the stabilisation of the atmospheric CO_2 concentration over the period 1991 to 2021 by calculating that the CO_2 emissions attributable to the UK housing sector would reduce by 10% every five years over the period 1991 to 2021. From this simple method, the UK housing sector would achieve the 60% CO_2 emission reduction target by 2021.

In 2000, Letherman and Samo investigated that achieving the UK government's 20% CO_2 emissions reduction target by examining three possible scenarios which are; (i) demolishing pre-1965 dwellings at 180,000 per year and building new dwellings with 1996 Building Regulations requirements; (ii) improving the fabric U-values of pre-1965 dwellings to the 1996 Building Regulations requirements at 400,000 per year; and (iii) same as scenario two but the rate changed from 400,000 to 200,000 per year and building new homes with the 1995 Building Regulation at 50,000 dwellings per year. The result indicated that the 20% reduction target could be only achieved by scenario two.

The Shorrock et al. (2001) study found that around 17–31% of CO_2 emissions could be achieved by introducing a range of energy efficient measures into the UK housing stock. In 2005, the three studies (BRE, 2007; Johnston et al., 2005; Boardman et al., 2005) were carried out and each study confirmed that 60% of the target could be achieved. This BRE study suggested that emissions reduction over 60% could be achieved by 50% solar thermal, solar photovoltaics (PVs) and heat pumps and 25% of centrally heated homes with biomass boiler installation. Boardman et al. (2005) explained the use of an average of two 'low or zero-carbon technologies' per home could make homes achieve 60% emission reductions and the technologies are 60% of dwellings installed solar thermal, almost 40% heat by micro-CHP, 30% had solar PV and 20% of heat from community heating.

In 2022, Ozarisoy (2022) reviewed the three studies and found that Johnston et al. (2005) were not able to achieve 60% emission reductions. The most efficient suggestions from Ozarisoy (ibid) is that solar PV, solar thermal or micro-CHP each would need to be installed in around 45% of all UK homes. Peacock et al. (2007) found that 60% emission reductions could be achieved from their studies, and it could only achieve emission reductions of over 60% through micro-generation technology with fabric improvements. The World Wildlife Fund (WWF) study found that 80% emission reductions could be achieved through the most extensive refurbishment with reduced energy demand and grid decarbonisation (WWF, 2007). The Energy Saving Trust (EST) study found that 80% emission reductions could be achieved by reducing energy demand, grid decarbonisation, maximal use of technical interventions and further reductions in appliance usage, as shown in Table 7.2.

There is general agreement within the various conducted studies to achieve carbon emission reductions over 60% in the UK housing sector. The essential premise to achieve these targets is an extensive government programme for housing stock improvements then most extensive technologies considered. None of the above studies, however, has indicated energy consumption and CO_2 emissions increased from cooling energy demand due to

160   *Young Ki Kim and Hasim Altan*

Table 7.2 Studies on emission cuts from UK housing scenarios.

Research	CO₂ Reduction Targets	Considering CoolingEnergy Demand
Evans (1997)	60% by 2021	**No**
Letherman and Samo (2000)	20% by 2020	
Shorrock et al. (2001)	17% to 31% by 2020	
BRE (2005)	60% by 2050	
Johnston et al. (2005)	60% by 2050	
Boardman et al. (2005)	60% by 2050	
Boardman et al. (2007)	80% by 2050	
Peacock et al (2007)	50% by 2030, 60% by 2050	
IPPR, RSPB & WWF (2008)	80% by 2050	
EST (2008)	80% by 2050	

climate change and global warming. Obviously, they mentioned improving energy efficiency of lighting and appliances but without considering cooling energy demand. If we add cooling energy demand with these studies, the government target should be changed or be carefully replanned to avoid dangerous levels of climate change due to greenhouse gases concentration into the atmosphere by human activities.

New Homes

Little more than a decade ago, few of us had considered the possibility of zero-carbon homes. The concept of modern homes was self-sufficient in terms of their energy use and had been limited to a handful of 'autonomous houses', not connected to mains services, designed, built and occupied by enthusiasts. That all changed in December 2006, with the launch of a government consultation proposing that, from 2016, all new homes should be built to a zero-carbon standard. The policy statement, 'Building A Greener Future', then followed in July 2007, confirming this proposal and its timetable. The extent of change required to deliver zero-carbon homes cannot be overstated. Figure 7.7 shows an illustrated figure that is based on the government's plan to achieve zero-carbon buildings in the UK.

Having a definition that is realistic, workable and has sufficient flexibility to enable compliance on all developments and for all kinds of homes is critical to achieving zero-carbon homes. Clearly, the challenge of developing a high-density urban infill site, where there may be less opportunity to exploit renewable energy resources is quite different from that of building a single detached home on a large south-facing plot where there is scope for using a variety of renewable technologies. The consequence of an inflexible definition of zero-carbon, which did not recognise these limitations and allowed

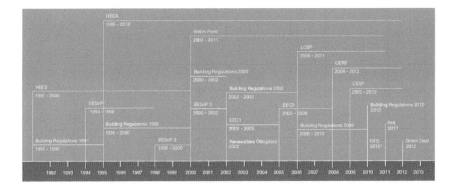

Figure 7.7 Current zero-carbon timeline for England. Source: Zero-Carbon Hub, 2008.

no scope for the use of renewable energy produced offsite, would be to prevent the development of a significant proportion of sites. Evidently that would run counter to government policy of improving the supply of new homes in the UK.

The commitment to build zero-carbon homes was one of several government strategies and initiatives at the time, which aimed to reduce the causes and adapt to the effects of climate change. In October 2008, the government also announced the creation of a new Department of Energy and Climate Change as part of its commitment to a wide range of strategies to reduce energy consumption, conserve water, reduce waste, manage flood risk, provide renewable energy sources, reduce risk of overheating, reduce fuel poverty, and so on. In December 2008, following on from work undertaken by the UK Green Building Council (UKGBC) earlier in the year, the government launched a second consultation, which deals specifically with the definition of zero-carbon and how it is assessed.

Zero-Carbon New Homes by 2016

To reduce UK domestic carbon emissions, the government at the time had set an ambitious target for new homes to be 'Zero-Carbon' by 2016. The government's definition of zero-carbon is as follows in Table 7.3. This means that new homes will need to reduce the energy that is used for activities such as space heating, water heating, lighting, cooking and running electrical appliances. Once that energy is reduced to a minimum, homes will need to supply the remaining energy required from renewable or zero-carbon energy sources, so that over a year there are no net carbon dioxide emissions because of the activities within the home. The government has also introduced a stamp duty land tax exemption for new zero-carbon homes

162　*Young Ki Kim and Hasim Altan*

Table 7.3 What does zero-carbon home mean?

<table>
<tr><td>

Building a Greener Future (July 2007) set out that all new homes are to be built from 2016 in such a way that, after taking account of:

- Emissions from space heating, ventilation, hot water and fixed lighting;
- Expected energy use from appliances;
- Exports and imports of energy from the development (and directly connected energy installations) to and from centralised energy networks;

the building will have net zero-carbon emissions over the course of a year.
The present consultation retains the approach of looking at net emissions (including from appliances) over the course of a year. It proposes that, to meet the zero-carbon homes standard, homes should:

- Be built with high levels of energy efficiency;
- Achieve at least a minimum level of carbon reductions through a combination of energy efficiency, onsite energy supply and/or (where relevant) directly connected low carbon or renewable heat; and
- Choose from a range of (mainly offsite) solutions for tackling the remaining emissions.

</td></tr>
</table>

Source: HM Government, 2008.

costing less than £500,000. From October 2007, to qualify, a zero-carbon home must be certified and calculated in accordance with the approved method, set out by the Stamp Duty Land Tax (Zero-carbon Home Relief) Regulations 2007 (OPSI, 2007).

However, CO_2 emissions associated with production and transport of building materials are not considered in this definition, nor is the energy used during the construction process. With the construction of each new home thought to be responsible for 20 to 40 tonnes of carbon dioxide there is growing concern that the present definition of a zero-carbon home does not reflect the 'true' carbon footprint. It may be argued that the definition of zero-carbon home should also address carbon emissions associated with the lifestyle of the occupant (de Dear & Brager, 2002). The location of the home will greatly influence the mode of transport, how and where food is bought from, travel to work and school, and interaction with their local community. All these activities have associated CO_2 emissions, which were not necessarily factored into the actual carbon emissions.

How Zero-Carbon Is Required or Encouraged

The three mechanisms were in place for requiring or encouraging zero-carbon standards for new homes, which are the building regulations, the CfSH and the Stamp Duty Land Tax Relief. The concept for zero-carbon was first introduced in the 'Building A Greener Future: Towards Zero-Carbon

Housing and Policies in the United Kingdom 163

Development' consultation document, published by the Department for Communities and Local Government in December 2006 (DCLG, 2006). It laid out a proposed timetable for changes to the building regulations for all new homes to achieve zero-carbon by 2016 and defined zero-carbon as follows:

> Notably, it will need to deliver zero carbon (net over the year) for all energy use in the home. These consisted of cooling, washing and electronic entertainment appliances as well as space heating, cooling, ventilation, lighting and hot water
>
> (DCLG, 2006).

This consultation marked a turning point because it was the first time that it was suggested that the CO_2 emissions from appliances, cooking and cooling within the home, might be brought under control using the building regulations. A policy statement was issued by DCLG in July 2007 (DCLG, 2007), which also confirmed the government's intention to press ahead with the policy to the following timetable in England and Wales, as shown in Table 7.4.

It was proposed that by 2010, new housing should achieve a 25% carbon improvement relative to the 2006 Building Regulations and then this would be increased to a 44% improvement in 2013 and leading to zero-carbon housing by 2016. Figure 7.8 represents Table 7.5 graphically. Note that zero-carbon represents an improvement in the order of 150% over the ADL1A.

Table 7.5 shows a summary of the range of the UK minimum building fabric standards needed for the respective certification at the time. From this, we could imagine how the home's fabric efficiency would be improved to achieve the Zero-Carbon home by 2016. It also made it clear that the building fabric's thermal properties would increase progressively, which meant less heat loss through the building fabric, and the buildings would be more airtight.

Code for Sustainable Homes

Launched in December 2006, the CfSH is an environmental assessment method for rating and certifying the performance of new homes. The code

Table 7.4 Proposed future changes to the Approved Document L1A (ADL1A).

Year	Improvement over the ADL1A 2006 (%)
2010	25
2013	44
2016	Zero-carbon (150)

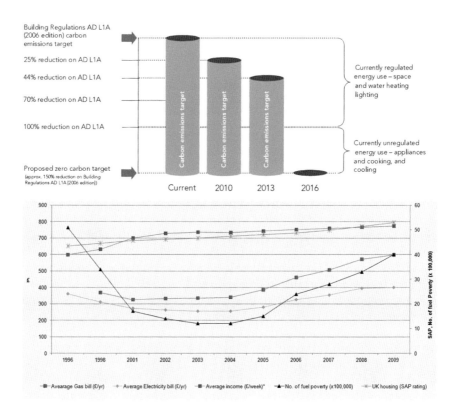

Figure 7.8 Reduction of CO_2 emissions from new housing. (de Dear & Brager, 2002) Zero-Carbon Hub, 2008.

has nine categories of sustainable design and credits are earned under these categories when specified performance targets are reached. Based on the number of credits achieved, an overall rating is awarded, ranging from Level one (1 star) to Level six (6 stars). Amongst the nine categories of sustainable design is energy and emissions. Due to the importance of this category, mandatory levels of performance for energy and emissions are prescribed for each level of the code. Again, these are expressed as a percentage improvement in CO_2 emissions over the level of performance required by the ADL1A at the time, as shown in Table 7.6.

The percentage improvement required over the target emissions rate (TER) required by the Building Regulations Part L is shown in Table 3.7. Code Level 3 needs a 25% TER improvement (CO_2 emissions set at least 25% lower than the minimum Building Regulations 2006 Part L compliance). Similarly, the Code Level 4 needs a 44% improvement on the Part L and requires 10.4 points. The design measures needed to achieve the Code

Table 7.5 Building fabrics standards.

U-value and Airtightness	Building Standards						
	Building Regulations 2006	EST – Good Practice	EST – Best Practice	EST – Advanced Practice	AECB Silver	AECB Gold	Passive House (AC/hr)
Roof	0.25	0.16	0.13	0.15	0.15	0.15	0.1
Walls	0.35	0.3	0.25	0.15	0.25	0.15	0.1
Floors	0.25	0.22	0.2	0.15	0.2	0.15	0.1
Windows	2.2	2.2	1.8	0.8	1.5	0.8	0.8
Airtightness(m³/m²/hr@50)	10	10	3	0.75	3	0.75	0.6

166 *Young Ki Kim and Hasim Altan*

Table 7.6 Anticipated mandatory improvement in CO_2 emissions.

Code Level	Percentage improvement over TER required by Part L1A (2006)	Points required	Government target for regulatory introduction
1	10% (EST 'Good Practice' level)	1.25	–
2	18%	3.77	–
3	25% (EST 'Best Practice' level)	6.28	2010
4	44% (Similar to 'Passivhaus' standard)	10.04	2013
5	100% (Zero emissions: heating, hot water, ventilation and lighting)	17.57	–
6	≈150% (Zero net emissions from all energy use in the home)	18.83	2016

Source: The Callcutt Review, 2007.

Level 5 and 6 about energy are essentially the same for all types of construction, requiring significant use of renewable energy in conjunction with a very high standard of fabric performance. The definition of zero-carbon that the code uses is essentially the same as that used in the 2006 DCLG consultation document (ibid), but two additional criteria are set as (DCLG, 2008):

- To ensure homes are built to excellent standards of fabric energy efficiency – this prevents homes heated using fuels with low or zero CO_2 emissions from being built with poor fabric performance;
- To allow the use of renewable energy generated offsite to be counted, only where it is directly connected by means of a 'private wire' – this prevents the developer from simply paying towards a wind turbine away from the site that would have been constricted in any case.

Since May 2008, it has been mandatory for a code rating certificate to be provided for all new homes built in England. For publicly funded new homes and those built on public land, achievement of Code Level 3 is the minimum requirement. The existing housing stock is responsible for an average of around 72 CO_2kg/m²/yr. After Code Level 5, carbon emissions from heating and hot water would be zero due to using renewable sources to provide the heating demand by solar thermal, district heating, biomass and CHP, and only remaining would be from cooking and appliances. These would be also removed by the energy provided from renewable energy sources, which are mostly coming from PVs and wind turbines. It is estimated that the new homes built between then and 2050 could account for up to one-third of the total stock of housing in 2050. Logic dictates, therefore, that if those new homes are built to high standards of energy efficiency, the amount of CO_2 they will emit would add less to total housing emissions than if they were built to lower standards. And so, it follows that if homes can be built to zero-carbon design standards, they would not in theory add to overall emissions at all. Importantly, the zero-carbon target provides certainty to the industry on what is needed and when, allowing time for progressive up-skilling and development of the new approaches required.

Construction of Zero-Carbon Houses

A wide range of new technologies are appearing to meet low- and zero-carbon standards, not just for creating renewable energy, but also in terms of constructing new houses. Many of these techniques are hybrids of tried and tested solutions, but many are highly innovative. In the main, the new forms of construction are more expensive than traditional buildings, but the incorporation of much higher specification windows and doors, ventilation systems and substantially more insulation will inevitably increase costs. To increase efficiency and keep costs within limits, there has been encouragement for more prefabrication, offsite construction and other new techniques. These range from 'high-tech' materials using steel and synthetic components, to timber frames and the use of low impact renewable crop-based materials.

Many of these innovations have been encouraged by the government at the time, and some were showcased at the BRE's Innovation Park. These showcase buildings have highlighted major challenges facing house builders aiming to achieve zero-carbon performance. Only 6% of homeowners surveyed by the National House Building Council Foundation (NHBC) felt that the £35,000 extra cost to achieve a zero-carbon home is reasonable (NHBC, 2008). For example, the Lighthouse, in BRE Innovation Park, built by Kingspan costs an estimated £180,000, compared to the average £100,000 for a building regulation-complaint home (McCarthy, 2008). A slightly lower cost of £150,000 has been estimated for Bill Duster's Rural Zed house to achieve Code Level 6 (Building Sustainability, 2008). However, this is a major investment that many homeowners were unwilling to make, even with possible savings in running costs of £400 per year. This was a serious concern for house builders surveyed by NHBC at the time, who believed that Code Level 6 homes cannot be built profitably by 2016.

The UK is one of the world's developed countries, yet a large proportion of its population suffers from fuel poverty. Despite numerous initiatives, the issues remained prevalent, enduring and serious. At the time, one in five UK households (21%) were fuel poor, but around the constituent nations the picture varies; the figure is as high as 44% in Northern Ireland, one in three homes (33%) in Scotland, a quarter of households in Wales (26%) and 18% in England (BRE/DECC, 2011).

168 *Young Ki Kim and Hasim Altan*

Fuel poverty is the term applied to households that spend more than 10% of their income on energy bills. As such, the proportion of people in fuel poverty varies as incomes rise or fall, as energy prices fluctuate and as the amount of energy consumed changes. For the period early in the 2000s when competitiveness in the liberalised energy market led to falling prices, combined with a period of rising benefits for low-income households, those in fuel poverty fell. From 2004 onwards, though, the trend has been upwards. In the year 2000, the UK government made a commitment to low-income households. By 2016, it was said, fuel poverty in the UK would be history. At that time, 2016 seemed a long way away; the target appeared reasonable and achievable. However, up to date figures showed that the government's target to eliminate fuel poverty by 2016 was not possible within their timeline.

Fuel Poverty in the UK

A household's income, the price it pays for its energy and the quality of its housing, heating and other equipment will determine whether the household is in fuel poverty. The quality of housing and equipment will have a major impact on the energy bill of low-income households generally. Fuel poverty is largely a problem of the existing housing stock and is not an issue in newer housing because of the comparatively higher standards of energy efficiency. The largest concentration of fuel-poor households is to be found in pre-1975 dwellings (BERR, 2005).

At the beginning of the century, the former government published the Warm Homes and Energy Conservation Act 2000 that promised to eliminate fuel poverty by 2016. The following year, the Fuel Poverty Strategy committed the government to removing vulnerable households from fuel poverty by 2010 and all households by 2016, as shown in Table 7.7. With 4 million households in the UK trapped in fuel poverty in 2009, that target was certainly missed. Indeed, those estimates showed that fuel poverty then was much more than twice as prevalent as it was in 2009 when targets for 2010 and 2016 were set (DECC, 2011).

The reduction in fuel poverty between 1996 and 2003 was very substantial. Since 2003, however, there were marked increases in the numbers

Table 7.7 Statutory obligation to eradicate fuel poverty in the UK.

Region	Vulnerable Households	All Households
England	2010	2016
Wales	2010	2018
Scotland	N/A	2016
Northern Ireland	2010	2016

Source: The UK Fuel Poverty Strategy, 2007.

Housing and Policies in the United Kingdom 169

in fuel poverty, thus in 2006 there were about 2.4 million households in England in fuel poverty. Reductions in the number of fuel-poor households over the period 1996–2005 were driven by energy price decreases, as the combined product of world trends and the introduction of competition in the UK energy market. Household incomes also increased significantly during this period, especially with the introduction of Pension Credit and Tax Credits. Furthermore, programmes for improving the energy efficiency of low-income households, such as Warm Front, also made important contributions.

The government, in its 2009 annual report on fuel poverty (BERR/DEFRA, 2009), estimated that – of the reduction in overall fuel poverty between 1996 and 2005 – three-quarters was due to income improvements and around one-fifth to energy efficiency improvements, with the rest resulting from energy price reduction. It is generally recognised that the best way to protect people against fuel poverty is with energy efficiency improvements. Nonetheless, in the last two decades, all the progress made in tackling fuel poverty through energy efficiency has been undone through rising fuel prices. Electricity bills rose by 13% in the five years to 2011, and gas bills rose by 25% over the same period (DECC, 2011). The result was that levels of fuel poverty were then estimated to be about the same as they were when the government committed to abolishing the problem. The need to tackle cold, unhealthy homes did not go away. The government's own Hills Review then estimated that more people die because of cold homes than die on the nation's roads (John Hills, 2011).

Dwelling Characteristics and Efficiency

7.8 shows the fuel poverty rate in households with varying numbers of bedrooms. In households with 1, 2 or 3 bedrooms, the fuel poverty rate is broadly similar at around 19–21%, whereas in households with 4 or more bedrooms, the fuel poverty rate is lower at around 12%. This is because households living in properties with four or more bedrooms tend to have a greater household income than those households living in smaller properties, as shown in Table 7.8.

Table 7.8 Average annual income by number of bedrooms in 2009.

Number of Bedrooms	Average Annual Income (£)
1	17,000
2	21,900
3	26,700
4 or more	44,200
All households	27,900

170 *Young Ki Kim and Hasim Altan*

The energy efficiency level of the dwelling is another key driver in the propensity to fuel poverty. Table 7.8 shows the fuel poverty rate by different SAP ratings, illustrating again that the least energy efficiency households are the ones most likely to be fuel poor. Most of the fuel poverty dwellings rate in EPCs as F and G, and these are mostly built before the introduction of modern building regulations. These dwellings are also commonly called 'hard-to-treat homes', and these homes commonly had solid walls, electric heating system, old boiler, minimum/or no loft insulation, no floor insulation, no completed double glazing and even off-the-grid systems.

Table 7.8 shows the distribution of SAP ratings for both the fuel-poor households and the non-fuel-poor households. The average SAP rating amongst fuel-poor households in 2009 was 43.9, lower than the average SAP rating of 55.3 amongst non-fuel-poor households. However, the distribution of SAP rating in the fuel-poor group is more spread than that of the non-fuel-poor group. The 5th and 95th percentile of the fuel-poor group is 8.7 and 67.8, respectively, whereas the 5th and 95th percentile of the non-fuel-poor group is 32.3 and 74.8, respectively.

Existing Programmes and Policies

Our homes need to be heated to a comfortable temperature, but some people cannot afford to heat them to achieve a comfortable temperature. To tackle fuel poverty, it is necessary to address its three causes as shown previously: high fuel prices, low incomes, and poor energy efficiency. Of these three, poor energy efficiency is the most cost effective to address. Improving home energy efficiency has other benefits too: it makes homes comfortable, and it helps to tackle climate change due to less heating energy demanded and less fossil fuel burning.

Government Funded Programmes

There are very sizeable schemes that provide energy efficiency measures free of charge for low-income households, and these measures can significantly reduce fuel bills.

Warm Front: This programme provided free insulation and heating system upgrades to people in England on means evaluated benefits who owned their own homes or who rented from private landlords. It also checked that vulnerable households did not miss out on their full benefits entitlements. In 2006/7, the Warm Front programme secured an average improvement in SAP ratings per household from 40 to 56, a fall in CO_2 emissions from 6.97 MtC per annum per household to 6.16 MtC and the potential to save an average £190 per annum for each household in energy running costs. However, having helped more than 2.3 million vulnerable households since its inception in 2000, Warm Front ended in 2013. This meant that, for the first time in 35 years, no publicly funded programme to improve the energy efficiency of vulnerable households existed in England. Grant schemes in Scotland (the Energy Assistance Package or EAP) and Nest in Wales continued at the time.

Raising Incomes (Winter Fuel Payments): This provided between £150 and £300 paid to approximately 12 million UK households that have residents over the age of 60. Costing £2.7 billion a year, as a universal benefit, it did not target the fuel poor. Additional Cold Weather Payments were made to households on specific means-tested benefits during periods of very cold weather lasting more than a week.

Programmes to Improve Rented Homes: Decent Homes in England, the Scottish Housing Quality Standard and the Welsh Housing Quality Standard set minimum levels of thermal comfort to tackle social housing in poor condition. Many homes in the private rented sector are highly energy inefficient. The Landlords Energy Saving Allowance gave landlords a £1,500 tax allowance each year for energy saving improvements. The Housing Health and Safety Rating System is a risk management system used by local authority environmental health officers in England that aims to minimise hazards in homes. It was used to regulate standards in the private rented sector. Cold homes are seen as a serious hazard, and although it is loosely defined, some official guidance – and many local authorities – classified all homes in the F and G banding on an energy performance certificate as representing a serious cold hazard. Two-thirds of G-rated properties were occupied by fuel-poor households at the time (DCLG, 2006).

Energy Supplier Funded Programmes: Supporting lower tariffs for vulnerable households, the Warm Home Discount was introduced in April 2011 and was paid for by energy providers at a cost of £250 million p.a. and subsidised electricity bills of selected vulnerable households – usually pensioners – by up to £140 a year. By the time the initiative was due to end in March 2015, it was expected to have helped more than two million households, although not all of them would be fuel poor.

The Carbon Emissions Reduction Target: This £1bn per year scheme obliged energy suppliers to fund energy efficiency improvements in homes. It was the government's main policy for improving energy efficiency across the UK housing stock. Investment in the scheme was considerable and, whilst it generally only funded basic cost-effective measures, it had provided insulation in more than 1.8 million cavity walls, 2.4 million lofts and 42,000 solid walls. CERT funds measures in all homes, but 40% of the target must be achieved in the homes of a group of 'priority' customers assumed to be at risk of fuel poverty; those in receipt of certain income-related benefits, and pensioners aged over 70. Within that 40%, since 2010 suppliers have been further obliged to target 15% (of the total target) at a 'super-priority' group on a more restricted set of benefits, and who were deemed to be at particular risk of fuel poverty at the time. Some energy suppliers have struggled to identify customers in this super-priority group.

The Community Energy Saving Programme (CESP): CESP brings energy companies, local authorities and third-sector organisations together to introduce a 'whole house' approach to energy efficiency measures in low-income areas. Introduced in 2009, it obligated energy suppliers to install energy saving measures in harder-to-treat, especially solid-wall properties – the homes that they had not found cost-effective to target under CERT. By the time the scheme ended in October 2012, it was expected to have delivered more than £350 million of energy efficiency measures to about 90,000 homes, which was equivalent to 1.6% of the total number of households in fuel poverty.

The Future: ECO and Green Deal: In 2013, the Energy Company Obligation (ECO) replaced supplier obligations under CESP and CERT. Costing the suppliers around £1.3 billion per year, ECO had two elements, the affordable warmth obligation and the carbon-saving obligation. The first, affordable warmth, proposed to target the current CERT super-priority group, but only in privately owned or privately rented accommodations. This would help low-income and vulnerable households to heat their homes adequately. The second element, carbon saving, would work with hard-to-treat homes where households cannot fund energy efficiency improvements fully through the Green Deal. The government predicted at the time that, by 2023, ECO would alleviate fuel poverty in 350,000–550,000 households – around 10 per cent of those currently affected – and, at the most optimistic level, 1.7 million cavity walls would be insulated – less than 30% of the potential (DECC, 2011).

The Green Deal was the government's flagship energy efficiency policy at the time. It provided households with access to finance for energy efficiency improvements. They would make repayments through the electricity meter, but there was a 'golden rule' for eligibility; annual repayments must be no more than the savings achievable by installing the improvements. The golden rule was based on the 'required' fuel use of the property, rather than the actual use. As many poor households use less than the required amount of fuel and are thus likely to achieve smaller savings, this poses a risk because the golden rule would have not applied to them (ibid). In July 2015, the UK government scrapped the Green Deal because it had 'failed to live up to expectations' and that its implementation had been poor, stating 'rather than facilitating access to energy efficiency measures and creating momentum in the market, the Green Deal has caused frustration and confusion for both consumers and the supply chain' (BBC News, 2015).

Conclusions

It is likely that housing, both existing and new buildings, will need to contribute more to the overall strategy to reduce CO_2 emissions in the future. The UK government has stated that 80% of GHGs emissions will be reduced by 2050 from 1990 levels in the Climate Change Act 2008. If CO_2 cannot be cut sufficiently from other sectors, such as shipping and aviation, then higher standards will be required elsewhere to make up the shortfall.

To combat climate change, the energy efficiency of the housing stock will need to be increased and the associated carbon emissions be reduced. Through the various national policies to improve energy efficiency of homes, schemes are working for existing and new-build homes and have helped to reduce heating demand from homes by providing better internal comfort for occupancy. However, the number of lighting and appliances has more than doubled since in terms of electricity consumption by households, which has also led to an increase in CO_2 emissions. Changing people's behaviours to adapt their lifestyle provides greater consideration for the environment rather than for their convenience.

The UK government meanwhile continues to increase the homes' energy efficiency through the building regulations and EPCs for existing homes and the code level for new homes. It was also pointed out that the fabric standards for new builds and existing dwellings would be significantly increased so that they are more airtight. These strategies helped to reduce heating energy consumption; however, in terms of climate change, summers got hotter, and more frequent heat waves occurred, such as those in 2003, 2006, 2018, 2019 and 2022. This meant that increasing the energy efficiency of dwellings through the building fabric efficiency measurements could be disastrous for the future summer overheating conditions for the UK homes. It could lead to the installation of air conditioning systems in every home in the country and contribute to increases in electricity consumption and CO_2 emissions, which may result in the government's target possibly failing.

Therefore, the direction of improving energy efficiency for both existing and new-build homes is the way forward, and we must do more for our energy inefficient homes such as fuel poverty and vulnerable households. However, when we design new homes, we should also consider that the designs are future-proofed, which means considering climate change and better performance of heating and cooling.

Notes

1 The Standard Assessment Procedure (SAP) is the UK government's approved methodology for rating the energy performance of dwellings. The SAP rating is based on energy costs and is expressed on a scale of 1–100, with a higher number indicating a lower running cost. The assessment takes into account a range of features of a building including construction materials, thermal insulation, heating, hot water, ventilation and lighting but assumes standard use by typical occupants.

2 In the UK residential market, the requirement is to provide an Energy Performance Certificate (EPC) when a property is sold or rented. Based on the familiar A–G rating displayed on domestic appliances, the EPC gives an indication of the current condition of the property along with its potential for improvement using cost-effective measures. The report accompanying the EPCs also lists a range of additional measures that could be adopted, including a small number of Low/Zero carbon technologies.

References

BBC News. (2015). Green deal funding to end, government announces. July 23, 2015. Retrieved from https://www.bbc.com/news/uk-england-gloucestershire-33638903.

Beizaee, A., Lomas, K. J., & Firth, S. K. (2013). National survey of summertime temperatures and overheating risk in English homes. *Building and Environment*, 65, 1–17. https://doi.org/10.1016/j.buildenv.2013.03.011

BERR. (2005). Fuel poverty 2005: Detailed tables, department for business, enterprise and regulatory reform. Retrieved from http://www.berr.gov.uk/files/file16567.pdf (last visited: 25.06.2011).

Boardman, B., Darby, S., Killip, G., Hinnells, M., Jardine, C. N., Palmer, J., & Sinden, G. (2005). The 40% house. Research report no. 31. Oxford: Environmental Change Institute, University of Oxford. Retrieved from www.eci.ox.ac.uk/research/energy/downloads/40house/40house.pdf (last visited: 25.08.2011).

Boardman, B., Darby, S., Killip, G., Hinnells, M., Jardine, C., Palmer, J., & Sinden, G. (2007). 40% house report. Oxford: Environmental Change Institute, University of Oxford. Retrieved from http://www.eci.ox.ac.uk/research/energy/downloads/40house/40house.pdf (last visited: 15.06.2013).

Building Research Establishment (BRE). (2007). Fuel poverty 2009 – Detailed tables; Annex to the annual report on fuel poverty statistics, BRE/DECC. Retrieved from http://www.decc.gov.uk/assets/decc/Statistics/fuelpoverty/2183-fuel-poverty-2009- detailed-tables.pdf (last visited: 15.06.2013).

Building sustainability. (2008). Rural zed explained, building, issue 12. Retrieved from http://www.building.co.uk/news/sectors/housing/zero-carbon-housing-kit-ruralzed- explained/3109716.article (last visited: 05.02.2011).

CIPHE. (2008). Taking control of carbon. Being comfortable at home, being kinder to the environment, Hornchurch, Chartered Institute of Plumbing and Heating Engineering. Retrieved from http://www.ciphe.org.uk/Global/PDF%20files/Taking%20Control%20of%20Carbon%20V2.pdf (last visited: 20.06.2013).

Department of Energy and Climate Change (DECC). (2008). UK leads world with commitment to cut emissions by 80% by 2050. Retrieved from http://nds.coi.gov.uk/environment/fullDetail.asp?ReleaseID=381477&NewsAreaID=2&NavigatedFromDepartment=False (last visited: 05.05.2010).

DCLG. (2007). Building a greener future: Policy statement. Retrieved from www.communities.gov.uk/documents/planningandbuilding/pdf/building-greener.pdf (last visited: 07.02.2009).

DCLG. (2008). Code for sustainable homes technical guide. Retrieved from www.planningportal.gov.uk/uploads/code_for_sustainable_homes_techguide.pdf (last visited: 07.02.2009).

DCLG. (2011). English housing survey: Housing stock report 2009. Retrieved from http://www.communities.gov.uk/documents/statistics/pdf/1937212.pdf (last visited: 30.06.2013).

De Dear, R., & Brager, G. (2002). Thermal comfort in naturally ventilated buildings revisions to ASHRAE standard 55. *Energy and Buildings*, 34(6), 549–561.

DECC. (2009). Climate change act 2008: Department of energy & climate change, DECC. Retrieved from http://www.legislation.gov.uk/ukpga/2008/27/contents (last visited: 04.06.2013).

Housing and Policies in the United Kingdom   175

DECC. (2011a). Average annual domestic electricity and gas bills, DECC. Retrieved from http://www.decc.gov.uk/en/content/cms/statistics/energy_stats/prices/prices.aspx December 2011 (last visited: 21.09.2012).

DECC. (2011b). Great Britain's housing energy fact file 2011, the Department of Energy and Climate Change. Retrieved from http://www.decc.gov.uk/assets/decc/11/stats/climate-change/3224-great-britains-housing-energy-fact-file-2011.pdf (last visited: 21.09.2012).

DECC. (2011c). The green deal and energy company obligation. Retrieved from http://www.decc.gov.uk/assets/decc/11/consultation/green-deal/3607-green-deal-energy-company-ob-cons.pdf (last visited: 12.06.2013).

Department for Communities and Local Government (DCLG). (2006). Building a greener future: Towards zero-carbon development consultation. Retrieved from www.communities.gov.uk/documents/planningandbuilding/pdf/153125.pdf (last visited: 21.06.2008).

Department for Environment, Food and Rural Affairs (DEFRA). (2009). The UK fuel poverty strategy: 7th annual progress report. Retrieved from http://www.decc.gov.uk/en/content/cms/funding/fuel_poverty/strategy/strategy.aspx.

Energy Saving Trust (EST). (2008). Towards a long-term strategy for reducing carbon dioxide emissions from our housing stock. London: Energy Saving Trust. Retrieved from http://s3.amazonaws.com/zanran_storage/www.eeph.org.uk/ContentPages/45617299.pdf (last visited: 30.06.2013).

Evans, P. (1997). Is there a marketable solution to sustainable housing? Draft MSc Thesis, Wolfson College, University of Cambridge. Retrieved from http://www.idbe.org/uploads/Evans,%20P.%20(1997)%20Is%20there%20a%20marketable%20solution%20to%20sustainable%20housing.pdf (last visited: 30.06.2013).

Guerra-Santin, O., Tweed, C., Jenkins, H., & Jiang, S. (2013). Monitoring the performance of low energy dwellings: Two UK case studies. *Energy and Buildings*, *64*, 32–40. https://doi.org/10.1016/j.enbuild.2013.04.002

Gupta, R., & Gregg, M. (2012a). Adapting UK suburban homes for a warming climate. In *Proceedings of the 7th Windsor conference: The changing context of comfort in an unpredictable world*. Windsor Conference Proceedings, Windsor, United Kingdom.

Gupta, R., & Gregg, M. (2012b). Using UK climate change projections to adapt existing English homes for a warming climate. *Building and Environment*, *55*, 20–42. https://doi.org/10.1016/j.buildenv.2012.01.014

Gupta, R., & Gregg, M. (2013). Preventing the overheating of English suburban homes in a warming climate. *Building Research and Information*, *41*(3), 281–300. https://doi:10.1080/09613218.2013.772043

Gupta, R., & Gregg, M. (2016). Do deep low carbon domestic retrofits actually work? *Energy and Buildings*, *129*, 330–343. https://doi.org/10.1016/j.enbuild.2016.08.010

Gupta, R., & Gregg, M. (2018). Assessing energy use and overheating risk in net zero energy dwellings in the UK. *Energy and Buildings*, *158*, 897–905. https://doi.org/10.1016/j.enbuild.2017.10.061

Hills, J. (2011). Fuel poverty: The problem and its measurement; interim report of the fuel poverty review, case. Retrieved from http://www.decc.gov.uk/assets/decc/11/funding-support/fuel-poverty/3226-fuel-poverty-review-interim-report.pdf (last visited: 09.09.2012).

HM Government. (2008). Definition of zero-carbon home and non-domestic building, department community and local government. Retrieved from http://www.zerocarbonhub.org/resourcefiles/1101177.pdf (last visited: 21.07.2010).

Johnston, D., Lowe, R., & Bell, M. (2005). An exploration of the technical feasibility of achieving CO2 emission reductions in excess of 60% within the UK housing stock by the year 2050. *Energy Policy*, *33*(13), 1643.

Letherman, K. M., & Samo, S. R. (2000). Energy conservation and carbon dioxide emission reduction in UK housing – Three possible scenarios. In *Proceedings of the international conference on technology watch and innovation in the construction industry*, April 2000, Brussels, Belgium, pp. 53–57.

McCarthy, M. (2008). On the market: The zero-carbon home with an affordable price. The Independent, February 27. Retrieved from http://www.independent.co.uk/environment/green-living/on-the-market-the-zerocarbon-home-with-an-affordable-price-787920.html (last visited: 30.08.2012).

Meier, H., & Rehdanz, K. (2008). Determinants of residential space heating expenditures in Great Britain. *Energy Economics*. Retrieved from http://mercury.ethz.ch/serviceengine/Files/ISN/93758/.../KaP_1439.pdf (last visited: 30.06.2013).

NHBC Foundation. (2008). Homeowners are not ready for zero-carbon homes. National Housing Building Council. Retrieved from http://www.zerocarbonhub.org/resourcefiles/1101177.pdf (last visited: 30.06.2013).

OPSI. (2007). Stamp duty land tax (zero-carbon home relief) regulations 2007. Office of Public Sector Information. Retrieved from http://www.legislation.gov.uk/uksi/2007/3437/contents/made (last visited: 30.06.2013).

Ozarisoy, B. (2022). Energy effectiveness of passive cooling design strategies to reduce the impact of long-term heatwaves on occupants' thermal comfort in Europe: Climate change and mitigation. *Journal of Cleaner Production*. https://doi.org/10.1016/j.jclepro.2021.129675.

Ozarisoy, B., & Altan, H. (2021a). Developing an evidence-based energy-policy framework to assess robust energy-performance evaluation and certification schemes in the South-Eastern Mediterranean countries. *Energy for Sustainable Development*, *64*, 65–102. https://doi.org/10.1016/j.esd.2021.08.001.

Ozarisoy, B., & Altan, H. (2022a). Significance of occupancy patterns and habitual household adaptive behaviour on home-energy performance of post-war social-housing estate in the South-Eastern Mediterranean climate: Energy policy design. *Energy*, *244*. https://doi.org/10.1016/j.energy.2021.122904.

Peacock, A., Banfill, P. F., Turan, S., Jenkins, D., Ahadzi, M., Bowles, G., ... Berry, A. (2007). *Reducing CO2 emissions through refurbishment of UK housing. ECEEE summer study*. La Colle sur Loup, France.

Shipworth, M., Firth, S. K., Gentry, M. I., Wright, A. J., Shipworth, D. T., & Lomas, K. J. (2009). Central heating thermostat settings and timing: Building demographics. *Building Research and Information*, *28*(1), 50–69.

Shorrock, L. D., Henderson, J., Utley, J. L., & Walters, G. A. (2001). Carbon emission reductions from energy efficiency improvements to the UK housing stock, BRE Report 435. Garston, Watford: Building Research Establishment.

Shorrock, L. D., & Utley, J. I. (2003). Domestic energy fact file 2003. Breast 457. Bracknell, IHS BRE Press, Retrieved from http://projects.bre.co.uk/factfile/BR457prtnew.pdf (last visited: 30.06.2013).

Tyndall Centre. (2005). Developing regional and local scenarios for climate change mitigation and adaptation, Part 2: Scenario creation. Retrieved from http://www.tyndall.ac.uk/sites/default/files/wp67.pdf (last visited: 20.08.2011).

WWF. (2007). 80% challenge: Delivering a low carbon UK. Retrieved from http://www.ippr.org.uk/publicationsandreports/publication.asp?id=573 (last visited: 08.09.2010).

Yohanis, Y. G., & Mondol, J. D. (2010). Annual variations of temperature in a sample of UK dwellings. *Applied Energy*, 87(22), 681–690.

8 Conclusions

Bertug Ozarisoy and Hasim Altan

Translations between Transgression and Utopia

This research aims for a 'Utopian Vision' approach to social, political and cultural relations, trends and tensions both locally and globally. It also seeks to inspire an awakening. This research is divided into six chapters: Analysis of the context in 12 terms, learning from a poem, searching a new diaspora for the buffer zone, transgression as a way of creating urban utopia, the event 'Creative Possibilities: Birds, Narratives and Artefacts' and constructing an urban utopian vision for Nicosia. Despite having points of connection, each chapter addresses the phenomenon from a different perspective: its philosophical background, its social construction, its experimental research process and its design implications on the city. The main research question is that can transgressive strategies rather than novel or radical design practices be more effective for unifying Nicosia?

Drawing is a reflective activity that at once generates and informs speculative design. The drawings here have the dual function of examining as well as narrating the spectacular qualities of the site for which they act as a proxy. The design takes lyrical as well as pragmatic directions and begins to pursue ideas evoked solely by the drawing itself.

Architecture is manifested in multiple states as ideas are overwritten by the palimpsestic nature of the design process. Although work at this stage is essentially more scenic than orthographic, the drawings contain information about scale and materiality and suggest ideas of contextual detail and structure. In this project the drawings are directly transformed into models and the spectacular nature of the site is fused into utopian urban vision strategy via technological devices. Three-dimensional form is created by elevating and layering duplicate copies of the drawings printed onto card, to create the space implicit in, or inspired by, the drawings. This process aims to stretch out and further define ideas already imagined for each of the layers of the utopian urban vision of Nicosia.

DOI: 10.4324/9781003243069-10

Transgression and Radical Practices Are the Concept

Transgression is a contextual term such as The Green Line and The UN Buffer Zone. In order to transgress, one walks across a line or acts in relation to an established code or order. There can be no transgression unless there is a boundary or a zone, against which any transgression can be measured. The historic evaluation of Nicosia, for example, has tracked the ways in which violence, occupation, separation and division of the island has been categorised against political power which has changed over the course of time, highlighting the fact that transgression has a temporal character. The social value shifts and transgression positions itself against both boundaries and time. For instance, the Ledra check point offers a temporary bridge between both communities rather than radical unification of the city. Moreover, transgression can occupy the space between modes, positioning itself in the gap between one condition and another.

Transgression is a social process and contestable contest of cultural practice. Transgression is that which transcends boundaries or exceeds limits. However, we need to affirm that cultural studies are the study of limits. Transgressive attitude therefore does not deny limits of boundaries rather it exceeds them and completes them in practice, experience, bringing its own fracture, penetration or impulse to dissidence. The point of investigating transgression is to demonstrate that the transgression is not a component of the rule. It is a dynamic force in cultural reproduction. It also prevents stagnation by breaking the rule, and it ensures stability by reaffirming the rule. In some cases, transgression could be said to occur because of a critical response to the circumstances of the physical site and the social, economic and institutional circumstances.

Bataille (1997) mentions that the space that transgression produces is therefore hybrid or heterogeneous (Bataille, 1997, 19–21). The heterogeneous space 'includes everything resulting from unproductive expenditure' (ibid, p.20). This consists of everything rejected by homogeneous society as a liminal border or real value of the city. Heterogeneity also indicates that it concerns elements that are impossible to assimilate which refers to the dead zones through the city thus defining the thresholds. Balletto (1996) describes that heterogeneity can be seen as the result of transgression or spacing, while emphasising the exclusionary function of architecture. Camus (1998) indicates architecture, as a whole, is an inclusive space. A space that does not exclude the other but as an apparatus of reform. Many of the examples of heterotopic spaces in the world, such as Nicosia, speak of 'other spaces' and convey this idea – as such heterotopia differs from heterogeneous space, since the other is made into a knowable, controlled and often reformed subject (Chen, 2011, 52). However, even in the most oppressive space, Foucault asserts that transgression can take place. Therefore, it can be concluded that both writers agree that any socio-spatial ordering, which architecture is or has the potential to be, is heterogeneous and, as such, contains the possibility of transgression (Chris, 2003, 29). This conclusion is asserted to understand the relationship between architecture and transgression (Foucault, 1963, 371). However, architecture becomes homogeneous only when we forget this foundation on which architecture is constituted or when the architect or the critic conceals this heterogenic background and contributes to community-led integrity. It is to these ends one must go to understand architecture.

Transgression is neither violent in a divided world nor a victory over limits, and exactly for this reason, its role is to measure the excessive distance, opens at the heart of the limit and to trace the Green Line that causes the limit to arise. As Feireiss (2011) advocates, there is no architecture without action, no architecture without events, no architecture without programme. By extension, there is no architecture without violence. Both these statements argue that a traditional historic method of analysis implies a distinguished relationship between action and space. It institutes a new order after the disorder of the original structure of the city. When it becomes necessary to mediate conflict and tension by political power, then there is no integrity between action and event.

Transgressions and Radical Practices versus Border

In architecture, transgressions are inevitably linked to borders, territories, boundaries and thus spatial conflicts. Hardt (2005) mentions that whether through literal or phenomenal transgression, architecture is seen as the momentary and sacrilegious convergence of real space and ideal space. Limits remain for transgression which does not mean the methodological destruction of any code or rule that concerns space or architecture. On the contrary, it introduces new articulations between inside and outside, between concept and experience. The metaphorical use of borders in everyday language, the emphasis on protective entities in political discourse and the border as a factual, has created a number of new borders which call for a spatial investigation.

The border is created by deterritorialization, the buffer zone between two territories, and the Green Line, the vectors of deterritorialization. The dead zone transgresses spatial and social boundaries, but they do not create new defined ones. Manaugh (2011) discusses in another context, 'they take place placeless'. This space is therefore, by definition, undefined and as such, Denison and Ren (2013) describe the dead space as heterogeneous. Because such space does not have defined boundaries, it cannot be autonomous and conversely, it cannot be revolutionary thus aiming to replace the existing space. As can clearly be seen with the dead zone and ideology (Sheil, 2005, 20–32), they are reluctant on the space which they transgress. In relation to this argument, the following statement from (Mosley & Sara, 2013, 14–19) 'Preface to Transgression' is important:

Hejduk (2007) suggests that transgression has its place at the limit or the border. But since the border is a dead zone, it is a conflict space. An obvious place to start is the actual border. Doron (2000) defines that articulation of the places of the border is defined as a non-place: 'If a place can be defined as relational, historical and concerned with identity, it will be a non-place'. The 'non-place' indeed depicts accurately the border, and while these are terrain vague, they are, in any other sense, identical to the border itself and not transgressive. Transgression, on the contrary, is always relational, acknowledges history and concerns identity which complicates but does not negate. Yet even though the dead zones are triggered by transgression, the transgression in these places is restricted by borders. Miessen (2006) admits that the liminal space has a 'precise and well-defined function within society'. On the contrary, it becomes a subject to be managed with the aim of preserving, if not regenerating, the social structure and tension and transgression (Miessen, 2007, 32).

The buffer zone is probably the most chaotic site for describing the space transgression which opens at the heart of the border (Sassen, 2004, 86). It is the city's threshold and the one that architectural characteristics sacrifice to maintain the city's future. This dead zone, as a liminal space, can be referred to as the generic term for uncertain urban spaces such as terrain vagues, derelict areas or urban voids (Shepheard, 2013, 67). These spaces are not easy to identify because they are not autonomous and consist of spatial and economic conditions that make them receptive to uses or events considered to be transgressive.

Transgression as such allows us to unify communities thus collectively reconfiguring the liminal spaces and borders within the city (Miessen, 2008, 124). This leads to power of presence, which grows only through inhabiting and 'being there', through activities and movement in urban situations in ways that go beyond the preconceptions of policymakers, developers and other owner Non-Governmental Organisations (NGOs) of power who appear to offer conceptual proposals thus shaping the city today (Tschumi, 1996, 78).

In the Nicosia case, such border conditions imply that at no moment can any part become an element or a structure totality. Each part leads to another, and every conceptual theory is off balance, constituted by the traces of another theory. It could also be constituted by the traces of an event, a programme and history. It can lead to new concepts, one radical objective, to understand a new concept for the conceptional vision of the future.

References

Balletto, L. (1996). *Ethnic groups, cross-social and cross-cultural contacts in Cyprus.* London: Cass Press, p. 56.

Bataille, G. (1997). Architecture. In N. Leach (Ed.), *Rethinking architecture* (p. 21). London: Routledge.

Camus, A. (1998). *The plaque*. New York: Penguin Publications, p. 45.

Chen, D. (2011). *On utopia and beyond: Productive dystopia*. Berlin: Gestalten Express, p. 52.

Chris, J. (2003). *Transgression*. London: Routledge, p. 29.

Denison, E., & Ren, G. (2013). Transgression and progress in China: Wang Shu and the literati mindset. *Architectural Design*, *83*(6), 38–43. https://doi.org/10.1002/ad.1672

Doron, G. M. (2000). The dead zone and the architecture of transgression. *City*, *4*(2), 247–263. https://doi.org/10.1080/13604810050147857

Feireiss, L. (2011). *On Utopia and beyond: This time tomorrow*. Berlin: Gestalten Express, p. 65.

Foucault, M. (1963). 'A Preface to Transgression', published in Language, Counter-Memory, Practice: Selected Essays and Interviews, Ed & *Translator*, *1963*, 371.

Hardt, M. (2005). *Multitude: War and democracy in the age of empire*. London: Hamish Hamilton Publications, p. 78.

Hejduk, R. (2007). Death becomes her: Transgression, decay, and eROTicism in Bernard Tschumi's early writings and projects. *Journal of Architecture*, *12*, 393–404. https://doi.org/10.1080/13602360701614672

Manaugh, G. (2011). *On Utopia and beyond: Utopia generator*. Berlin: Gestalten Express, p. 89.

Miessen, M. (2006). *Did someone say participate? An Atlas of spatial practice*. Cambridge, MA: MIT Press, p. 45.

Miessen, M. (2007). *The violence of participation*. Berlin: Architectural Association School of Architecture Bookshop Publishing, p. 32.

Miessen, M. (2008). *East Coast Europe*. Berlin: Sternberg Press, p. 124.

Mosley, J., & Sara, R. (2013). The architecture of transgression: Towards a destabilising architecture. *Architectural Design*, *83*(6), 14–19. https://doi.org/10.1002/ad.1668

Sassen, S. (2004). Afterword. In J. Gugler (Ed.), *World cities beyond the west* (p. 86). Cambridge: Cambridge University Press.

Sheil, B. (2005). Transgression from drawing to making. *Architectural Research Quarterly*, *9*(1), 20–32. https://doi.org/10.1017/S1359135505000059

Shepheard, P. (2013). *How to like everything: A Utopia*. London: Zero Books, p. 67.

Tschumi, B. (1996). *Architecture and transgression, published in architecture and disjunction, Bernard Tschumi*. Cambridge, MA: MIT Press, p. 78.

Part 2

Learning from the Globe

Urban Regeneration, Brand Identity and City Making

9 Introduction

Bertug Ozarisoy and Hasim Altan

Transgression between Architectural Design and Urban Regeneration Developments

This study is a remarkable contribution to architectural design as a practice and as a discipline. It brings clarity to what is often obtuse in visionary utopian urban design scenarios, while revealing the significance of tackling theory whether as a student, a teacher or a practising professional. Exemplar images and questions framed by equally thoughtful prose comprise a rich body of architectural theory and design thinking and experience. These series of international case studies can be seen as a core source in teaching and broadly could lead to an increase in the intellectual rigour of the discipline in architecture and urbanism. One of the strengths of this part is the diversity of case studies that are included, reinforcing the versatility of the urban design strategies as applied to different cultures, climates, landscapes and building typologies. This mix of old and new emphasises the importance of the identification of architectural discourse throughout time and lays the foundation for a discussion about why the implementation of effective urban design proposals in the decision-making process of architectural applications remains today as urban environments adapt to the challenges of sustainable urbanism.

This section proposes a successful route map for architects, urban planners, students, academics and other practitioners to close the gap between the notion of transgression and architectural discourse in the conflicted territories and the metropolitan city of London that have shown similar cultural paradox, diaspora and openness. The layout of this part aims, instead, to provide a practical and balanced view of a current novel epistemological approach developed and a road map of the way forward in a contested space that is rapidly changing in both its structures and processes as well as in the demands placed on its outputs and the solutions that are available.

This part introduces theoretical ideas to students without the use of jargon or an assumption of extensive knowledge in other fields, and in doing so, it links these ideas to the processes of design. In four thematic

DOI: 10.4324/9781003243069-12

case studies, this book presents: the theoretical groundings of the theory or philosophy, why it matters to design, an example of the theory in a work of urban regeneration development projects from the 20th and 21st centuries and debates surrounding the theory, particularly as they elaborate modern and post-modern thought. An extensive glossary of theoretical terms also adds a vital contribution for students' comprehension of theories relevant to architectural design and urbanism.

10 Case Study 1

King's Cross Regeneration Development, London, United Kingdom

Guillaume Delfesc[1] and Bertug Ozarisoy[2]

King's Cross: Past and Present

The regeneration project that one can witness in Southwark is part of a wider context. Many other redevelopments took place recently or are currently taking place across London. King's Cross is one famous example. To the north of King's Cross and St Pancras stations, 65 acres of brownfield of former railway lands are being redeveloped as shown in Figure 10.1. The project is a mixed-use programme of housing, offices and public spaces. Initiated in the 2000s with the move of the Eurostar international station from Waterloo to St Pancras in November 2007. In 2022 the redevelopment is nearing completion. This type of massive urban intervention doesn't get unanimous support. A large amount of online literature exists to make dissonant points of view visible. Inhabitants of the affected areas create websites, blogs and set up public meetings to make their voices heard.

What stands out of these media is people feeling not heard by the decision-makers.

> I've often wondered how the management of Argent would feel if a development the size of a small town happened within 300 yards of their front doors. If they had been positively engaged with their concerns properly given respect and real weight, they may well have welcomed it. If they had been effectively shut out with a massive outline planning application stopping real discussion of detailed plans perhaps, they would feel miffed.
>
> (Roberts, 2017, 123–150)

The results of such redevelopment are not only brand-new buildings and refurbished streets but also a change in the local populations. Higher rents of the newly built homes make living in the area more difficult for the historical inhabitants. Newcomers with higher purchasing power settle, changing the whole social character of the neighbourhood (Nord, 2022). This process is called gentrification. This gentrification phenomenon happened or is currently happening to many redeveloped areas across London (Agarez, 2019,

DOI: 10.4324/9781003243069-13

Figure 10.1 Location map of Kings Cross Regeneration Development area. Image credit: Delfesc, 2022.

950–981). The issue is being widely criticised by inhabitants. Southwark Notes is a blog created and maintained by locals of the borough of Southwark who feel affected by the new redevelopment in Elephant & Castle. This blog strongly criticises the regeneration project engaged by the council. The site informs us about three of the main reasons for this opposition. Firstly, gentrification, rising the properties prices and threatening the existing shops:

After the luxury flats market set the trend for our previously unfashionable and always snubbed part of London, the volume housing developers (like Wimpey or Countryside) came in on the act to throw up acres of cheaply built but expensive housing. Now, after nearly a decade of development, Walworth, one of the poorest areas in England has seen the first arrival of a yuppie housing market. Not only has this impacted on the local area, with vacant spaces being built on for new oddly coloured buildings, but the sale and market in ex-council houses has gone through the roof.

(Haddad, 2009)

Then, the destruction of the 1200 homes of the Heygate Estate and the eviction of its inhabitants. 'Heygate Estate had to be removed from the Zone 1 super transport-connected Elephant & Castle – a massive site of prime cheap land for new expensive private housing' (Haddad, 2009). Difficulties in relocating inhabitants in 16 new Housing Association-run blocks, some of them not yet built at the time of eviction, led to some council tenants being asked to find homes themselves through the Council's Home search waiting list.

Finally, among the 2300 new homes of the project, only a small fraction was reserved for social housing. Indeed, only 79 homes of the new programme will be social housing units (3.4%). In the meantime, the lowest price for a one-bedroom flat in the new development when hitting the market in 2014 is £310,000. The process of gentrification brings a controversial change to local communities and is a reason for the criticism that developed in recent years towards large redevelopment projects in London. In Elephant & Castle, the regeneration project supported by the council sees homes demolished and their occupants evicted, without being resettled nearby because of the lack of social housing included in the new programme (Tostoes & Ferreira, 2021, 1082–1106). As a result, the project has been called a 'rip off' by the inhabitants. It is in this complex context that the project is going to take place. We shall see now how luxury can further inform this endeavour.

Mapping Existing Physical Conditions

The site of study is focused on Caledonian Road. It is delimited on the south by Pentonville Road and on the north by the railways of the London Overground. Following the detailed study of Zones 1 and 2 in the 'Historical Analysis' part, the project site is in Zone 3. Thornhill Square is located on the east side of Caledonian Road and Barnsbury Estate on the west. The area of study extends towards the west to the King's Cross redevelopment programme. This cut section through the site helps reveal its organisation, as shown in Figure 10.2.

First, one can observe an important contrast between the different parts of the site. Thornhill Square on the east, is a large and relatively open

190   *Guillaume Delfesc and Bertug Ozarisoy*

Figure 10.2 Cross cultural section of Caledonian Road. Image credit: Delfesc, 2022.

space, with a park in the centre. It is also wealthier than the rest of the area. Terraced houses of Thornhill Square and Caledonian Road are arranged back-to-back; therefore, one can notice a lack of connection between them. Caledonian Road used to be a busy shopping street, as the analysis suggests. As seen during our research in 2014, although many shops can be found, they are not always open, consequently the street today is lethargic, as shown in Figure 10.3.

As shown in Figure 10.3, bordered on both sides by its terraced houses, Caledonian Road also acts as a physical and visual border between Thornhill Square and Barnsbury Estate. Finally, Barnsbury Estate in the western part, is a well-maintained and quiet social housing complex. However, it doesn't contain any shops, and the residents need to go to Caledonian Road for shopping. This photographic analysis is to reveal the hidden context of Caledonian Road and its shops and buildings. At first, one can notice the many different shops, cafes and restaurants. Furthermore, many different communities have settled here. By looking inside one can see the differences in the appropriation of space by the individuals. A physical mapping has been conducted on Zone 3, the northernmost part. This study compares the built environment since 1874 until today.

Figure 10.3 Mapping of shops across Caledonian Road. Image credit: Delfesc, 2022.

192 *Guillaume Delfesc and Bertug Ozarisoy*

Design Proposals: Through Mapping, Prospective Analysis and Drawings

The research site is located between King's Cross Central Development in the western part and Upper Street in the eastern part. These two areas play a crucial role in physical, social, cultural and historical terms. However, Caledonian Road, the central part of the area nicknamed 'Cally', doesn't get benefits through the circulation on the site, as shown in Figure 10.4. According to our research, we demonstrate that in Caledonian Road, communities live separately and do not use all the potential of the site, such as the terraces of the row houses, the variety of shops and the existing green spaces (Davidi, 2020, 203–229). This project aims to create a linkage within the communities, made of different nationalities, genders and demographic structures, by making them part of an urban agriculture (Hawkes & Lawrence, 2021, 861–892).

Figure 10.4 A new 'Cally' with its green nature. Image credit: Delfesc & Ozarisoy, 2022.

The urban agriculture city model aims to create a new hybrid space devoted to transversal circulations (Hejduk, 2007, 393–404) of the inhabitants and the visitors, keeping in mind the great qualities and potential of the site. In this, there is a disarming reasonableness about urban agriculture, with attempts to keep the city viable in an era of rapid change. It is an expression of solidarity and polemical contradiction, with other mega structures nearby such as the King's Cross Central redevelopment as an urban future (Oldfield et al., 2009, 591–613). Urban agriculture offers voids and alternative routes more marked than the existing ones which have derived from the construction of Thornhill Square followed by the Barnsbury Estate Development, as shown in Figure 10.5.

The vegetated zones characterise the sustainable urban planning act to develop an 'urban linkage' through Caledonian Road and through a broader area (Jacoby et al., 2022, 1–33). Urban experience would consequently be less determinate, physically and mentally, as shown in Figure 10.6. If city planning had traditionally encouraged contemplation of the fixed and ideal architectural object, the collective garden city model promoted architecture as a part of social and cultural events that could only be realised by the active involvement of its inhabitants (Calder & Bremner, 2021, 79–115).

The dynamic processes of collective urban agriculture city model and its ethic has to be made visible and become an aesthetic by creating alternative routes, e bridges, walkways, parks, roof gardens or terraced gardens and bigger architectural objects, such as multistorey buildings (Lueder, 2021, 1031–1053). An urban hybrid turns architecture inside out to make its interior life exterior as well, and expandable apartments are slung down to the outside of the tallest vertical garden structures, rearranged by the bridges to control circulation between the vegetated surfaces (Chang, 2016, 1171–1202). The urban agriculture model must show that the frame and unit method would eventually aggregate into urbanism of equivalent quality to what it would supplant functionally and artistically (Le Roux, 2003). This research vision brings the feverish bustle of the metropolis to all places willing to connect to the collective gardening network (Grubbauer, 2019, 469–486). It tackles global issues that would become local ones by the migrations of the inhabitants. It finally tackles the problem of isolated communities, land use and pedestrian circulation (Coleman, 2013, 135–166).

Greening the City

The early proposals were focused on Caledonian Road after observing that the terraces of the terraced houses were not used. Agriculture was seen to bring communities together, to recreate social links, to attract new visitors and then revitalise Caledonian Road. Plantations and community gardens are located on the terraces for the inhabitants to use, as shown in Figure 10.7. In some places, greenhouses can house some specific plant

194 *Guillaume Delfesc and Bertug Ozarisoy*

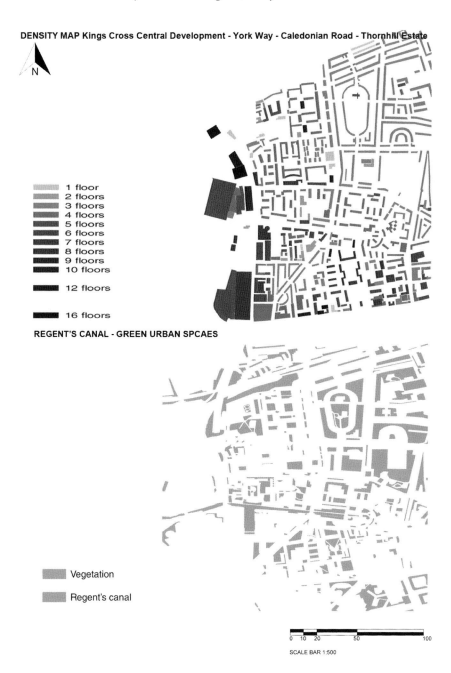

Figure 10.5 Mapping of density and green areas. Image credit: Delfesc & Ozarisoy, 2022.

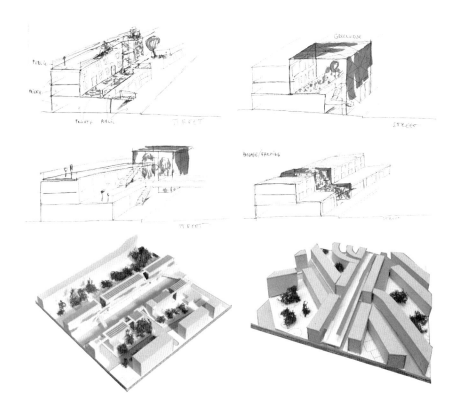

Figure 10.6 Green urbanism approach for the regeneration of the area. Image credit: Delfesc, 2022.

species. The terraces can also be used as walkways for pedestrian traffic – above the ground and therefore separated from the road. Finally, urban sections are created by removing some buildings in order to connect physically and visually Barnsbury Estate and Thornhill Square. The gable walls are then used as vertical support for urban agriculture.

This conceptual model represents the connections that are to be created in this project. On the east side is Upper Street, and on the west side is King's Cross and its new development project, as shown in Figure 10.8. The aim is to revitalise Caledonian Road by making it attractive for the people who used to go to Upper Street shops and visit King's Cross. In addition, more locally, the aim is to connect the different communities together: young, elderly and communities from different countries and origins.

This final proposal aims to take the best of the previous two concepts. The goal is to provide an opportunity for residents of different communities to gather around a common collaborative project. Harvested produce

196 *Guillaume Delfesc and Bertug Ozarisoy*

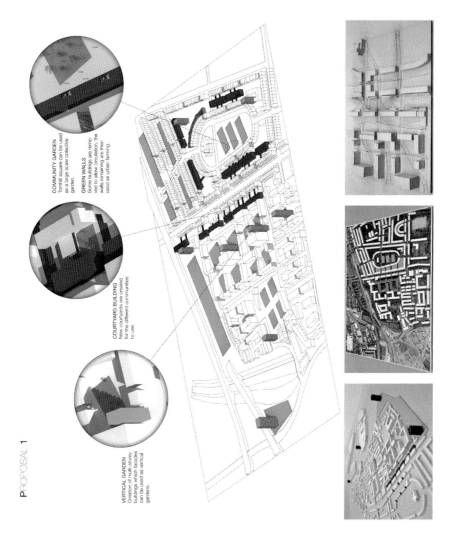

Figure 10.7 Experimental analysis of existing urban conditions. Image credit: Delfesc & Ozarisoy, 2022.

Case Study 1 197

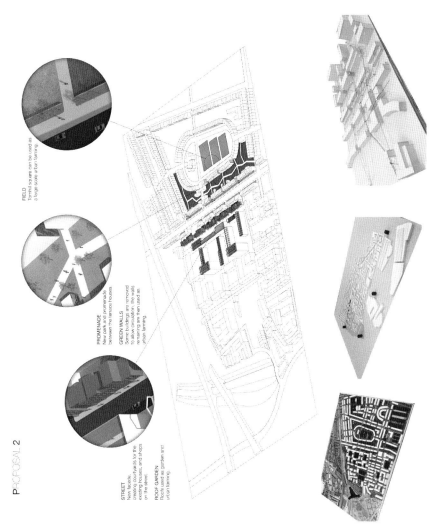

Figure 10.8 Green urbanism approach and its integration with the Caledonian Road. Image credit: Delfesc & Ozarisoy, 2022.

can then be consumed locally, sold along Caledonian Road in shops or during pop-up markets or finally processed in the multistorey buildings created (Shonfield, 2000). Urbans sections are cut out through the buildings to visually and physically connect the east and west of the district and make it permeable to traffic between King's Cross and Upper Street. Rooftops of the Barnsbury Estate social housing are used for greenhouses and plantations. A public park is designed between the terraced houses of Caledonian Road and Thornhill Square to create a north-south linkage. New buildings are created behind the terraced houses, offering a facade with shops facing Barnsbury Estate and inner courtyards for the ground floor.

Two new multistorey buildings host social programmes for the communities, such as libraries, community centres, etc. as well as light industries and craftsmen capable of transforming the products harvested in the area, to export them nationally and internationally, taking advantage of the railways (Jung & Cinn, 2020, 736–758). Finally, a new green route is created on the northern part of the site and creates a link between the King's Cross redevelopment project and Caledonian Road.

Urban Linkage: Reclaiming Urban Agriculture

This proposal offers agriculture programmes across the area. The aim is to provide an opportunity for residents of different communities to gather around a common collaborative project, as shown in Figures 10.9 and 10.10.

The project site is truly complex and, at the same time, metropolitan (Caledonian Road, Upper Street), national (London, King's Cross), European (Saint Pancras station, Eurostar) and International (Communities from African, Asian and European origins). At the same time, as seen here, Caledonian Road has a great potential for development. Answering Caledonian Road issues is just the first step of a broader architectural and urban project.

Many communities live in Caledonian Road and the surrounding area. As our research suggests, those communities do not mix and barely interact. The elderly do not interact with the younger generations, as there is a lack of community centres for them to meet. The owners of the Ethiopian restaurants never visit their Chinese counterparts, etc. Therefore, creating social links is a priority. That is what the 'Urban Linkage' project proposes. Through a common project of urban agriculture, this objective is to be tackled. Then, Caledonian Road must face the issue of being underused and not competitive compared to the two major venues nearby that are King's Cross and Upper Street. Its shops are not always open, and the street is rarely busy with pedestrians. The new urban sections associated with the urban agriculture programmes and market aim to answer this problem. The project answers these issues by considering the local issues of London as a

Case Study 1 199

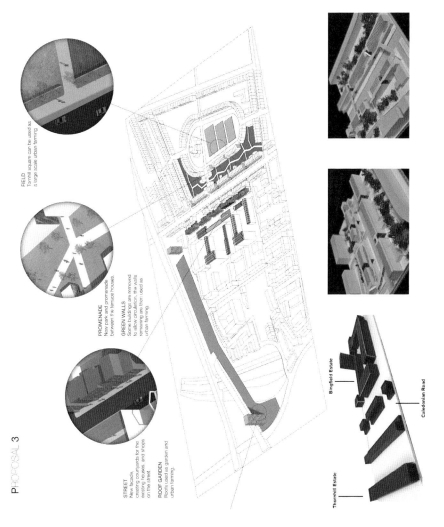

Figure 10.9 Urban agriculture towards sustainability. Image credit: Delfesc & Ozarisoy, 2022.

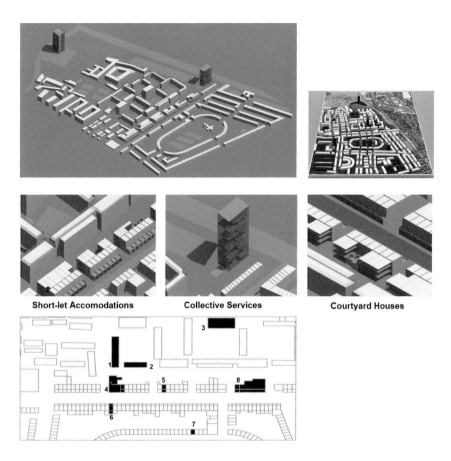

Figure 10.10 Urban skyscrapers are vegetated spaces. Image credit: Ozarisoy, 2022.

city, and the global issues of London as an international and multicultural metropolis.

Architectural Design Interventions: Courtyard Houses

Siheyuan is a type of courtyard house that has been built in Beijing since 600 B.C. up until the 20th century. Their spatial organisation comes from a grid plan following Confucian principles (Chiu et al., 2020, 513–557). The house is an enclosed courtyard with several peripheral buildings. This modular character is an important feature of the Siheyuans; it enables them to accommodate almost all social classes. The courtyard house is a typology that can also be found in many places around the world (Margalith, 2020, 602–627). What is relevant here, is how this typology can evolve to adapt to a different urban context. The next part will demonstrate an example of such an adaptation.

'Machiya' literally means 'blockhouse' and indicates that the existence and form of these timber houses is directly linked to the urban environment and its building blocks. Kyo-machiya is the specific name for these houses in Kyoto. Founded in AD 794, Kyoto became the second permanent capital city of Japan. Its urban organisation follows the Chinese principles, and therefore adopts a strictly orthogonal grid structure (Jackson, 2013, 167–195). At that time, and until the Edo period, machiyas were a mix of commercial and residential use. The houses were in the form of a closed square, with an inner courtyard hosting several amenities.

With the enforcement of high taxes on facade length, this spatial logic changed. The plots became long and narrow, nicknamed 'eel houses', and were closed on the two lateral sides as well as on the rear. As a result, the house has a narrow facade on the street, a smaller courtyard hosting a traditional Japanese garden, metaphors of a smaller inner world, and several amenities located at the end of the plot.

The Rue des Suisses apartment building located in the centre of Paris is a residential building built in the place of a long courtyard within the urban plot. Kyoto's Machiyas help us to explain this feature (Short, 1998). The residence in Rue des Suisses was designed by Swiss architects Herzog & de Meuron (Ripatti, 2020, 873–900). It shares many similarities with the traditional Japanese model, there is an offset in height that separates the natural ground of the corridor, from the floor of the residential area. The exterior facade has movable wooden elements that remind us of Shoji panels. Private and collective areas thus interact. By opening the partition walls of the Kyo-machiyas, the hierarchy between the rooms is lifted. In the Paris example, the facade acts as a threshold between the privacy of the home and the common area of the courtyard. This example of courtyard development and use will be considered in the following proposal.

Following the creation of the new buildings on Carnoustie Drive, the following sketches are possible designs for the new courtyards. Each one being specific to a row house, their design can be different, depending on the programme on the ground floor. Barnsbury Estate is a social housing complex. The flat roofs of those buildings can be used for urban farming, with the creation of plantations, community gardens and greenhouses.

How to revitalise the street facing Barnsbury Estate? How to provide new housing without creating oversized multistorey buildings? The project aims to create new buildings behind the terraced houses of Caledonian Road. These buildings form a new facade along Carnoustie Drive and contain housing and shops. The shops on the ground floor revitalise the street the same way the narrow shops do in the streets of Kyoto. And the newly created inner courtyard acts in the style of Kyo-machiyas and benefits the shops, cafes, restaurants, located on the ground level, as well as the neighbours.

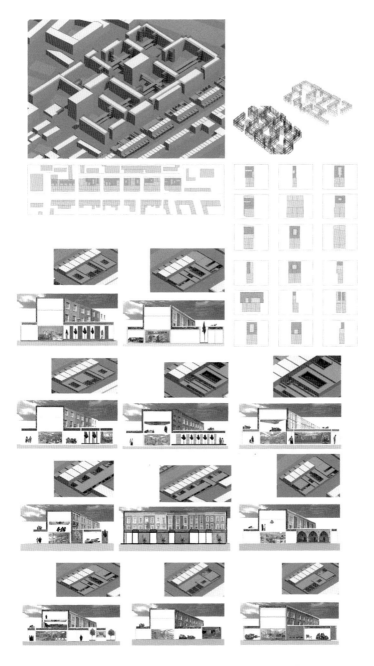

Figure 10.11 Intervention of Victorian houses by adopting a green urbanism approach. Image credit: Ozarisoy, 2022.

References

Agarez, R. C. (2019). Philanthropy, diplomacy and built environment expertise at the Calouste Gulbenkian Foundation in the 1960s and 1970s. *Journal of Architecture*, *24*(7), 950–981. https://doi.org/10.1080/13602365.2019.1698637

Calder, B., & Bremner, G. A. (2021). Buildings and energy: Architectural history in the climate emergency. *Journal of Architecture*, *26*(2), 79–115. https://doi.org/10.1080/13602365.2021.1891950

Chang, J. H. (2016). Thermal comfort and climatic design in the tropics: An historical critique. *Journal of Architecture*, *21*(8), 1171–1202. https://doi.org/10.1080/13602365.2016.1255907

Chiu, C. Y., Goad, P., Myers, P., & Yılgın, C. (2020). Ideas and ideals in Jørn Utzon's courtyard houses: Dwelling, nature, and Chinese architecture. *Journal of Architecture*, *25*(5), 513–557. https://doi.org/10.1080/13602365.2020.1788115

Coleman, N. (2013). Building in empty spaces: Is architecture a degenerate Utopia? *Journal of Architecture*, *18*(2), 135–166. https://doi.org/10.1080/13602365.2013.783225

Davidi, S. (2020). Caring for parents: Modern dwellings for elderly German-Jewish immigrants in Mandatory Palestine. *Journal of Architecture*, *25*(3), 203–229. https://doi.org/10.1080/13602365.2020.1758953

Grubbauer, M. (2019). Postcolonial urbanism across disciplinary boundaries: Modes of (dis)engagement between urban theory and professional practice. *Journal of Architecture*, *24*(4), 469–486. https://doi.org/10.1080/13602365.2019.1643390

Haddad, E. (2009). Charles Jencks and the historiography of post-modernism. *Journal of Architecture*. https://doi.org/10.1080/13602360902867434

Hawkes, D., & Lawrence, R. (2021). Climate, comfort, and architecture in Elizabethan England: An environmental study of Hardwick Hall. *Journal of Architecture*, *26*(6), 861–892. https://doi.org/10.1080/13602365.2021.1962389

Hejduk, R. (2007). Death becomes her: Transgression, decay, and eROTicism in Bernard Tschumi's early writings and projects. *Journal of Architecture*, *12*, 393–404. https://doi.org/10.1080/13602360701614672

Jackson, I. (2013). Tropical architecture and the West Indies: From military advances and tropical medicine, to Robert Gardner-Medwin and the networks of tropical modernism. *Journal of Architecture*, *18*(2), 167–195. https://doi.org/10.1080/13602365.2013.781202

Jacoby, S., Arancibia, A., & Alonso, L. (2022). Space standards and housing design: Typological experimentation in England and Chile. *Journal of Architecture*, 1–33. https://doi.org/10.1080/13602365.2022.2045340

Jung, Y., & Cinn, E. (2020). Conflicting ideals and realities: The architecture of South Korea's first high-rise housing complex. *Journal of Architecture*, *25*(6), 736–758. https://doi.org/10.1080/13602365.2020.1802613

Le Roux, H. (2003). The networks of tropical architecture. *Journal of Architecture*. https://doi.org/10.1080/1360236032000134835

Lueder, C. (2021). Corbusian space and urban corpus: The Unité d'Habitation in Marseille And the Bastide town of Monpazier. *Journal of Architecture*, *26*(7), 1031–1053. https://doi.org/10.1080/13602365.2021.1976813

Margalith, D. (2020). Memory enabling dwelling: Remembrance and amnesia in Louis I. Kahn's design for the Salk Institute for Biological Studies in La Jolla,

California. *Journal of Architecture*, 25(5), 602–627. https://doi.org/10.1080/13602365.2020.1791931

Nord, C. (2022). Post-colonial architecture: Deterritorialisation of apartheid township housing and mass-housing. *Journal of Architecture*. https://doi.org/10.1080/13602365.2022.2054015

Oldfield, P., Trabucco, D., & Wood, A. (2009). Five energy generations of tall buildings: An historical analysis of energy consumption in high-rise buildings. *Journal of Architecture*, 14(5), 591–613. https://doi.org/10.1080/13602360903119405

Ripatti, A. (2020). Printing a new architectural style in mid nineteenth-century Sweden. *Journal of Architecture*, 25(7), 873–900. https://doi.org/10.1080/13602365.2020.1828995

Roberts, D. (2017). Make public: Performing public housing in Ernő Goldfinger's Balfron Tower. *Journal of Architecture*, 22(1), 123–150. https://doi.org/10.1080/13602365.2016.1276096

Shonfield, K. (2000). The use of fiction to interpret architecture and urban space. *Journal of Architecture*. Routledge. https://doi.org/10.1080/13602360050214395

Short, T. (1998). Of mice and madness: Questions of occupation interpreted through Disneyland and Parc de la Villette. *Journal of Architecture*. https://doi.org/10.1080/136023698374260

Tostões, A., & Ferreira, Z. (2021). Social endurance at the Barbican Estate (1968–2020). *Journal of Architecture*, 26(7), 1082–1106. https://doi.org/10.1080/13602365.2021.1978523

11 Case Study 2
Elephant & Castle Regeneration Development, London, United Kingdom

Guillaume Delfesc

Introduction

Luxury fashion brands are well known for having their shops in the most expensive streets of world capitals. Louis Vuitton, Hermès, Chanel are just a few examples of those brands, and you can find them in Paris, Tokyo as well as in London. In the past 30 years, we have seen more and more of those shops opening on the high street in western countries and, largely, in Asia. The growth of the luxury market, as well as the Asian economies, explain this phenomenon. Firstly, we need to understand those spaces better. By using the work of the philosopher Michel Foucault, we can ask ourselves relevant questions beforehand. In 1966, Foucault conceptualised the idea of 'Heterotopia' (*Hétérotopies*) for spaces (Sara & Littlefield, 2014, 295–304). Heterotopias are utopias found in actual spaces (Hejduk, 2010). He defines them as spaces out of time: these are spaces of otherness, neither here nor there, simultaneously physical and mental. Examples of heterotopias are hospitals, prisons, retirement houses, etc. When speaking about luxury shops, it would be incorrect to qualify them as heterotopias in the way Michel Foucault did. First, as these spaces serve the purpose of shopping, the activity there is clearly defined and is therefore not 'out of time'. However, one can ask if those spaces are 'out of space'. A luxury brand being in many countries, their shops must have similarities, so they can carry the same message (Stepnik, 2020, 127), the same brand identity. What is the result of such a global phenomenon on local identities? When a Chanel, Hermès, or Louis Vuitton shop is built somewhere, does it overlay the local identity of the street, the city, the country where it is built? If so, is the brand identity more important than the local identity? Those are the questions we are going to discuss here.

To do so, we will first try to define what luxury is, and what the luxury identity means. Then we will move to the economical and marketing concept of brand identity. We will then use the works of Robert Venturi and Denise Scott Brown on *Learning from Las Vegas* to see how brand identity can cross the local identity. After this we will study in greater detail the case of Japan in particular, and its large amount of luxury shops, as shown in Figure 11.1.

DOI: 10.4324/9781003243069-14

Figure 11.1 Luxury brand samples in Japan and London. Image credit: Delfesc, 2012 & 2014.

As an architect, many of the cities and buildings that I saw during my stay in Japan provoked my curiosity – among them, flagship stores of luxury and fashion brands. The standards of quality in the land of the rising sun seemed higher than in western countries. And the field of construction is no exception to this rule. The quality of construction is extreme whether concrete, glass, or wood, and the attention to detail is impressive to a Western eye. As an example, Japanese carpenters are renowned for having developed dozens of advanced joineries without using any nails to connect the beams. This notion of quality struck me and was even more striking in the case of some luxury and fashion brand flagship stores in Tokyo. Many of those flagship stores have been designed by renowned Japanese and foreign architects. But these are only examples, among many others, of what architecture for luxury brands can look like in Japanese cities. These buildings are not just shops, they host many other functions: cafes, offices, exhibition spaces, etc. And these many programmes contribute to giving the brand a certain image and a certain status.

'It was in Japan that the perfect storm arose when the high disposable income of a homogeneous society met the age-old quest for perfection. Thanks to these ingredients, the luxury industry exploded' (Altay, 2013, 102–109).

Therefore, to follow the aim of this exercise, the community studied here could have been the Japanese one. I could have met and interviewed Japanese-born people, expats, migrants, established in London for a long or short period. But I didn't. The community I decided to study here is not a group of people that we could easily classify in accordance with their country of birth, ethnicity, or religion (Cunningham, 2001). As I described here, my interest lies in what is made well, made beautifully – as it can be found typically in Japanese architecture and craftsmanship. And in luxury shops. This is the reason why I choose to study the field of the architecture of luxury as a community.

The Architecture of Luxury: Key Questions

We've been talking about the luxury brands, their shops, and their design, as shown in Figure 11.2. All this is only focused on the building itself. But so far, we have not discussed the context where those boutiques are located (Lohtaja, 2021, 499–515). Of course, they are everywhere in the world, in cities with local identities that we can assume are different from one another (Dawes & Ostwald, 2014). Then one can wonder how those shops are integrated. Indeed, we have seen previously throughout the example of Louis Vuitton and Chanel boutiques, that the brand identity dictates the architecture of its branches, as well as their visual identity. Therefore, this fact can make one ask this question: Does a brand identity become more important than the local identity of the place it is built in?

In 1972, Robert Venturi and Denise Scott Brown wrote the well-known book, *Learning from Las Vegas*. The architects studied the famous 'Strip' in Las Vegas. Being a large highway, commercial buildings around installed signs to grab the attention of potential customers, lost among hundreds of other signs. That is what is relevant to our study. On the Las Vegas Strip, buildings exist for themselves, they must be the biggest, the most impressive, to be visible from the highway and attract customers.

The following questions arose: When luxury or fashion brands bring their own identity to a place, are they purposely overlaying local identity? Is this done in a provocative manner, neglecting the context? This leads us to what is happening in Japan, where we have seen that large parts of the population are potential buyers of luxury products. What is it like to show luxury retail in architecture, in opposition to traditional retail? One idea that animated me when I chose this subject in connection with this Master was to analyse those luxury brand boutiques established in Japan and elsewhere, and to see how they were designed. My assumption was that the notion of cultural identity of a place could be overlayed by the identity of a globalised brand.

It is necessary to ask another question: Is this phenomenon specific to luxury brands? Isn't it just as fair to say that Starbucks or McDonalds embody the same similarities and try to carry the same message anywhere they are? Not to mention the products sold: those shops feature the same colours, the same logo and a similar interior design wherever they are. Thus,

208 *Guillaume Delfesc*

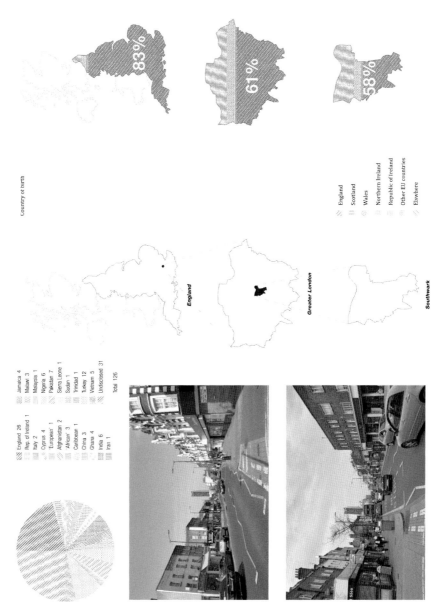

Figure 11.2 Mapping shops in Walworth Road, London. Image credit: Delfesc, 2014.

the emerging question would be to know what it is like to show luxury retail in architecture, in opposition to traditional or more ordinary retail (Sachs, 2019, 925–949). How is the brand putting its own image and values in many places, in many different locations? When we step into a luxury or fashion shop, we step into a very particular world. A world inhabited by *products* and arranged in a methodical manner. From the floor on which we walk, the lights that brighten the shelves, the uniforms of the employees, to the music we hear – all of this contributes to the atmosphere of the place.

Littlefield (2013) explains the case of the luxury brand he was director of in Japan: Louis Vuitton. In the 1990s, the company commissioned the American architect Peter Marino to design the Louis Vuitton flagship store on the Champs-Elysées in Paris (Lending, 2018, 797–819). After the building was completed, the company asked the architect to create a design guideline for the shops. That guideline was used to elaborate the design concept of all the new Louis Vuitton shops being built across the world over the next few years. When designing a new building for the brand, local architects must refer to that guideline and integrate it into their work. This is another question I would like to explore through this work: How is the brand putting its own image and cultural values in many places, in many different locations? Is this a matter of concepts, guidelines, colours, materials? Finally, another way to deal with this question would be to see what happens during the process of displacement. In other words, what happens when we take all those concepts and put them in another place? This should help us to understand more clearly how those concepts work, what their effects are, how they are implemented and the difference with other types of retail shops. Finally, the last part could be to displace an actual luxury shop into an environment where we would not usually find it.

Brand Identity versus Local Identity

What is brand identity?

> 'The outward expression of a brand – including its name, trademark, communications, and visual appearance – is brand identity'
> (Kimmel, 2020, 659–678).

Brand identity is how the owner of a brand wants the customer to perceive it. Brand image, however, is how the customer perceives the brand, its mental image. A gap can exist between those two definitions, and it is the owner's goal to reduce the gap between the brand image and the brand identity.

> 'Identities with high yields of added value have to be protected. Brands, copyrights, trademarks and patents are all mechanisms for safeguarding the added value vested in products'
> (Doron, 2000, 247–263).

210   *Guillaume Delfesc*

Trademarks can be registered at the World Intellectual Property Organization, a specialised agency of the United Nations. Those trademarks are created to protect and maintain them against abuse or infringement. Brands seek to protect themselves from copies or external influences that could alter their image, their identity. But what is a brand identity?

In ever more saturated markets, however, brands depend increasingly on symbolic added value. The advertising agency Leo Burnett speaks of the 'personality' of the brand to explore visibility of luxury. In his statement, he identifies that there are variations in, its 'functions', its 'differentiators', and its 'source of authority'. Anecdotally, he also stated that each market has its own 'brand statement' to justify the research gap. This help can boil down to two or three words. It provides definition to the Burnett parlance and it also identifies the brand's 'essence' (Graham, 2008, 100–101).

Selling images as much as products, brands need their own venues, 'mini-temples in the service of "brand deities"' to replace more secular environments like the department store. The first international luxury brand stores were opened by Louis Vuitton in London (1885) and by Cartier in London (1906) and New York (1907). A large increase in brand store number occurred in the 1980s, when luxury stores started to leave the limited space of the department stores to open their own boutiques on the High Street. This coincides with the establishment of Louis Vuitton Japan, and the rapid growth of the luxury market from the 1980s, as we will discuss later. This study is not the study of a community in the sense of a particular ethnic group. Indeed, to carry out this exercise, I decided to take a more conceptual approach on the notion of community, while still following the key issues developed above. Thus, communities are the architect, the shops he designed and the location of displacement.

I contacted an architecture and interior design office based in London. The company was established in 2002 by its current owner and director and they have been working since then on luxury and fashion brand stores worldwide. They count among their clients' international brands such as Esprit, Hermès, Jimmy Choo, etc. I got in touch with the director, and I had the chance to interview him. Knowing the shops that have been designed by this office, my aim was to try and visit some of them and maybe engage with some of the people working there. Finally, the last part could be to displace an actual luxury shop into an environment where we would not usually find it. Looking at some famous high streets such as Regent Street or New Bond Street in London, Ginza in Tokyo, or the Champs-Elysées in Paris, what would happen if one of these shops was moved to a more popular area like Green Street, or Walworth Road in London?

Transgression between Luxury Brand and Architecture

We all already have an idea of what luxury is. A luxury item is often seen as an expensive one, for many reasons: it can be rare, made of expensive

Case Study 2   211

materials, of very high quality, requiring skilled craftsmanship, etc. Still, this definition seems incomplete. One must have in mind the idea that a luxury product can embody a certain social status. As we will see later, a luxury object can make its owner part of a certain social group.

After working for more than ten years as a director of the luxury Spanish brand Loewe, Maria Eugenia Giron wrote her own definition of luxury in her book, *Inside Luxury: The Growth and Future of the Luxury Industry: A View from the Top* (2010).

> 'A luxury watch must not only tell the time, but the mechanism must also be extremely accurate. But technical perfection alone is not enough to give rise to a luxury product'
>
> (Sanchez-Verdejo Perez, 2021, 67–89).

The technical quality, or 'perfection' as it is stated, is the first thing that comes to mind but is not enough to define what we are talking about. Because luxury has also to do with the concept of beauty.

> 'Luxury brands are built up around a certain aesthetic concept [...] so that every person who possesses one feels imbued with those values'
>
> (Hejduk, 2007, 393–404).

> Luxury is a quest of technical perfection as well as beauty. And through her activities, the author experienced 'the pleasure of being close to that which is beautiful'
>
> (Dovey, 2013, 82–89).

The same object can be not considered luxurious by everyone, by every society, and moreover in every place of the world. This point will be discussed later.

> The history of Victorian furniture was dominated by the sale of some candidly tasteless items. Many of them were the work of the London firm of Jackson & Graham. This firm was offered the most flamboyant stage design principles to the various shop owners. For example, many of items were a carved cabinet of pollard oak, decked out with figures of boys gathering grapes, two female caryatids and a set of carved pilasters. The whole was crowned by a majestic 60-centimetre-high gold-plated bull.
>
> (Faustino, 2013, 120–123)

Before mocking the people who would buy such a piece of furniture, the author of *Status Anxiety* tells us about the wider context in designing luxury brands. In fact, he explains to us about what luxury can serve in terms of social status of buyers. Indeed, in the Victorian era, the owner of such a furniture would have [...] felt psychologically necessary and rewarding.

(Lawrence, 2020, 419–443)

It should be noted that the history of luxury could more accurately be read as a record of emotional trauma. It is the legacy of those who have felt pressured by the disdain of others. Additionally, it is an extraordinary amount of architectural philosophy to their bare selves in order to signal the built environment.

(Littlefield, 2013, 124–129)

Luxury has long been associated with the idea of social status, of a signal, and one way to define the concept of luxury is scarcity. Scarcity could be easily achieved for example by using a certain type of material for the design of a product, by the outstanding quality of the work or by the time needed to make it. Today, things have changed. Scarcity could make the simplest things luxury, which in our age of abundance is harder to achieve. Therefore, the term 'luxury' became more and more complicated to define. Today, luxury has become an industry, in which major groups like LVMH and Kering employ thousands of people throughout the world. Thus, as any other industry, it needs to sell its products to be profitable. A pen used to be a possession that could be passed from father to son, as part of a coming-of-age rite and because the quality of the product would allow it to last for generations. And as the Dutch architect Rem Koolhaas once claimed: 'Luxury is stability. Luxury is "waste". Luxury is generous. Luxury is intelligent. Luxury is rough. Luxury is attention'. And concluded, unarguably, that 'Luxury is not "shopping"'. How then does the industry manage to stay profitable, and even to grow? That is where fashion and trends are considered. Architecture can be used as a way of achieving this industry goal, as Deyan Sudjic suggests in *The Language of Things*. 'The well-known luxury brands – Dior and Prada – hire Pritzker Prize-winning architects to build stores on the scale of grand opera to reduce shoppers to an ecstatic consumerist trance.'

The Birth of the Brand Street

When we step into a luxury or fashion shop, we step into a very particular world. A world inhabited by *products* and arranged in a methodical manner. From the floor on which we walk, the lights that brighten the shelves, the uniforms of the employees, to the music we hear, all of this contributes to the atmosphere of the place. And what is happening in other parts of the world? Is this kind of atmosphere similar in a shop in New York, London, or Tokyo?

If we consider a luxury brand with shops worldwide, it is likely that we would feel the same atmosphere in any of those brand shops, the reason being that most of the interior design in such places has been thought out and developed in advance. One cannot deny that the kind of interior design we experience when visiting those shops is done on purpose. The atmosphere we may feel in those places leaves nothing to chance.

An Interview with the Architect

In February 2014, I visited an architecture and interior design office. I had been in contact via e-mail with its director, and I was invited to assist with a presentation scheduled with his colleagues that day. This talk was the same he did the previous month at *Interiors UK*, 'an event on interior design and furniture', and it described the recent fusion of art, fashion, and architecture in the luxury retail sector with reference to some of their recent projects. It was a good opportunity for me to understand this office's works, their collaborations and point of view regarding the luxury and fashion retail industry.

I arrived in this office, on the fourth floor of a London building with large windows overlooking the area. There, a dozen people were working on CAD programmes on their computers, like in any other architecture office. We then all sat in a small meeting room where the owner/director gave us his speech. The presentation lasted around 30 minutes, and I decided to show here some of the key examples. The first example is the art installation *Prada Marfa* by the Scandinavian artist duo Elmgreen & Dragset: a Prada shop in the middle of the Texas desert commissioned by the brand in 2005.

The collaboration between fashion brands and artists is becoming more and more common since the past decades. It coincides with the establishment of this office in the beginning of the 2000s. This example of art installation introduces an important notion about luxury and fashion brands. These brands no longer communicate exclusively through classical advertising. Indeed, fashion and luxury brands today are used to go beyond the field of retail, to do some patronage operations such as the Prada one here above. This phenomenon can be explained by several factors as we will see below.

During the last decade, LVMH (Louis Vuitton Moët Hennessy) and Kering (previously known as PPR), the two main luxury groups in the world, both acquired many existing luxury brands. With few exceptions like Hermès, it is still family run. When those two groups are owning all the major luxury and fashion brands, the question that arises for the companies is how to differentiate their brands. Art and patronage are one way for the brands to achieve this differentiation, by bringing another dimension to their image. After this presentation, I didn't have the chance to talk with the architect and ask him the questions I had in mind. Fortunately, we scheduled a second interview for the week after. My questions were targeted at three key points I wanted to explore: 1) the relationship between the

214 *Guillaume Delfesc*

architect and the client (the brand); 2) the idea of quality that can be found in a luxury shop; and 3) how architecture can be used in a marketing way as part of the brand strategy.

The first item I wanted to discuss was the relationship with the client:

GD: In your office, how is the discussion with the client during the design process?

The Architect: Well, the interesting thing, when you are working with a fashion company as a client, which is different I think to virtually any other type of client, is that the client is a designer. And they themselves are in the process of making something creative and designing clothes and products and selling those. It means that they are also merchants. So, they are artists, but they are merchants. So, these three things are the creative process, the commercial process and the temporal process, because fashion is very temporal and changes all the time. So, these come together in a specific way with fashion, which I really like. So, the discussion with the client really is first about … For me, what is the individual, cause really all the best brands, the brands I like the most are ones where there are people you can identify the brand with. Most fashion houses have somebody you can identify.

GD: Like the family?

A: Like the family or the creative director or, you know, a key person that is in that brand. […] whether it's Johnathan Ive at Apple, or it's Nicolas Ghesquière at Balenciaga (2014), they are making a design and a product that are basically what they are interested in, that they find fascinating themselves, and then they are making an invitation to people to say: 'this is what I do, this is how I do it. If you like it, please come in, take part'. So, it's very much a kind of discourse of that time. And when we are working with the client, the first thing I am trying to do is to identify that personality in the business. What are they trying to communicate, what are they interested in?

Quality and craftsmanship:

GD: How is the question of quality addressed in your work? Would you consider it different from an architectural project for clients who are not in the field of fashion or luxury?

A: Yes, it's very different from when we don't have fashion or luxury. Clearly because so much to do with luxury is to do with the craftsmanship and the kind of skill and history and tradition and artistry that goes into making the product. And the same must be in the creation of the store. When we very first started to work with Hermès, many years ago, the first brief that I had from Pierre Alexis Dumas, who is the son of the owner, said that 'our store has to be as beautiful as one of our wallets', and that was the brief, this is what you need to achieve. And what that means is we are seeking out craftsmen, the best leatherworkers, the best plaster workers. We are seeking out craftsmen that are often no

Case Study 2   215

longer working in general buildings. If you build The Shard for example, you are not really working with craftsmen, you're working with systems, you're working with components, you're working with putting something together. There may be some craftsmanship in some of the fitting out, but not in the actual general building. Most craftsmanship in general building has been lost. Shop fitting, and luxury shop fitting is one of the few places where it still exists. It's becoming more and more rare, but it still exists, and it's very enjoyable to work with those people because they are unusual.

Marketing and brand identity:

GD: What's the role of marketing during the design process? Knowing that marketing is an important part of any brand strategy, does the client consider architecture as part of its brand strategy?

A: Some of them do, some of them don't; it depends on their own sensibility and their interests. When we did this project for a luxury furniture maker in Shoreditch last year, they were very interested in, for example, social media as a way of informing the design process and also communicating the design process, so throughout the project of designing they would be taking photographs of our workshops and of our mood boards and they would be tweeting to their customers, to give them an idea of the process, to include them in the process, they also were asking for feedback, […] I think there is an interesting quote that says 'the customer should be a participant in your brand, not just a victim of your campaign'. And I think the same goes in architecture today, it's not simply interesting to say to the customer: here is our product finished, you know. I think the product becomes more interesting if the customer is participating somehow in the process.

GD: How is the issue of brand identity considered during the design process? Does the client come with his own specifications beforehand?

A: Mostly, I mean basically the logo and the signature colours of any brand, unless it's a new brand, are already existing, and the client would have a kind of guidelines of how the logo and the colours, and the brand identity elements need to be used. It depends on, you know, some of the clients are much stricter about those things, some of them are more fluid. It depends also when they come to us, some of them are coming to us because they want to rebrand. If we are working as a part of a rebrand, then everything might begin to start again. When we were doing a rebrand two years ago with this sports brand, everything was different. After 6 years of working with a particular set of guidelines, everything was different, the logo changed, the spacing in the logo changed, the materials changed, the signature materials changed, everything was new. […]

GD: Sometimes architects already designed guidelines for brands, such as Peter Marino for Chanel; did it happen to you to have this kind of guideline to work with?

216 *Guillaume Delfesc*

A: Yea, sometimes from another architect who has already done it, or more often from an actual branding company that is working for the client or inside the client business.

Our conversation then moved on to an interesting point that I had not thought about so far: The question of guilt. Guilt is in fact sometimes associated with luxury. Through this conversation we discussed this notion in Japanese society.

GD: Would you say there is a luxury architecture vs an ordinary architecture? Or are there only luxury clients?
A: I think there is a luxury architecture, and there are luxury clients, there are a whole kind of things around luxury which need to be defined, and they can be defined in many ways. [...] I think it's complex, I think that question doesn't really deal with the complexity of the situation. It's working on many different levels, the architecture that goes with luxury brand stores, retail, is working on many different levels. I think some of the analysis Koolhaas did in the Harvard guidebook to shopping is interesting in the way that he is speaking about luxury architecture. Because what he is talking about is how luxury architecture must deal with the guilt that comes from luxury. There is a kind of shame attached to luxury, people don't feel completely straightforward and happy about luxury. You know, you can enjoy luxury at one level because you think this is beautifully made, but at the same moment you're enjoying it, you're also feeling discomforted because you know there is inequality in it. You know there is exclusivity in it, and you know that it's not available to anybody. So, Koolhaas is interesting, he says the white box for example became so popular, was a way of kind of blanking out the guilt. There is a representation of trying to make it as clean and straightforward as possible. [...]

The Architect then proceeds to read a passage from the book, *Delirious New York*:

According to Koolhaas, 'minimalism has become the signal signifier of luxury'. Minimising the shame of consumption, he maintained that the historic association of luxury with guilt, and sin can now be avoided by redefining the concept of luxury. So, these ideas of being indulgent, of being selfish... You know lots of interesting ideas culturally. You're talking about the difference between cultures where you're starting. So maybe an interesting thing is that Japanese people have a different relationship with sin, with the idea of guilt and shame, when it comes to luxury.
GD: I think that luxury for them is not associated with the same thing. It should be noted that this is a phenomenon in western countries. One of the main reasons is that owning a Louis Vuitton bag is every women's desire. It doesn't have the same meaning as here. It's considered more as an ordinary product for them. A: So that's an interesting point. How

come? They don't feel conflicted, you know. The western attitude is more ambivalent towards luxury, why is the Japanese idea less ambivalent, more direct towards luxury, that's an interesting story. […]

The Shops

As the next step in my study of the communities, I decided to visit some luxury brand shops on Regent Street and New Bond Street. Among them some were designed by the office of the architect I interviewed. My goal was to engage with the salesperson there, talk about the brand identity and how they feel the architecture of the place brings a message that helps to carry the brand identity. My questions were kept simple and aimed to understand the architecture of luxury as seen from the client point of view. However, these visits didn't go as I expected, as we will see further.

Hermès New Bond Street and Louis Vuitton New Bond Street were the first two boutiques I went to, with the idea of conducting some interviews. However, the staff there didn't want to answer my questions, and they suggested I get in touch with the PR department or marketing department of their brand. The answer was similar in all of the luxury shops I have been to on the street. Luckily, the manager of an American fashion brand shop on Regent Street was happy to answer my questions. The interview was very brief and informal.

GD: How would you define the image of that brand?
M: It's strong, I think. It's a strong image.
GD: Do you consider it being luxury?
M: Hum high-end I would say. High-end.
GD: Do you think the architecture of the place corresponds to the image of the brand?
M: Yes, I think there is something. With the colours. And you can see the waves. The brand comes from California, so you can see the waves.
GD: What would you change or add to make it better?
M: I would use more marble, I think. The floor is in marble here [on the ground, but downstairs it's wood].
GD: Have you ever worked in another shop before?
M: Yes
GD: How would you consider it different?
M: Yea, it's different. I think there is more attention to details. The smell for instance, we have perfume diffuser here. So, I think more details, yea.

The Displacement between the Green Street and Walworth Road

The next step in my study of this community was to visit Green Street, a popular street located in the London borough of Newham. The road is

218   *Guillaume Delfesc*

known to have a strong South Asian community and hosts an array of shops specialising in primarily South Asian goods. There is, of course, not any luxury shop on that road where I could conduct an interview. The shop I went to belongs to a value footwear retail brand. And I had the chance to have a quick interview with one of the saleswomen of the shop.

GD: How could you describe the area here, Green Street?
S: The area? Hum, it's okay, you've got your fish, you've got your drug addicts. And it's 90% Asian community, they're very pleasant, they are very nice customers.
GD: Do you have a lot of customers in this shop?
S: We're doing okay.
GD: Are there many new shops that opened here recently in this street?
S: There is one 2 doors away, that has been renovated and rebuilt, and I am not sure if it's a butcher or something else.
GD: Okay, and do you know if there will be any other projects in the future?
S: Hum, there could possibly be an ASDA, trying to apply for Westham football ground. And then people are talking about a mosque as well, so we don't know.
GD: And about the shops that are coming, what do you think about it, do you think it will work well?
S: Well, it will attract … It will bring more people, but it will also bring congestion of traffic. Hum, and obviously with that it will bring more shoplifting and …
GD: And the final question: How would you react, and what would you think of a luxury shop that would come here?
S: Hum, that's never going to happen! And if it did it would look like …
GD: Weird?
S: Yes, it would be weird. It wouldn't suit here. The best place for that would be either Westfields, or in the city, but along here …
GD: Okay.
S: So, who are you working for?
GD: The University of Westminster.
S: Alright, so is it a project?
GD: Yes, I am studying the architecture of shops. Previously I've been studying the architecture of luxury shops in the centre of London, and now I am coming to other areas of London to see …
S: I mean, don't get me wrong. A lot of the Asian community and a lot of women do like nice things. So, if you had a shop with shoes and handbags and … and things like Chanel Gucci, Louis Vuitton, that do very well. But you would also get an impact of thieving problem that goes with it so … Okay!
GD: Thank you very much.

Urban Regeneration in Elephant and Castle

It becomes interesting then to discuss the question of displacement further by comparing this case of Green Street with another high street, Walworth Road. Located in the South Bank, it runs between Elephant and Castle and Camberwell Road, as shown in Figure 11.3. This road shows many similarities with Green Street, especially in terms of 'ethnic retail' (Jewell, 2001), shops owned by people from the different communities living in the area and that offer merchandise from various countries. Before visiting the site, I came across this interesting article 'High Street adaptations: Ethnicity, independent retail practices and localism in London's urban margins', published in *Environment and Planning A* in 2011. The author Suzanne M. Hall describes the case of 'multi-ethnic high street in London's urban margins (Hall, 2011, 45–47)'.

According to the author, the high street has an important role. As two-thirds of Londoners are living within 500 metres of a high street, its role is not only economical but also social and cultural. Indeed, two-thirds of the trips to the local street appear to be made to access forms of exchange and interaction other than retail. At the same time, small independent shops must face a marked, severe and continued decline across Britain: 'retail is either large, affiliated and growing; or small, independent and on the rapid demise' (Hall, 2011, p.3). Chains, including large international brands, are establishing where small shops used to be, therefore changing the local identity. This local identity was paradoxically the agglomeration of cultural identities from a multitude of different countries and backgrounds.

One may think that luxury has no place in such a street. However, it appears that one shop offers high-end products:

> Kid's Brand is an upmarket clothing store for children. It was opened by the proprietor 'Sayeed' in 1993. [...] Kid's Brand supplied the upper end of children's clothes and stocked Armani Junior, DKNY kids and Baby Dior labels. Many of the clothes had prominent external labels. It has provided a clear indication of the related status and expense of the items.
> (Roberts-Hughes, 2017, 157–168)

Thus, luxury products are not incompatible with the popular high street. Talking about the origins of the different shops, both locations have interesting features that I tried to explore in the creative piece of this work. Hermès shops can be found worldwide, thus each shop is connected in a sense to many other shops of the same brand in multiple locations. Through the products sold, the brand identity, and the interior design, they are in a way connected. And stepping in a Hermès shop in Tokyo is virtually like stepping in a Hermès shop in Dubai. In the meantime, Walworth Road hosts shops owned by people from all over the world, displaying a large variety of traditional food or groceries. All those shops also relate to other

Figure 11.3 Map of Walworth Road and its retail spaces, along with the country of origin of the shops. Image credit: Delfesc, 2014.

locations worldwide. And this is what the creative piece of this work tries to represent.

Design Proposal: Through Mapping, Prospective Analysis and Drawings

Luxury phenomenon coincides with the historical context in which luxury and fashion brands developed themselves in the 1990s – since architecture and the architects started to be seen as helpful for the brand's image.

> The great luxury brands have chosen architects and designers. One of the main reasons is the reputation and prestige of having a luxury brand. Their work is not on sale. On the contrary, it helps to display the product by converting it into a symbol of power and a permanent link with culture.
>
> (Sara & Littlefield, 2014, 295–304)

More recently, especially since the 2000s, collaboration between fashion brands and artists is becoming more and more common. Indeed, not only do luxury brands value their shops' architecture, but they also invest in patronage of artists. These brands no longer communicate exclusively through classical advertising. Fashion and luxury brands today are used to go beyond the field of retail, and patronage is one way to do so. The main idea behind these patronages is for the brand to relate to its customers through art, giving the brand a more cultural status.

Among all the luxury and fashion brands that have a patronage programme, Prada is an interesting one. It developed its own foundation for contemporary art: Fondazione Prada, based in Milano and designed by OMA. The examples of luxury boutiques we have seen so far can be found throughout the world, bringing with them the identity of the brand. Thus, the brand identity of Prada, Louis Vuitton or Hermès that can be found inside of their shops is the same regardless of the location. As mentioned before, one can find these shops in Paris, New York or Tokyo. The only common point among these locations is the high disposable income of the people visiting the areas. In other words, these are areas where you can find potential customers, not only in terms of wealth but also in terms of the values they share with the brand. What else could architecture do for luxury brands, and what could luxury brands potentially do for architecture? This is something we will explore through this work.

The Elephant & Castle Shopping Centre: A Focal Point for London

One option would be to create an actual luxury shop in an environment where we would not usually find it. Looking at some famous high streets,

222   *Guillaume Delfesc*

such as Regent Street or New Bond Street in London, Ginza in Tokyo or the Champs-Elysées in Paris, what would happen if one of these shops was moved to a more popular area like Walworth Road? This is what I want to explore throughout this project. Furthermore, the street is currently facing some changes and challenges, as the Elephant & Castle area is undergoing a massive regeneration, with large-scale projects like the Strata Tower, as shown in Figure 11.4.

Walworth Road is located in the South Bank, in the borough of Southwark. The street runs between Elephant and Castle and Camberwell Road and hosts a multitude of 'ethnic retails' (Suzanne M. Hall, 2011) in other words, shops owned by people from the different communities living in the area that offer merchandise and goods from various countries. According to the author, the high street has a crucial role. The street offers chances and opportunities to breach social and spatial divisions. This point becomes even more important in an environment that brings together individuals with different cultural backgrounds. But how exactly does it work? How can the street act as a catalyst for interaction between people? The book suggests that the experiences of the street are likely to create a local identity. This local identity is then shared by its inhabitants and therefore creates a 'collective membership' (Malone, 2020, 679–696).

The retail spaces are the architectural and physical elements responsible for this phenomenon. Research has shown the 'significant economic and social role of small shops' on high streets across the UK. Therefore, the role of the different shops on Walworth Road can inform the project. We shall begin our exploration with a particular shop: Nick's Caff, a typical London caff located on the Walworth Road. Born in Cyprus and emigrated to London in the 1950s, Nick's father established the cafe in the 1960s.

On Walworth Road, the caff is the shared space where 'newcomers' and 'established residents', or migrants, come to know each other. The question the author tried to answer was to know whether an array of individuals can recreate a sense of being local and in what kind of space. Through the study of this space, its role of a local meeting place became clear. One can explain this situation through two points of view. For the owner, there is the question of gaining the support of a varied clientele. One can explain this situation through two points of view. For the customer, the point is to appropriate a space by regularly occupying it, 'while observing established code of conduct' (Manning et al., 2018). Nick's Caff is just an example, but one can understand its role and implication among the retail fabric of Walworth Road (Short, 1998).

The northern part of the Walworth Road ends on a major road junction, the Elephant & Castle. This location is also situated near the shopping centre that bears the same name. This shopping centre built in the 1960s became the first covered shopping mall in Europe.[1] It imported concepts from American shopping malls in a fashion that was completely new to the UK. In

Case Study 2 223

Figure 11.4 Ethnographic study in Walworth Road, London. Image credit: Delfesc, 2014.

224 *Guillaume Delfesc*

2014, it hosted around 80 shops, with an important representation of Latin American and Caribbean communities among them. Despite its architectural novelty, or perhaps because of it, the Elephant and Castle Shopping Centre has never been as successful as it was expected, as shown in Figure 11.5.

It's worth mentioning that when this work was first written, in 2014, the Elephant and Castle Shopping Centre was still in use. It closed in 2020 after 55 years, and has been consequently dismantled, despite protests from the shop owners and the local community.[2]

> Largest and most ambitious shopping venture ever to be embarked upon in London. In design planning and vision, it represents an entirely new approach to retailing, setting standards for the sixties that will revolutionise shopping concepts throughout Britain.
>
> (Amini-Behbahani et al., 2016, 348–374)

During the 1990s it underwent some quick fixes and refurbishments and was soon decided to be demolished. A master plan had been drawn in 2004 by MAKE architects and would see the shopping centre demolished in 2010. However, no demolition works have begun. Recently, the Southwark Council sold two major areas located on both sides of the Elephant & Castle to a developer to create new homes as part of a massive regeneration project. This project is spread on two sites of respectively 22 acres. On the smaller part, the developer created a 37-storey tower adjacent to a four-storey building offering around 300 high-end flats and studios. The larger part is located on the site of the former Heygate estate, on the east side of the current shopping centre. Completed in 1974, the Heygate estate was a large housing estate of neo-brutalist architecture, housing around 3000 people in 1200 socially rented units. It is currently under demolition. This whole regeneration project is strongly criticised by a group of local inhabitants who fear gentrification. At the intersection of a street with a strong identity, and two new redevelopment programmes bringing new inhabitants to the area, is the Elephant & Castle shopping centre. On this very site, how can an architectural project accommodate all these factors? Then how can retail spaces in general, and luxury shops, take part in such a project?

A Manifesto – Urban Development Proposal: The New Elephant & Castle

Elephant & Castle is a complex site. Its complexity lies in the fact that its history is shared with the histories of the many communities established there, and their future is closely connected. The fascinating sociological and ethnographic study of the Walworth Road by Suzan Hall taught us about the social role of the street in complex displacement processes, identity and the reappropriation of a local identity. The Walworth Road is rich in many different shops, inhabitants and cultural backgrounds. The

Case Study 2 225

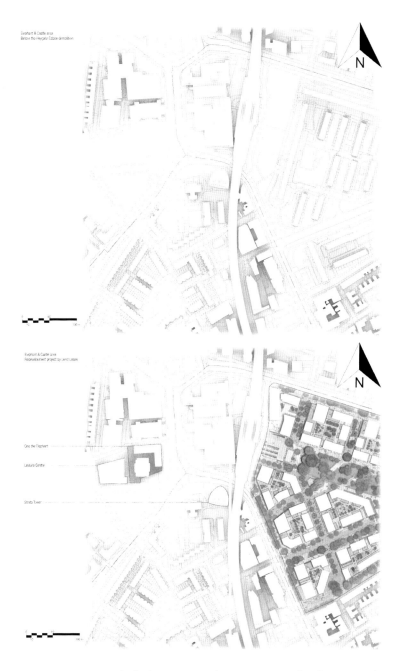

Figure 11.5 Map of Elephant & Castle regeneration development scheme. Image credit: Delfesc, 2014.

226 *Guillaume Delfesc*

Elephant & Castle shopping centre is an extension of this street. Large-scale regeneration projects have been transforming London for years, although often facing protests from residents fearing gentrification. It is the duty of the architect to understand what is happening in a particular site, and to consider its human features. Architecture itself has a role to play in integrating communities in the processes of urban change, as shown in Figure 11.6.

Luxury industries are no longer mere goods retailers. They embody various features, such as a brand image and values, which attract their customers. Earlier, we were asking the question whether these brands could contribute in a new way. In other words, if they could become patrons in a new way.

> The market is the place where goods and utilities meet.
> (Mumford, 2009, 237–254)

A traditional meeting place in the city is the market. One of the main issues of this project is to bring together newcomers of the redevelopment programmes and historical inhabitants. The natural site for such a project would be the Elephant & Castle shopping centre. Therefore, I aim to create in this central area a new meeting point, a new market, in fact a new shopping centre. Based on my previous research on brands, the project will offer a new 'brand identity', a 'rebranding': The New Elephant.

Thanks to the data gathered by Suzan Hall on the shop's ownership, we can imagine what the programme of The New Elephant could look like. The shopping centre would offer a mix of shops from different locations. The goal is to allow newcomers and migrants who first settled in the area to open a business and become part of the community. These shops would have the opportunity to settle in a place with cheap rents. Indeed, the project aims to create a 'social patronage' as mentioned earlier, and brands can be part of this scheme. Luxury brands would have some boutiques on The New Elephant, and by paying a higher rent, they would help to finance the low rents of the other shops. Luxury for these brands would be to settle in the heart of a vast regeneration programme, where they will have access to wealthy customers. In the meantime, luxury for the shops of the newcomers would be to have an affordable place to settle and make business in an extremely well-located and connected area of London. The New Elephant can then act as an incubator for these small shops, allowing newcomers and migrants to settle in, grow their business, and move to other parts of the city or the country. Figure 11.7 displays the mass plan of the building.

Conclusions

The luxury brands have strong identities. We have seen here that these identities are materialised in the design concepts of the shops. Boutiques are

Case Study 2 227

Figure 11.6 Mapping social housing estates in Elephant & Castle, London. Image credit: Delfescc, 2014.

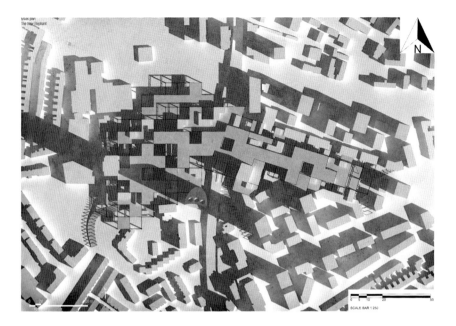

Figure 11.7 A New Elephant & Castle multi-purpose urban habitation with its multi-diversity and culture. Image credit: Delfesc, 2014.

designed by architects, sometimes famous, to serve the cultural status of the brand. Anywhere in the world, those luxury brands adopt similar design guidelines and concepts to serve their image. Sometimes those buildings appear to neglect the context of the local identity – more accurately, they seem to overlay their brand identity above it. In those situations, they do create 'Heterotopias', where the customer is inside of a brand image, instead of being in a street of New York, Tokyo or Paris. Then what would be the solution for a design acknowledging the local identity and supporting the brand identity?

> What needs to be emphasised is that the general tendency to try to shout more loudly than neighbours usually results in everyone shouting and no one person being heard at all.
>
> (Birch et al., 2017, 245–260).

This quotation from *Design in the High Street*, a book commissioned by the Royal Fine Art Commission on how to design shops in the high streets of Britain, is still very accurate. This is particularly true in Tokyo and other cities of Asia, where building regulations regarding height and context can be lighter than in European cities.

Notes

1 The information is extracted from: https://www.theguardian.com/cities/2018/jul/03/save-the-elephant-and-castle-the-fight-to-protect-south-londons-anti-westfield (accessed on 03/06/2019).
2 The information is extracted from: https://www.theguardian.com/uk-news/2020/sep/24/were-going-to-miss-the-community-elephant-and-castle-shopping-centre-closes-after-55-years (accessed on 03/06/2019).

References

Altay, C. (2013). Transgression in and of the city. *Architectural Design*, *83*(6), 102–109. https://doi.org/10.1002/ad.1682

Amini Behbahani, P., Ostwald, M. J., & Gu, N. (2016). A syntactical comparative analysis of the spatial properties of Prairie style and Victorian domestic architecture. *Journal of Architecture*, *21*(3), 348–374. https://doi.org/10.1080/13602365.2016.1179661

Birch, J., Parnell, R., Patsarika, M., & Šorn, M. (2017). Creativity, play and transgression: Children transforming spatial design. *CoDesign*, *13*(4), 245–260. https://doi.org/10.1080/15710882.2016.1169300

Cunningham, D. (2001). Architecture, Utopia and the futures of the avant-garde. *Journal of Architecture*. https://doi.org/10.1080/13602360110048195

Dawes, M. J., & Ostwald, M. J. (2014). Testing the wright space: Using isovists to analyse prospect-refuge characteristics in Usonian architecture. *Journal of Architecture*. https://doi.org/10.1080/13602365.2014.965722

Doron, G. M. (2000). The dead zone and the architecture of transgression. *City*, *4*(2), 247–263. https://doi.org/10.1080/13604810050147857

Dovey, K. (2013). Architecture the challenge of informal. *Architectural Design*, *83*(6), 82–89.

Faustino, D. (2013). In praise of transgression: The work of Didier faustino/bureau de mésarchitectures. *Architectural Design*, *83*(6), 120–123. https://doi.org/10.1002/ad.1685

Graham, G. (2008). Art and architecture: A place between. *British Journal of Aesthetics*, *48*(1), 100–101. https://doi.org/10.1093/aesthj/aym048

Hall, S. (2011). *City, street and citizen: The measure of the ordinary*. London: Routledge.

Hejduk, R. (2007). Death becomes her: Transgression, decay, and eROTicism in Bernard Tschumi's early writings and projects. *Journal of Architecture*, *12*, 393–404. https://doi.org/10.1080/13602360701614672

Hejduk, R. (2010). Step into liquid: Rites, transcendence and transgression in the modern construction of the social sacred. *Culture and Religion*. https://doi.org/10.1080/14755610.2010.505476

Jewell, N. (2001). The fall and rise of the British mall. *Journal of Architecture*. https://doi.org/10.1080/13602360110071450

Kimmel, L. (2020). Walter Benjamin's topology of envelopes and perspectives. *Journal of Architecture*, *25*(6), 659–678. https://doi.org/10.1080/13602365.2020.1800791

Lawrence, R. (2020). Halls, lobbies, and porches: Transition spaces in Victorian architecture. *Journal of Architecture*, *25*(4), 419–443. https://doi.org/10.1080/13602365.2020.1767176

Lending, M. (2018). Negotiating absence: Bernard Tschumi's new acropolis museum in Athens. *Journal of Architecture*, *23*(5), 797–819. https://doi.org/10.1080/13602365.2018.1495909

Littlefield, D. (2013). Ashes thrown to the wind: The elusive nature of transgression. *Architectural Design*, *83*(6), 124–129. https://doi.org/10.1002/ad.1686

Lohtaja, A. (2021). Henri Lefebvre's lessons from the Bauhaus. *Journal of Architecture*, *26*(4), 499–515. https://doi.org/10.1080/13602365.2021.1923551

Malone, P. (2020). Bourdieu in London. *Journal of Architecture*, *25*(6), 679–696. https://doi.org/10.1080/13602365.2020.1800792

Manning, J., Rifkin, A., Noble, G., Garofalakis, G., & Elsea, D. (2018). RIBA president's awards for research 2017 winner, cities and community category: London's local character and density. *Journal of Architecture*. https://doi.org/10.1080/13602365.2018.1427377

Mumford, E. (2009). CIAM and the communist bloc, 1928–59. *Journal of Architecture*, *14*(2), 237–254. https://doi.org/10.1080/13602360802704810

Quinn, B. (2008). Exhibition review: AngloMania: Tradition and transgression in British fashion. *Fashion Theory - The Journal of Dress Body and Culture*. https://doi.org/10.2752/175174108X332341

Roberts-Hughes, R. (2017). Transgression and conservation: Rereading Georges Bataille. *Journal for Cultural Research*, *21*(2), 157–168. https://doi.org/10.1080/14797585.2016.1239608

Sachs, A. (2019). Research and democracy: The architectural research division of the Tennessee valley authority. *Journal of Architecture*, *24*(7), 925–949. https://doi.org/10.1080/13602365.2019.1698636

Sánchez-Verdejo Pérez, F. J. (2021). 'It [the castle] is old, and has many memories': Transgression and cultural, literary idiosyncrasy of space in gothic tradition. *Revista Thélos*, *1*(13), 67–89. Retrieved from https://thelos.utem.cl/articulos/essay-it-the-castle-is-old-and-has-many-memories-transgression-and-cultural-literary-idiosyncrasy-of-space-in-gothic-tradition/

Sara, R., & Littlefield, D. (2014). Transgression: Body and space. *Architecture and Culture*, *2*(3), 295–304. https://doi.org/10.2752/205078214X14107818390513

Short, T. (1998). Of mice and madness: Questions of occupation interpreted through Disneyland and Parc de la Villette. *Journal of Architecture*. https://doi.org/10.1080/136023698374260

Stępnik, M. (2020). The house that lars built: The architecture of transgression. *Arts*, *9*(4), 127. https://doi.org/10.3390/arts9040127

12 Case Study 3

Berlin: The State of Power, Kreuzberg, Berlin, Germany

Guillaume Delfesc

Berlin: Past and Present

In 1987, Wim Wenders directed 'Wings of Desire'. In this film, invisible and immortal angels listen to the thoughts of the human inhabitants of Berlin and comfort those who are in distress (Pullan, 2011). Those supernatural characters also can move freely across the border between East and West Berlin and the buffer zone (Walker, 2015). It is also known as the 'death strip' a massive no man's land in the heart of the city, circled by walls and walkways and heavily guarded. After the fall of the wall in 1989, the vast empty spaces of what used to be the buffer zone, suddenly became available. These spaces were affordable and well located at the heart of the city and the Potsdamer Platz was one of them. The Potsdamer Platz then underwent a massive redevelopment, as shown in Figure 12.1.

Big companies, such as SONY or the Deutsche Bahn, bought some land on this site and had their headquarters designed by famous architects. The Pariser Platz is one of the city's main focal points and is known worldwide for its neoclassical triumphal arch, the Brandenburg Gate. During the last years of World War II, most of the buildings around the Pariser Platz were destroyed by air raids. None of them would be rebuilt until after the reunification. In fact, the square remained empty, as it was located inside of the buffer zone. Only the Brandenburg Gate remained, facing the Reichstag, the Tiergarten and the rest of West Berlin.

When the city was reunited in 1990, it was decided that the Pariser Platz should be made into a fine urban space again. The French and American embassies were established around the square and the British embassy on a street nearby. Prestigious firms were encouraged to build here. Under the rules of reconstruction, eave heights had to be 22 metres, and buildings had to have a proper termination against the sky. Stone cladding was used as much as possible. Interpretations of these constraints, however, varied to a great extent. In 1951, in this loop of the river Spree, immediately north of the Tiergarten is a space left empty after World War II. Most of the buildings were destroyed or heavily damaged by bombings, amongst them the German parliament (Reichstag). For decades, the Reichstag was unused,

DOI: 10.4324/9781003243069-15

232 *Guillaume Delfesc*

Figure 12.1 Aerial view of Potsdamer Platz. Image credit: the author, 2014

as the West German capital was moved to Bonn in 1949 (Wimmelbcker, 2012, 407–432).

In 1999, following a referendum, Berlin was designated as the capital city of Germany. The parliament, chancellery and ministries were to move back to the historical capital. It was decided to move to this very loop of the river near the Reichstag, the chancellery, Bundestag and library of the Bundestag. The Reichstag was refurbished some years before, by British architect Norman Foster (Boyarsky, 2021, 639–658).

Before being reunited, East Berlin was the ideal place where the East could display its power. It became an architectural showcase for the communist government of the time, as the following projects suggest. Hereafter are examples of the 'Seven Sisters' project initiated by Stalin in 1947: dual skyscrapers implemented on both sides of a major avenue or square (Stanicic, 2021, 371–393). Indeed, dual towers, flanking major city squares, can be found from Berlin to Siberia. In Berlin, those towers were part of a larger urban development project, the Karl Marx Allee.

Berlin's famous motto 'Poor but Sexy' doesn't make it the most popular of German cities according to an online survey: the capital is ranked 45/71. In the meantime, it makes it a relatively affordable city to live in.

Existing Urban Conditions: Identification of Leftover Urban Space in Kreuzberg

The borough of Kreuzberg is one of the best-known areas of Berlin. Kreuzberg has emerged from its history as one of the poorest quarters of the city in the late 1970s (during which it was an isolated section of West Berlin) to one of Berlin's cultural centres in the middle of the now reunified city (Sheil, 2005, 20–32). Its situation, close to the wall, made it the cheapest district to live in West Berlin as shown in Figure 12.2.

It then became home for many migrants, especially from Turkey. Today, there is still a large percentage of immigrants and second-generation immigrants in Kreuzberg, many of whom are of Turkish ancestry. Some famous illegal settlements can be found, as squares and empty spaces offer the opportunity to set up tents and temporary housing. Although this situation is illegal, it's mostly tolerated by the authorities, thanks to the counterculture tradition of Kreuzberg. Figure 12.2 shows one of those settlements, located on a public square.

Kreuzberg is also one of the trendy districts of Berlin, as many bars, pubs and nightclubs can be found in the area. It is still one of the symbols of Berlin's 'club culture' that attracts many young European tourists to the city. At the corner of Skalitzer Straße and Marianenstraße, the project site is located in a Volkswagen garage and car park. It faces an elevated metro line (U-bahn) on its south side, and a small park on its east side, as shown in Figure 12.2.

A Manifesto: Conceptual Stages of a Mix-Use Development Project Proposal

Berlin has several faces. Today's capital of Germany, the most powerful European economy, it was widely destroyed during World War II, separated by the wall, reunited and rebuilt. Not only a major European capital but Berlin is also a World City (Sharp, 2022). Embassies, international organisations and corporate headquarters are located there. Its power is also cultural, as Berlin attracts countless tourists and artists in its streets every year (Pilav, 2020, 697–716). Berlin is famous for its art scene and club culture, and many of these activities happen in the vast and unused spaces of the city, whether it's in the eastern or western part. The borough of Kreuzberg is an example of this counterculture (Garcia-Vergara & Pizza,

234 *Guillaume Delfesc*

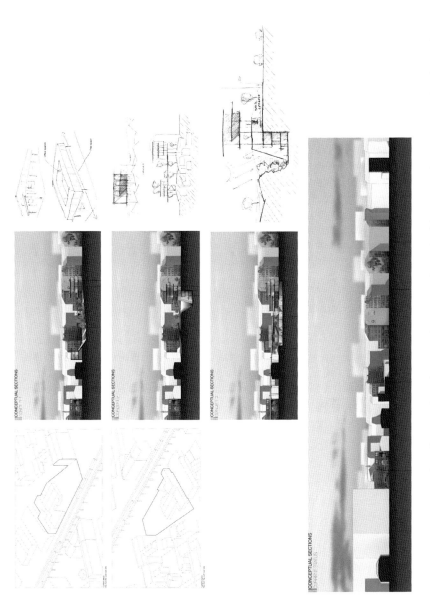

Figure 12.2 Conceptual analysis and renderings of a new embassy building in Berlin. Image credit: the author, 2014

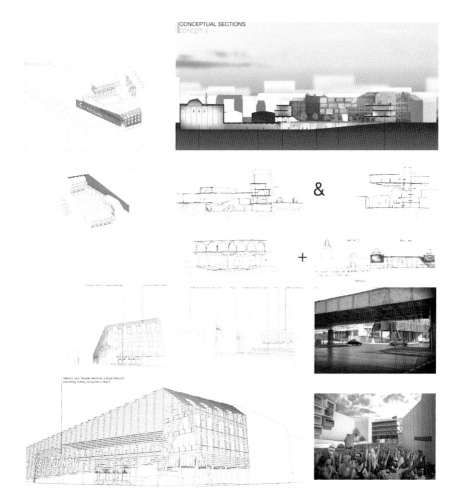

Figure 12.3 A new Turkish embassy building in Berlin. Image credit: the author, 2014

2021, 1117–1145). A home to many migrants, its squares sometimes host illegal settlements and some of its building's squats. The district also has a vibrant art scene. Kreuzberg nowadays faces the issue of gentrification, the cheap rents are increasing and new expensive constructions are built on the empty plots. Some of its historical inhabitants protest this issue. The project here is to design a new Turkish consulate building located in Kreuzberg.

The Turkish community is by far the most represented in Kreuzberg, and some of them can't speak German. The idea is to bring to these people a sense of pride and citizenship by creating a consulate that would allow gathering and create a connection with their homeland. In that sense, the

236 *Guillaume Delfesc*

project embodies the Turkish concept of 'meydan' or public square. In the meantime, small temporary housing is incorporated into the programme, finding its inspiration in the Turkish 'cappadocias' to tackle the issue of gentrification. The nearby mosque is moved directly into the space of the central courtyard, or 'meydan', making the space ideal for gathering and socialising. Finally, the offices and other security-sensitive programmes are set above the ground, letting the ground floor open and free as is the case for many other places throughout Berlin, as shown in Figure 12.3.

Consulates and embassies are buildings that need a particular level of security. There have been attempts to make those programmes more open to the public, such as the British Embassy in Berlin by Michael Wilford, but the originally open spaces had to be closed to the public after the events of 9/11. The first concept was then to separate the diplomatic and security-sensitive spaces above the ground while letting the ground floor free for people to use.

By following the Turkish concepts of 'cappadocia' and 'meydan', the building would be divided into three spaces: an elevated space for offices and diplomatic uses; an intermediate space on the ground floor that could be used for gatherings, events, art exhibitions or freely, as many other spaces in Berlin; and finally, an underground space resembling the cappadocias, to host programmes that do not need a high level of security.

This last concept combines all the previous ideas and connects to the mosque currently under construction by a subway. Thus, making the central meydan space an extension of the traditional courtyard found in traditional mosques.

In the final project, a new mosque is designed in the land plot of the project. This way, the idea of having the courtyard of the mosque in the 'meydan' space is used, and the central space becomes a truly multipurpose area.

References

Boyarsky, N. (2021). Auto portraits and the enigmas of self: Geometries of distraction and detection in the work of Peter Wilson. *Journal of Architecture*, 26(5), 639–658. https://doi.org/10.1080/13602365.2021.1942136

García Vergara, M., & Pizza, A. (2021). The Mediterranean and modern architecture: The dissemination of a myth in architectural media. *Journal of Architecture*, 26(8), 1117–1145. https://doi.org/10.1080/13602365.2021.1980419

Pilav, A. (2020). 'Architects in war': Wartime destruction and architectural practice during the siege of Sarajevo. *Journal of Architecture*, 25(6), 697–716. https://doi .org/10.1080/13602365.2020.1800793

Pullan, W. (2011). Frontier urbanism: The periphery at the centre of contested cities. *Journal of Architecture*. https://doi.org/10.1080/13602365.2011.546999

Sharp, D. (2022). Concretising conflict. *Journal of Architecture*. https://doi.org/10 .1080/13602365.2022.2029026

Sheil, B. (2005). Transgression from drawing to making. *Architectural Research Quarterly*, 9(1), 20–32. https://doi.org/10.1017/S1359135505000059

Staničić, A. (2021). Media propaganda vs public dialogue: The spatial memorialisation of conflict in Belgrade after the 1999 NATO bombing. *Journal of Architecture*, 26(3), 371–393. https://doi.org/10.1080/13602365.2021.1897645

Walker, J. (2015). Islands-in-the-City: Berlin's urban fragments. *Journal of Architecture*. https://doi.org/10.1080/13602365.2015.1075226

Wimmelbcker, L. (2012). Architecture and city planning projects of the German Democratic Republic in Zanzibar. *Journal of Architecture*, 17(3), 407–432. https://doi.org/10.1080/13602365.2012.692610

13 Case Study 4

Undercliffe Social Housing, Bradford, United Kingdom

Hasim Altan and Young Ki Kim

Introduction

The main construction site of the case study homes is located in the Undercliffe area, Bradford (53°45′00″N 01°50′00″W) and is roughly 60 metres above sea level. Bradford is a city in West Yorkshire in Northern England and about eight miles away from west of Leeds. The construction site is about two miles north-east from Bradford city centre. When the case homes were completed, 'Undercliffe Health Care Centre' was not constructed next to the case study homes. The housing estate comprising six case study homes (or units) are shown in Figure 13.1.

Figure 13.1 shows the simplified floor plans for case study homes where both the monitoring and simulation studies were undertaken in each home's selected bedroom and living room. The case study homes, which formed the basis of a pilot study of an energy efficient social housing project that was completed by the Accent Group Ltd in conjunction with the University of Sheffield. The main aim of this pilot study was to inform the development of flexible affordable energy efficient domestic properties. The case study homes consist of a terrace of four domestic buildings, which were designed and built by the Accent Group for social housing tenants using modern building and procurement methods and sustainable materials, based on extensive research from the adaptable and grow home principles of Avi Friedman (2003). The Building Environments Analysis Unit (formerly known as Building Energy Analysis Unit) (BEAU, 2007) in the School of Architecture at the University of Sheffield have worked with the Accent Group and their architects, the Goddard Wybor Practise, and consulting engineers, Mott MacDonald, to evaluate and modify the Canadian designs to produce these housing developments as environmentally friendly and low energy designs for the UK climate (Accent Group, 2007).

Within this terraced social housing, the two middle units are family homes, and the two end units are divided into two separate flats. The mid-terraced houses have four bedrooms, the ground-floor flats have one bedroom, and the first-floor flats have two bedrooms and the first-floor flat with mezzanine floor has three bedrooms. Ground flats and terraced houses have

DOI: 10.4324/9781003243069-16

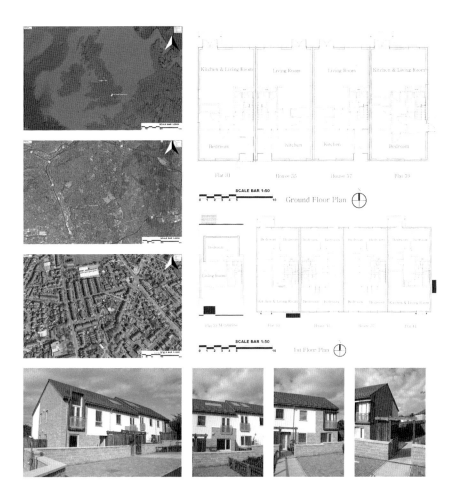

Figure 13.1 Site and external appearance of case study homes; ground floor plan; first floor plan. Image credit: Altan & Kim, 2022.

north-facing living rooms and the first-floor flats have south-facing living rooms. A mix of different heating systems is used in the units, including gas central heating radiators, electric panels, and underfloor heating. Table 13.1 shows a detailed summary of the case study homes.

As can be seen in Table 13.1, mixed generation and families live(d) in the case study homes, which range from a single person flat (in the later period of monitoring, another person with a baby moved into this flat) to family houses with children and teenagers. This household variation was considered when the Post Occupancy Evaluation (POE) study was carried out, especially about the relationship between household pattern and

Table 13.1 Detailed summary of the case study homes.

Unit	31	33	35	37	39	41
Sign	Flat 1	Flat 2	House 1	House 2	Flat 3	Flat 4
Description	1 bedroom ground floor	3 bedrooms with mezzanine	4-bedroom house	4-bedroom house	1-bedroom, ground floor	2-bedroom, first floor
Floor area[m^2]	49,62	85,64	127,56	127,56	53,73	55,26
Volume[m^3]	119,6	206,4	307,4	307,4	129,5	133,2
Occupancy	1 (1 adult)	3 (1 adult + 2 children)	5 (1 adult + 4 teenagers)	5 (parents + 3 children)	2 (pensioners)	2 (2 adults)

energy consumption (Altan et al., 2015). The occupancy input data for the simulation studies were also developed based on these occupancy patterns and room occupancy input data as well (Ozarisoy, 2022). This helped to improve the accuracy of the simulation input data and to make the simulation more realistic rather than just based on assumptions (Ozarisoy, 2021).

Construction Detail

The properties are of timber frame light-weight construction and built using off-site manufacturing techniques. The concept for the Accent Home makes use of a high degree of prefabrication and modular construction techniques, resulting in an increase in speed of construction along with substantial reductions in labour and wastage during the site installation phase. At the heart of the construction method is a panelised timber frame with blown cellulose insulation. The structural panels give exceptional insulation and airtightness values – even for sound reduction in partitioning wall units. Timber for the panels is sourced from verified sustainable sources accredited by the World Wildlife Fund (WWF) Forest Stewardship Council. Total external walls are built up to achieve a U-value of 0.21 W/m²K and a minimum Standard Assessment Procedure (SAP) rating of 100 (BRE, 2005), as shown in Figure 13.2. The chosen insulation material, cellulose, is made from 100% recycled newsprint and is particularly suited for use in ventilated or breathing constructions.

At the design stage for the homes, the homes are provided with airtight, durable, and visually pleasing external cladding. Due to their airtight, well insulated and timber framed construction, these units have exemplary standards in energy efficiency for UK housing. The homes were designed to require only a small amount of heating, which was required only during the very coldest parts of the year. Heat gains from equipment and cooking will be sufficient to meet space heating needs for most of the year. For similar reasons, rejection of excess heat during mild and warm weather periods would become an issue to be addressed. Figure 13.3 shows the details of the case study homes' construction.

Figure 13.3 shows a comparison between the standards of three super-insulated homes; the 2006 Building Regulations Part L minimum requirements; and the case study of homes. It shows the six units' fabric standards, which were better than the Building Regulations 2006 Part L except for the windows and doors. Hence, windows, doors and walls, rest fabric elements' thermal properties were closed to AECB's 'Gold' Standard which is proposed to be 'Code Level 6' home by AECB (Bertoldi & Mosconi, 2020). When designing the case study homes, it was aimed to meet the 'Code Level 3' and to satisfy the Level 3 home, the building fabric standards would be required as 'Best Practice' level. From this, it was concluded that the case study homes are super-insulated, light-weight timber frames with airtight

242 *Hasim Altan and Young Ki Kim*

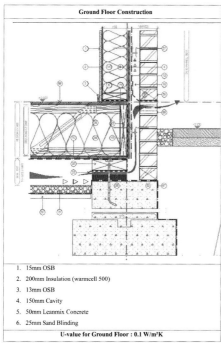

1. 15mm OSB
2. 200mm Insulation (warmcell 500)
3. 13mm OSB
4. 150mm Cavity
5. 50mm Leanmix Concrete
6. 25mm Sand Blinding

U-value for Ground Floor : 0.1 W/m²K

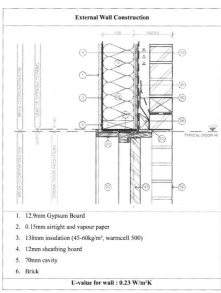

1. 12.9mm Gypsum Board
2. 0.15mm airtight and vapour paper
3. 138mm insulation (45-60kg/m³, warmcell 500)
4. 12mm sheathing board
5. 70mm cavity
6. Brick

U-value for wall : 0.23 W/m²K

Figure 13.2 Case study homes' construction detail; ground-floor and external wall construction joint details. Image credit: Altan & Kim, 2022.

Case Study 4 243

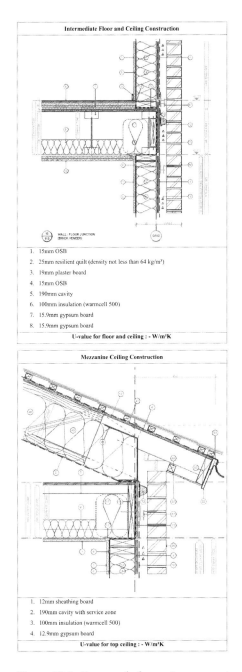

Figure 13.3 Case study homes' construction detail; intermediate floor and ceiling-mezzanine ceiling construction details. Image credit: Altan & Kim, 2022.

244 Hasim Altan and Young Ki Kim

Table 13.2 Comparison between case study homes and national standards.

Elemental U-value (W/m²K)	Accent Home	BedZED[a]	EEBPH 'Advanced' Standard[b]	Proposed AECB 'Gold' Standard[c]	Building Regulations 2006 Part L[d]
Walls	0.23	0.1	0.15	0.15	0.35
Roofs	0.14	0.11	0.08	0.15	0.25
Floors	0.1	0.1	0.1	0.15	0.25
Windows, Doors	2.26	1.2	1.5	0.8	2.2
Air permeability m³/m²hr@50Pa	0.9@50Pa	2.0@50Pa	1.0@50Pa	0.75@50Pa	(No greater than 10@50Pa accepted)

[a] Bill Dunster Architects, the ZED Factory, 2003. Achieving sustainable communities – the ZED challenge; using a value engineered version of BedZED and its supply chain.
[b] General Information LEAFLET 72 (UK Best Practice Programme, Energy Efficiency Best Practice for Housing (EEBPH), www.housingenergy.org.uk.
[c] AECB Energy Standard(S) 'Prescriptive' Version 2005.
[d] UK Building Regulations Part L1 2006 Edition.
[e] UK Building Regulations Part L1A 2006 Edition – for all new dwellings' air tightness standard.

homes (see Table 13.2 for more detailed comparisons with national building standards).

Heating System

The primary objective of the chosen heating system was to provide space heating to the case study homes. Given the low energy nature of the homes, its aim was that operation of the heating systems in winter will be minimal. Heating will therefore be such that it can be easily controlled and in keeping with the low thermal capacity of the structures. To meet this primary aim of the Heating, Ventilation and Air Conditioning (HVAC) system for the case study homes, each unit was carefully fitted with its own type of heating as follows: (i) **Flats 1 and 2, and Home 1** were fitted with domestic gas-fired condensing boilers. The boilers provide heating to a tank hot water cylinder for hot water heating. Space heating is provided by good quality round top radiators fitted with Thermostatic Radiator Valve (TRV) devices fed from a factory assembled heating manifold; (ii) **Home 2** is fitted with a High Efficiency Ventilation system with electric heater battery and additional top-up electric panel heaters; (iii) **Flats 3 and 4** are fitted with electric panel heaters in the ground floor unit and electric underfloor heating in the first-floor unit. Temperatures for internal spaces are designed to achieve the following minimum temperatures at –4°C external ambient temperature. The boiler shall be a fully automatic, wall-mounted, room-sealed condensing, high efficiency standard boiler for central heating and domestic water.

Table 13.3 Target internal temperature for heating.

Internal Spaces	Set Temperature
Living Spaces	21°C
Bedrooms	18°C
Toilets and Bathrooms	25°C
Stairs Lobbies and Circulation	18°C

As shown in Table 13.3, the boiler is rated to the Seasonal Efficiency of Domestic Boilers in the UK (SEDBUK) Band A and has a dimension no greater than 300mm from front to back to enable it to be in the ventilated riser (Cuerda et al., 2020). The boiler will be manufactured from materials such that 90% of the unit can be recycled when the unit reaches the end of its service life. Radiators are fitted on adequately supported radiator brackets on the timber walls. Each radiator will have bottom opposite end connections and be complete with a lock shield valve and a good quality TRV suitable for space temperature control in the range of 18°C to 28°C. Underfloor heating is a 3mm thick mat manufactured by Creda Applied Energy Products Limited. The mat comes complete with a Creda Net main borne signalling control system and local room temperature control stats.

Ventilation System

Due to the exceptional airtightness of the timber frame construction, ventilation systems would be necessary to alleviate problems of heat and moisture buildup, elevated CO_2 buildup, odours, or any potentially harmful pollutants. As with the heating systems, it is intended that each demonstration home has its own unique ventilation system. The ventilation system is operated at all the times of occupancy and would be designed to maintain a minimum CO_2 level of 1000 ppm, and/or maximum relative humidity of 70% saturation in all spaces. Table 13.4 shows target ventilation flowing minimum rates for each room, which was adopted in the computer simulation studies. To achieve this target ventilation rate, kitchen and bathrooms have mechanical ventilation for some space to achieve the target ventilation rate for each room with a heat recovery unit. For example, on activation of the kitchen canopy hood or a bathroom light, the system would provide a 25% boost in flow rate to all areas.

All systems would be arranged for quiet operation. Noise levels from the system would not exceed NR25 in bedrooms and NR30 for living spaces. More detailed explanation of ventilation systems as follows: (i) **Flat 1 Ground-Floor Apartment**: Extract System from bathroom and kitchen with replacement through window trickle ventilators. This system provides a low-cost installation but with higher anticipated heating costs. The system

246 *Hasim Altan and Young Ki Kim*

Table 13.4 The flowing minimum rates for ventilation.

Internal Space	Set Ventilation Rate
Living Spaces	8 litres per second per person
Kitchen/Diners	10 air changes per hour
Kitchens	10 air changes per hour
Bathrooms/En Suite WC	10 air changes
Whole House	Minimum of 0.5 air changes at all times
Halls/Common Areas	1 air change per hour

would operate on detection of high humidity in the living spaces, or operation of the kitchen hood canopy or light in the bathroom; (ii) **Flat 2 First-Floor Apartment**: Whole-house ventilation system to provide fresh air to all living spaces and bedrooms balanced by extract from all wet areas and the kitchen. The system will operate during all occupied periods to provide 0.5 air changes per hour of the total dwelling's volume. On activation of the kitchen canopy hood or a bathroom light, the system would provide a 25% boost in flow rate to all areas. The system provides a medium capital cost against a lower running cost solution; (iii) **House 1 – 4-Bedroom House**: Heat Recovery Ventilation (HRV) system to provide fresh air to all living spaces and bedrooms balanced by extract from all wet areas and the kitchen. In addition, the system is fitted with a Solar Thermal Collector to provide a renewable energy heating source in winter. The ventilation system will operate during all occupied periods to provide 0.5 air changes per hour of the total dwelling's volume (Borelli et al., 2020). On activation of the kitchen canopy or a bathroom light, the system would provide a 25% boost in flow rate to all areas.

In addition, the solar-thermal panels will provide a free source of hot water for domestic uses. The system provides a high capital against low running costs solution; (iv) **House 2 – 4-Bedroom House**: HRV to provide fresh air to all living spaces and bedrooms balanced by extract from all wet areas and the kitchen. As well, the house incorporates electric heater batteries for zone heating of ground and first floors. The system would operate during all occupied periods to provide 0.5 air changes per hour of the total dwelling's volume. On activation of the kitchen canopy hood or a bathroom light, the system will provide a 25% boost in flow rate to all areas; (v) **Flat 3 – Ground-Floor and Flat 4 – First-Floor Apartments**: Both apartments are fitted with their own Positive Input Ventilation (PIV) system. The system would supply fresh air to the hall space in the apartment to positively pressurise the whole of the dwelling. Air relief paths would be via window trickle ventilators in living spaces and unitary extract fans in the kitchen canopy hood and bathroom. Incoming fresh air to the supply fan would be taken from the relatively warm floor cavity, or the roof terminal. The intelligent on-board controls will decide on the most appropriate source of fresh air to provide adequate temperature and ventilation for the home. The system represents a low installation cost with a medium running cost solution; (vi) **Heat Recovery Ventilation Unit**: The unit is manufactured by Nuaire Limited model MVHR system 6, and the units would be manufactured from materials such that 90% of the unit can be recycled when the unit reaches the end of its service life. The contractor would provide the appropriate ISO 14001 certification to this effect; (vii) **Positive Input Ventilation Unit**: The unit is manufactured by Nuaire Limited model Drimaster 365, and the units would be manufactured from materials such that 90% of the unit can be recycled when the unit reaches the end of its service life. The contractor would provide the appropriate ISO 14001 certification to this effect; (viii) **Unitary Extract Fans**: The unit is manufactured by Nuaire Limited model Genie X (continuous ventilation with boost), and control of the boost function is via a light switch. The units would be manufactured from materials such that 90% of the unit can be recycled when the unit reaches the end of its service life (Ozarisoy & Altan, 2022a). The contractor would provide the appropriate ISO 14001 certification to this effect. Table 13.5 shows the summary of the heating and ventilation systems for the case study homes, which were explained above.

It should be mentioned that the heat recovery and solar thermal systems were not considered within the computer simulation study due to lack of data gathering and access to information, and no capability or less accuracy of the simulation software (later, the 2012 version of the simulation tool could do this). Furthermore, during the validation studies, with and without having a heat recovery unit with mechanical ventilation system in simulation, studies showed less than ±2% difference in simulation results but 1.5 times more duration of running simulation (Ozarisoy & Altan, 2022b). Therefore, the heat recovery ventilation unit was removed from the simulation models.

Monitoring Study

Data is needed for three purposes: for building the simulation model, for validating the model, and for performing experiments with the validated model (Kalluri et al., 2020). Additionally, one more purpose was added (i.e., the POE study) in which the data were used as input data for developing simulation models. This monitoring data was used to analyse and understand occupancy patterns and improve simulation model accuracy by reducing the uncertainty of input data (Altan & Ozarisoy, 2022c). Furthermore, this data was used for a comparison study of how well the case study homes compared with the typical UK homes by using the national rating systems such as SAP.

To build a simulation model, it was necessary to have sufficient data to make it as close to a real building as possible with construction data, indoor environment data, energy performance data and user behavioural data

Table 13.5 Summary of heating and ventilation systems.

Unit	31	33	35	37	39	41
Sign	Flat 1	Flat 2	House 1	House 2	Flat 3	Flat 4
Heating	Gas central heating with radiators + 1 electric panel heater	Gas central heating with radiators + electric panel heater in bathroom	Gas central heating with radiators + electric panel heaters in bathrooms	Electric panels (no storage)	Electric panel heaters	Underfloor electric heaters
Ventilation	Mechanical extract only with heat recovery	Mechanical extract only with heat recovery	HRV Supply + extract with thermal roof (Nuaire MVHR4)	HRV Supply + extract with electric heater battery for space heating	PIV ventilation system with heat recovery	PIV ventilation system with heat recovery
Gas usage	s	Heating, oven and boiler	Heating, oven, and boiler	Oven	–	Oven
Hot water preparation	Unvented hot water calorifier with power shower	Unvented hot water calorifier with power shower	Unvented HW with power shower and solar thermal collector with drain down	Electric unvented HW with power shower and solar thermal collector with glycol	Simple unvented electric immersion calorifier with 2 stage heaters	Simple unvented electric immersion calorifier with 2 stage heaters

(Theodosiou et al., 2021). If one of these data was not available, high confidence in the simulation results usually cannot be obtained because sufficient operational validity cannot be achieved. Therefore, having monitoring studies and analysing the data could help to reduce the level of uncertainty of the simulation studies and to validate the model for carrying out the next simulation studies, as shown in Figure 13.4.

There were three parts to the monitoring studies, namely, (i) 'Indoor Environments', (ii) 'Energy Consumption', and (iii) 'Occupant Survey'. With such studies, data gathering was possible and utilised for further analysis using computer simulations. In particular, the energy consumption monitoring was utilised for validating the simulation model against actual case study homes performance, which was also supported by an occupant survey designed for analysis on end user behaviour and for further improving the computer model input data with better understanding the occupancy, which would also help in improving accuracy of simulation models. The following subsections explain the data acquisition methods and what kinds of data were recorded and how these data would be used for further studies.

Indoor Environments

The indoor environments monitoring data were obtained from HOBO data logger through the POE study where the data of indoor air temperatures and relative humidity (RH) levels were recorded over a 2-year monitoring period (2007–2009) with 20-minute intervals (see Table 4.6), which was then also converted into hourly data.

Figure 13.4 shows the location of the HOBO data logger in a selected housing unit, i.e. the case study home's bedroom and living room spaces. Once the POE monitoring was completed, the data were then analysed to develop the simulation model input data, such as the heating system's set temperature and natural ventilation's set temperature. When selecting rooms for monitoring, two factors were considered: (i) orientation of the room and (ii) size of the window, as shown in Table 13.7.

These two factors are generally effective on the solar gains for the room and the solar gains through the window that could affect heating energy consumption and overheating during the summer. In Figure 13.4, there is an external HOBO data logger, which was installed at the very early stages of the monitoring to provide outdoor conditions from the area as a weather station. However, for some unknown reasons during the early stage of the monitoring period, it was removed. Therefore, the external weather data were obtained from the British Atmospheric Data Centre (BADC) for Bradford for the monitoring studies. The nearest weather station from the site is near Lister Park, which is almost three miles north of the actual site and 134 meter above the mean sea level that is almost double the height of the site.

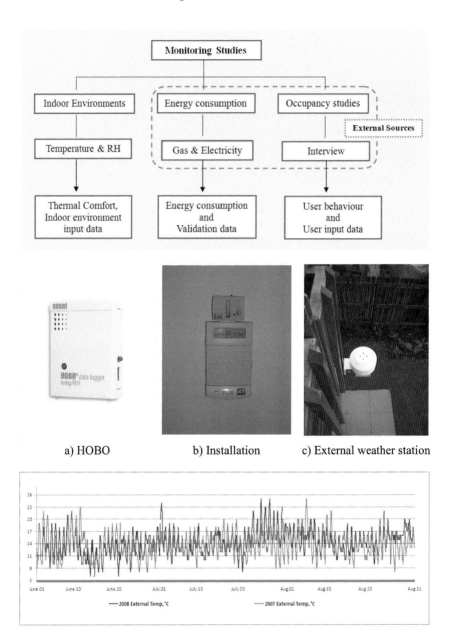

Figure 13.4 Overview of monitoring studies. Image credit: Altan & Kim, 2022.

Case Study 4   251

Table 13.6 The monitoring periods for the case study homes.

Home	Room	Dates
Flat 1	Bed	2007.08.17 to 2009.02.27
	Living room	
Flat 2	Bed	2007.10.12 to 2009.02.27
	Mezzanine	2007.10.12 to 2009.2.12
House 1	Bed	2007.05.04 to 2007.09.23
	Living room	2007.05.04 to 2008.08.05
House 2	Bed	2006.12.15 to 2009.02.27
	Living room	
Flat 3	Bed	2006.12.15 to 2008.03.07
	Living room	
Flat 4	Bed	2006.12.15 to 2009.02.27
	Living room	

Table 13.7 Case study homes' monitoring studies.

Unit	31	33	35	37	39	41
Sign	Flat 1	Flat 2	House 1	House 2	Flat 3	Flat 4
Bedroom	South facing with small window	North facing with small window	South facing with large window	North facing with small window	South facing with small widows	North facing with large widow
Living room	North facing	South facing mezzanine floor	North facing	North facing	North facing	South facing

As shown in Figure 13.5, the external weather data, especially the outdoor temperatures, were provided hourly and daily by the BADC. These hourly and daily outdoor temperatures were used to generate the upper limits of thermal comfort temperatures by 'Adopted Method' for the analysis. Figure 13.5 shows the external temperatures from the BADC for 2007 and 2008, from June to August. The purple line represents the summer external temperatures in 2008 and the green line shows the temperatures for 2007 summer conditions. From this data, it shows that 2007 summer was warmer than 2008, especially from late July to early August.

Energy Consumptions

The utility data (gas, electricity and water consumptions) was obtained from the POE study of the dwellings, measuring the energy usage in the first 3 years (2007–2009) of occupancy. In the case study homes, a remote monitoring system was used (Databird), which was installed by the Energy Metering Technology (EMT) in all 6 units to measure and record all energy

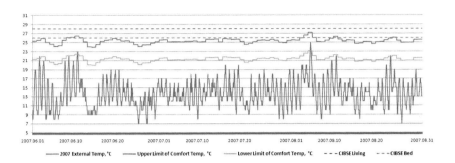

(a) 2007 thermal comfort upper limit temperatures

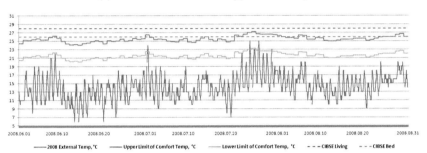

(b) 2008 thermal comfort upper limit temperatures

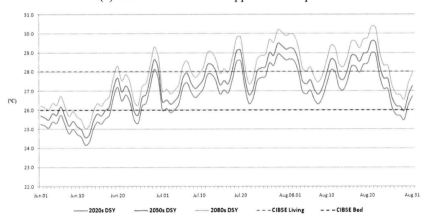

(c) Thermal comfort upper limit temperatures under future climatic data

Figure 13.5 Overview of monitoring study findings. Image credit: Altan & Kim, 2022.

consumption (electricity and gas) and water usage. The utility data were stored on a server in the BEAU research centre and were then evaluated using a Monitoring and Targeting programme for Automatic Utilities Auditing (DYNAMATplus) (DYNAMATplus Training Manual, 2007), as shown in Figure 13.6. The energy consumption data were used to validate the simulation model, which then helped to compare the case study homes against the typical UK homes.

Occupant Survey

This survey was carried out by Dr. Tracey Crosbie and Dr. Hasim Altan as part of the research project undertaken by the Carbon Reduction in Buildings (CaRB), a five-university consortium. The interviews were designed to explore the experience of living in the case study homes and helped to understand how these properties function from the resident's point of view. The interviews were carried out on four out of six units, which were Flats 3 and 4, and Houses 1 and 2.

From their report, it helped to improve the understanding of these units and user behaviour especially, in the way they were managing their heating and mechanical ventilation systems. These data were used for creating model input data for a simulation study to reduce the uncertainty of input data and to improve the accuracy of simulation studies. Table 13.8 shows some of the findings from this survey study and is used for creating input data for simulation models. From the interviews, it was confirmed that households do not know how to use their heating and ventilation systems properly. They do not know how to set the programmable heating system. Therefore, sets for the heating and ventilation set temperatures were based on monitoring data.

Without the validation of the simulation model, it would have not been possible to carry out further simulation studies. At the most basic level validation, the actual long-term energy usage of a building is compared to that calculated by the simulation tool, which is why this method was adopted (Thonipara et al., 2019). Hence, the energy consumption was more considered than using the internal temperature for simulation model validation. This could be one of the limitations of this study, having less confidence in the thermal comfort prediction study. However, to improve the studies for simulation and accuracy, the simulation model input data for controlling heating and ventilation set temperature and user behavioural data were created using the monitoring studies (Ballarini, Corgnati, & Corrado, 2014). Therefore, the authors believed that the simulation models and the associated results would be more reliable than they would have been without any input data validation and model validation from the case study homes' data.

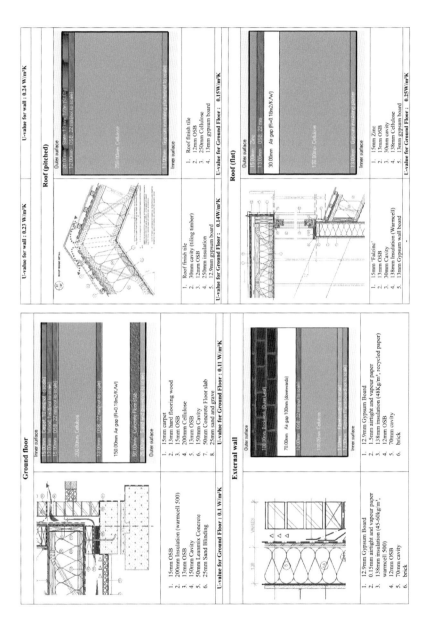

Figure 13.6 Construction details and building energy simulation set input parameters. Image credit: Altan & Kim, 2022.

Table 13.8 The findings from the occupant survey.

Home	Feedback
House 1	*This respondent lives in a household of five persons (four children and one adult). Mid forty years of age and not in employment. The income is less than 10 thousand per annum.* *The back of her house becomes 'chilly' in the evenings, while the front of* *her property gets too warm during the day.*
House 2	*This respondent lives in a household of two adults and three children. The respondent is between 31 and 40 years. One adult is in full-time employment. The respondent is on dependency leave looking after her youngest daughter with serious health problems.* *Open the windows in her children's bedrooms to cool them down in the winter because she lacks the knowledge to turn down the heating system.*
Flat 3	*This respondent lives in a household of two married adults both between* *60 and 65 years of age and both retired. The household income is between 10 and 15 thousand pounds per annum.* *Her hallway and bedroom are cold in the evenings and uses the towel rail in the bathroom to heat these areas in her home.* *She is confused over how to use her heating system and complains that her heating does not work in her bedroom and the use of a mobile electric heater.*
Flat 4	*These respondents are a married couple, male aged 59 and female aged 47. Both are full-time employment. The household income is between 25 and 30 thousand per annum.* *He honestly would not know if he was using his heating system properly.*

Conclusions

In general, as the floor area and number in the household increased, the energy consumption and CO_2 emissions increased. Regarding the influence of the main energy source, homes' heating systems using electricity as a main energy source showed better performance than those using gas central heating systems. However, in terms of CO_2 emissions and the influence of the main energy source, it seems that homes with more electricity consumption were at a disadvantage. In terms of the correlation between internal temperature and number of children for energy consumption, homes with children showed higher internal temperatures and higher energy consumption than homes with no children.

The applied building standard to the case study homes is better than the '2006 Building Regulations'. However, two of the case study homes performed worse than the 2006 Building Regulations' homes. From this result, it could be concluded that it is the occupants who determine how energy efficient a dwelling will be, even if the building is well-insulated and the dwelling has an efficient energy source. Therefore, reducing energy use depends not only upon improving building performance, but also understanding the relationship between how occupants use the unit and their personal circumstances. For example, House 1 and House 2 units have an identical floor plan, floor area and size of household, but the energy consumption showed large variations due to user behaviour.

As a result of the winter comfort study, it shows that the occupants in the case study homes prefer a higher internal temperature for the bedroom than the 'CIBSE Guide A' recommendation, however, not in the living room. With regard to overheating, some of the case study homes showed overheating during the monitoring periods due to the fact that they had south-facing living rooms and bedrooms with large windows. It is also seen that solar gains through windows and exposed walls influence thermal comfort.

References

Accent Group. (2007). The accent home. Retrieved from http://www.accentgroup .org/Housing/Accent+Home/ (last visited: 15.07.2010).

Altan, H., Gasperini, N., Moshaver, S., & Frattari, A. (2015). Redesigning terraced social housing in the UK for flexibility using building energy simulation with consideration of passive design. *Sustainability (Switzerland)*, *7*(5), 5488–5507. https://doi.org/10.3390/su7055488.

Altan, H., & Ozarisoy, B. (2022c). An analysis of the development of modular building design elements to improve thermal performance of a representative high rise residential estate in the coastline city of Famagusta, Cyprus. *Sustainability*, *14*(7), 4065. https://doi.org/10.3390/su14074065.

Ballarini, I., Corgnati, S. P., & Corrado, V. (2014). Use of reference buildings to assess the energy saving potentials of the residential building stock: The experience of TABULA project. *Energy Policy*, *68*, 273–284. https://doi.org/10 .1016/j.enpol.2014.01.027.

BEAU. (2007). *Accent homes project, internal report*. BEAU, United Kingdom: Sheffield University Press.

Bertoldi, P., & Mosconi, R. (2020). Do energy efficiency policies save energy? A new approach based on energy policy indicators (in the EU Member States). *Energy Policy*, *139*. https://doi.org/10.1016/j.enpol.2020.111320.

Borelli, D., Cavalletti, P., Marchitto, A., & Schenone, C. (2020). A comprehensive study devoted to determine linear thermal bridges transmittance in existing buildings. *Energy and Buildings*, *224*. https://doi.org/10.1016/j.enbuild.2020 .110136.

BRE. (2005). The government's standard assessment procedure (SAP) for energy rating of dwellings 2005 edition. Retrieved from http://projects.bre.co.uk/ sap2005/pdf/SAP2005.pdf (last visited: 01.05.2010).

Cuerda, E., Guerra-Santin, O., Sendra, J. J., & Neila, F. J. (2020). Understanding the performance gap in energy retrofitting: Measured input data for adjusting building simulation models. *Energy and Buildings*, *209*. https://doi.org/10.1016 /j.enbuild.2019.109688.

Friedman, A. (2003). *The adapted house: Designing for choice and change.* New York: McGraw-Hill.

Kalluri, B., Seshadri, B., Gwerder, M., & Schlueter, A. (2020). A longitudinal analysis of energy consumption data from a high-performance building in the tropics. *Energy and Buildings*, *224*. https://doi.org/10.1016/j.enbuild.2020.110230.

Ozarisoy, B. (2022). Energy effectiveness of passive cooling design strategies to reduce the impact of long-term heatwaves on occupants' thermal comfort in Europe: Climate change and mitigation. *Journal of Cleaner Production*. https://doi.org/10.1016/j.jclepro.2021.129675.

Ozarisoy, B., & Altan, H. (2021). A novel methodological framework for the optimisation of post-war social housing developments in the South-Eastern Mediterranean climate: Policy design and life-cycle cost impact analysis of retrofitting strategies. *Solar Energy*, *225*, 517–560. https://doi.org/10.1016/j.solener.2021.07.008.

Ozarisoy, B., & Altan, H. (2022a). Significance of occupancy patterns and habitual household adaptive behaviour on home-energy performance of post-war social-housing estate in the South-Eastern Mediterranean climate: Energy policy design. *Energy*, *244*. https://doi.org/10.1016/j.energy.2021.122904.

Ozarisoy, B., & Altan, H. (2022b). Bridging the energy performance gap of social housing stock in South-Eastern Mediterranean Europe: Climate change and mitigation. *Energy and Buildings*, *258*. https://doi.org/10.1016/j.enbuild.2021.111687.

Theodosiou, T., Tsikaloudaki, K., Kontoleon, K., & Giarma, C. (2021). Assessing the accuracy of predictive thermal bridge heat flow methodologies. *Renewable and Sustainable Energy Reviews*, *136*. https://doi.org/10.1016/j.rser.2020.110437.

Thonipara, A., Runst, P., Ochsner, C., & Bizer, K. (2019). Energy efficiency of residential buildings in the European Union – An exploratory analysis of cross-country consumption patterns. *Energy Policy*, *129*, 1156–1167. https://doi.org/10.1016/j.enpol.2019.03.003.

14 Conclusions

Bertug Ozarisoy and Hasim Altan

Introduction

These case studies seek to demonstrate the means and the techniques of architectural drawings deployed for uptake delivery of visionary utopian urban design scenarios. The research is not therefore detached from the essence of the project but informs our view on the city's existing categorisations, on the patterns of spatial occupation and practices that define a series of architectural archetypes and protocols. This book presents several architectural drawings, writings on architectural manifestos and urban design proposals and investigates the materiality, the actuality, the present and past of the given reality of the research context under investigation.

In this exploratory study, the architectural scale presented is directly confronted with the territorial scale without any possible mediation of planning and economic management techniques. From this perspective, such a peculiar condition is the ideal environment where architecture as a project for the city is called to revert the paradigm of translation between the city and the way of community living (Mosley & Sara, 2013, 14–19). Rather than being conceived as an architectural discourse of undertaking visionary utopian urban visions in respect to the luxury and cultural identity, it embodies the possibility of an alternative model for social, political and economic development (Doron, 2000, 247–263). Confronted with reclaiming the local physical conditions such as existing infrastructure and buildings, Part 2 of this book explores the impact of international capitalism on luxury branding, and it also claims the local identity as a source of human energy, memories and relationships as a possibility for a different ethos of Europe within a global world (Altay, 2013, 102–109). One of the main reasons is that the hearsay research monograph contains visual illustrations and narratives of storyboards to reflect design proposals in architecture and promoting sustainability in urban design. Therefore, the book is only limited to the last divided capital of Europe – Nicosia in Cyprus, Berlin in Germany and several case studies in the United Kingdom but it could be generalised and used as a guideline for other conflicted

DOI: 10.4324/9781003243069-17

territories and metropolitan cities across the globe. The study focuses on understanding spatial design and its impact on implementing effective architectural interventions in conflicted cities, particularly in the context of Berlin. Throughout the case studies, the grounded theory approach was adopted to interpret the transactions in urban theory and architectural discourse.

Reviewing of Case Study Locations

This chapter raises the questions of how to spatialise architectural design in the conflicted territory in Europe and consider international scales that define the research context in terms relevant to urban design. It demonstrates the scale of architecture, its spatial configuration and typological analysis but also the political and socioeconomic realities that organise it. In this study, the notion of transgression's role in the building of a nation-state or as a capital city both at the conceptual and national levels in the Mediterranean region and European Union is analysed.

The book presents a courageous, critical excursion in the implementation of visionary utopian urban design scenarios in line with the notion of transgression and architectural discourse (Roberts-Hughes, 2017, 157–168). It provides an overview of ideas that guide thinking through the design process in an explicit attempt to help students examine their design thinking and motivations (Cunningham, 2001). It manifests the roots of architectural design theory from philosophy to practice for identifying sources of normative theory in architecture and urbanism (Sharp, 2022). The exploratory case studies included in this part contain the utopian urban vision of contested spaces as a speculative architectural and urban project. They seek to explore the radical potential of architecture within the geopolitically shaped context of the city.

The study explores how architectural landscape as an idea, a visual medium and a design practice is organised, appropriated and framed in the transformation of places, from the local to the global (Jacoby et al., 2022, 1–33). It highlights how the development of the idea of visionary utopian urban design scenarios in architectural theory and practice can fundamentally change our engagement with future architectural design philosophy (Littlefield, 2013, 124–129). Including a wide range of international case studies as an informative precedent, each illustrated chapter investigates the many ways in which the relationship between the ideas and practices of architectural discourse and social and subjective formations and material processes are invested with effective implementation strategies. The study critically examines the role of contested spaces in the process of contemporary urban development, environmental debate and effective architectural interventions implemented for base case scenario development in sustainability and explores how these relations can be analysed and rethought through a dialogue between theory and practice.

260 Bertug Ozarisoy and Hasim Altan

This part contributes to exploring transatlantic fusion between the more critical architectural design milieu in North America and those in Britain and continental Europe, which both need a real shake-up. Likewise, it deliberately aims to address the more abstract theoretical positions in urban design and actual case studies on the ground. The array of case studies in this part of the book is lively and challenging. None try to be definitive but rather hope to provoke those involved in urban theory and architectural design practice to become more critically explicit about what they do – and asking main design principles of visionary utopian urban design scenarios, what are the forms of agency that architectural design-led research and projects might potentially have.

A Future Outlook

The case studies present an extensive illustration to inform the readers on the development of visionary utopian urban design scenarios in the conflicted territory in Berlin and vibrant and multicultural urban regeneration areas in London. Yet all these fragmented geographies' urban and cultural importance at different times and for different political and economic reasons is not fully understood without considering the formative role that architectural theory and discourse has played in establishing them as important intellectual, liberal and cosmopolitan centres (Faustino, 2013, 120–123).

In this exploratory case study represented throughout the practice-led case studies, the enquiries emerging from these different scales were the starting point to reconsider the dichotomy of public and private that underlies the discipline of urban design and led to an examination of how different reader groups get benefit from this book as part of their studies and practices in architecture and urban design. One of the main reasons is that this research monograph is also designed to reflect the cultural identity and practice of everyday lives of the Cypriot community by understanding cultural paradox and diasporas between sociology and architecture. This multicultural experience could be generalised to the wider context and will be entailed into other postgraduate taught programmes outside of architecture.

The study investigates the importance of the city as an urban formation inhabited by traces of both an ancient and a recent past in order to devise both architectural and urban manifestos. The objective of this part is to relate the research context's past and contemporary conditions with the technology of the existing urban conditions and infrastructure of agricultural trade. This constitutes a spatial strategy which uncovers fragments of the city's social and political activity. The design proposals inform the foundation upon which the grounded theory is built and demands a synthesis of material composed of these fragments as follows: the actual configuration of the city, its history and geology, its infrastructure and the architectural spaces that represent the subjects shaped within it.

Conclusions 261

Conclusion and Recommendations

The study establishes definitions of methodology, scope of work, outlook and design concepts for students and professionals alike. It touches succinctly and clearly into the history and evolution of the profession and the scale and typological architectural landscapes that professionals are committed to today. It also defines the amplitude and limitations of a profession difficult to define. It has been stressed that the aim of this study is much more than a source to inform readers considering the significance of visionary utopian urban design scenarios on sustainable development as a possible career choice. It is meant for professionals who wish to make a difference in their design projects, in the lives of others, and for the sustainable preservation of the environment through design.

Both the present study and the competitive book exploring contested spaces and culturally fragmented urban conditions have focused schemes with critical and timely studies that the manifestos built upon in detailed speculations with both quantitative and qualitative design strategies. This reference book is an example and doesn't claim any special design methodology; rather, it lays out the background and presents design manifestos with the most compelling visuals that communicate critical information, with clear verbal narratives. The high-quality drawings could help the readers to understand the theory and practice while imagining the narrative stories. They are exemplary as a whole set of reflecting critical thinking and analysis. It provides design students a critical lens to scrutinise emerging issues for researchers and practitioners. It offers quantified data at various scales.

The undergraduate and postgraduate taught programmes are open to a whole spectrum of graduates in architecture and cognate design fields. This book enables students to determine appropriate methodologies for research in architecture and design and to use these techniques to formulate intellectual and creative work which investigates specific aspects or issues within the broad field of architecture. In summary, there is a strong correlation between the scope of exploring conditions of utopian urban visions and architectural discourse concurrently.

References

Altay, C. (2013). Transgression in and of the city. *Architectural Design*, *83*(6), 102–109. https://doi.org/10.1002/ad.1682

Cunningham, D. (2001). Architecture, Utopia and the futures of the avant-garde. *Journal of Architecture*. https://doi.org/10.1080/13602360110048195

Doron, G. M. (2000). The dead zone and the architecture of transgression. *City*, *4*(2), 247–263. https://doi.org/10.1080/13604810050147857

Faustino, D. (2013). In praise of transgression: The work of Didier faustino/bureau de mésarchitectures. *Architectural Design*, *83*(6), 120–123. https://doi.org/10.1002/ad.1685

Jacoby, S., Arancibia, A., & Alonso, L. (2022). Space standards and housing design: Typological experimentation in England and Chile. *Journal of Architecture*, 1–33. https://doi.org/10.1080/13602365.2022.2045340

Littlefield, D. (2013). Ashes thrown to the wind: The elusive nature of transgression. *Architectural Design*, 83(6), 124–129. https://doi.org/10.1002/ad.1686

Mosley, J., & Sara, R. (2013). The architecture of transgression: Towards a destabilising architecture. *Architectural Design*, 83(6), 14–19. https://doi.org/10.1002/ad.1668

Roberts-Hughes, R. (2017). Transgression and conservation: Rereading Georges Bataille. *Journal for Cultural Research*, 21(2), 157–168. https://doi.org/10.1080/14797585.2016.1239608

Sharp, D. (2022). Concretising conflict. *Journal of Architecture*. https://doi.org/10.1080/13602365.2022.2029026

Index

Note: Italic page number refers to figures and bold page number refers to tables; Page numbers followed by "n" denote endnotes.

Accent Group Ltd 238
Agamben, G. 34
agriculture in RoC 82–83
Altay, C. 35–36
Annan, Kofi 10
Annan Plan 10
annual food festival 83–84, *84*
architectural design: critical 26–27, *27*; cultural diasporas for identifying main principles of 81–82; key principles of creating 76–80, *77–80*; marketing and 215; participant-led co-design 39–41; participant-led design 50–53, *53*; scenarios 100
architectural discourse 64
architectural education 5, 144
architectural philosophy 30, 35, 59, 62, 89, 123, 212, 259; *see also* transgression
architectural reconciliation process: decision-making of 51–52; exploratory case study design and its implications on 54–56; transgression, learning from 56–57
architectural theory 2–3, 5, 20; architectural transgression 27–32, 40–42, 65–68; case studies (*see* case studies); utopian ideas 30; utopian urban vision 34, 39, 49, 54–56, *55*, 73–90, *78*, 101–102
architecture 24, 26–27, 178; archipelago in 31–32; of buffer zone, UN 35; co-existence in 33; discourse of 3–5; of luxury 207–212; in marketing 214; of oppression 35–36, 48; politics in 33; power of 32–33,

46; state of conflict and 34–35; of transgression 27–33, 40–42, 65–68; of violence 32–33, 47
arts 97

Ballard, R. 135
Balletto, L. 179
Barnsbury Estate 191, 193, 195, 198, 201
Bataille, G. 179
Berlin: Kreuzberg 233–236; past and present 231–233; Turkish embassy building in *235*
birds, city of 84–85, *85*
border 180–181
brand identity *205*, 205–206, 215; *vs.* local identity 209–210
brand street 212–213
Brown, Denise Scott 205, 207
buffer zone, UN 4, 9–10, 14, *15*, 32, 50–60, *55*, 65, 69, 69–70, *71*, 100, 181; architectural archipelago throughout *31*; architecture of 35; design of 26; language of 18–20, 70–72; mapping invisibility of 105–108, *106–107*; new diaspora for 24–42; political space 35–36, 46–49; representational diaspora 18–20, *19*, 70–72; research design approach for reclaiming architectural discourse in 50–51; transgression and 25–26
built environment 4, 9, 34, 37, 56, 90, 123, 191, 212

Camus, A. 179
cappadocias 236

264 *Index*

carbon emissions reduction target (CERT) 171
Carbon Reduction in Buildings (CaRB) 253
case studies 2–5; Elephant & Castle regeneration development, London, UK 219–228; King's Cross, London, UK 187–202; State of Power, Kreuzberg, Berlin, Germany 231–236; Undercliffe Social Housing, Bradford, UK 238–256
CERT *see* carbon emissions reduction target
CESP *see* Community Energy Saving Programme
Chanel 205, 207, 215–216
city of birds 84–85, *85*
city of trees 83–84, *84*
city of watchtowers 85–86
Climate Change Act 2008 172
Code for Sustainable Homes (CfSH) standard 157, 163–167
Cold homes 171
'Collective Memories and Narratives' 50
colonialism 14, 140
Community Energy Saving Programme (CESP) 172
conflict 32, 37–38; participation and 39–41; state of 34–35
conflicted territories 1–2, 33–35, 185
counteractive urbanism 49–50
craftsmanship 214–215
creative ideas 26–27
'Creative Possibilities: Birds, Narratives and Artefacts' 49–50, 52–54, 57
'Creative Possibilities', event of 16–17, 24, 26, *38*, 39–42, 49–50, 53–54
critical design 26–27, *27*
critical thinking 24, 26, 30, 32, 36, 45, 49, 52, 57, 75, 88, 108, 128, 261
cultural identity 2–3, 12–13, 18, 68, 90, 105, 123, 132–133, 207, 258
culture 26, 105; hybridisation of 141; identity of 3, 132–133
Cypriot identity 12–13, 16–18, 20, 71, 82, 86, 104, 109, 111, 117–118, 140, 144–145
Cypriot immigrants 145n11

dead space 180
'death strip' 231

decision-making, architectural reconciliation process 51–52
democracy 35
Denison, E. 180
Department for Environment, Food and Rural Affairs (DEFRA) 156
diasporas 97–98
division 29–30
domestic space, Turkish Cypriot 127–143, *131*
Doron, G. M. 181
drawings 178

eel houses 201
Elephant & Castle regeneration development, London, UK (case study) 219–228; design proposal 221; as focal point for London 221–224, *223*; mapping social housing estates in *227*; urban development proposal 224–226, *225*; urban regeneration in 219–221, *220*
Energy Company Obligation (ECO) 172
energy consumption in UK 150–151, 172–173; anticipated mandatory improvement in CO_2 emissions **166**; carbon emission cuts from UK housing 158–160, **160**; and CO_2 emissions 150–152; code for sustainable homes 163–167; domestic 150–156, *151–152*; domestic energy efficiency measures **158**; dwelling characteristics and efficiency 169–170; dwellings in UK 152–156, *153*; energy efficiency of housing stock 153–154; government funded programmes on 170–172; for housing 150–156, *151*; new homes 160–163; policies, background on 156–158, *157*; profile of energy performance of domestic stock by age in 2004 *154*; programmes and policies on 170; SAP rating for 153–154; space heating 154–156; total *151*, 151–152; zero-carbon new homes by 2016 161–163, 167–168
energy efficiency of housing stock 153–154; *see also* energy consumption in UK
Energy Performance Certificate (EPC) 173n2

energy studies *see* energy consumption in UK
Energy Supplier Funded Programmes 171
ENOSIS 9, 21n7
EOKA-B 9, 21n5, 129
Europe 4–5
Evans, P. 158

Feireiss, L. 180
Ford, S. 33
Foucault, M. 27–30, 35, 48, 68, 127–128, 134, 179–180, 205
Friedman, Avi 238
fuel poverty in UK **168**, 168–169

gentrification 187–188
Giron, Maria Eugenia 211
globalisation 24
graphical illustrations 4–5
Greek Cypriots 9–10, 50
Green Deal 172
greenhouse gas (GHG) emissions 150–151
Green Line 9, 13–14, *25*, 32, 62; language of 70–72; representational diaspora 70–72; *see also* New Green Zone of Nicosia
green religion 118–121
Green Street 217–218

Hall, Suzan 226
Hall, Suzanne M. 219
Hardt, M. 180
Heating, Ventilation and Air Conditioning (HVAC) system 244–245
Heat Recovery Ventilation (HRV) system 246
Hegglund, J. 127
Hejduk, R. 98, 181
Hermes 205, 210, 213–214, 217, 219, 221
heterotopias 205
Heygate estate 224
house 127–129; *see also* case studies
Housing Health and Safety Rating System 171
hybridisation 140–141

Inside Luxury: The Growth and Future of the Luxury Industry: A View from the Top (Giron) 211

Jakobsen, J. 42
Japan *205*, 205–207
junta 9, 21n6

Kering (previously known as PPR) 213
King's Cross, London, UK (case study) 187–202; courtyard house 200–202; cross cultural section of Caledonian Road *190*, 190–191; design proposals *192*, 192–193; greening of 193–198, *194–197*; location map of *188*; past and present 187–189; physical conditions, mapping existing 189–191, *190–191*; redevelopment 187–202; as urban agriculture city model 193–200; urban linkage 198–200, *199–200*
Koolhaas, Rem 212
Kucukcan, T. 137
Kyo-machiya 201

Landlords Energy Saving Allowance 171
Language of Things, The (Sudjic) 212
Las Vegas Strip 207
Learning from Las Vegas (Venturi and Brown) 205, 207
Ledras Street checkpoint 14–16
Lefebvre, H. 140–141
Letherman, K. M. 158–159
liberalism 35
Littlefield, D. 209
living space culture 127–129
local identity *vs.* brand identity 209–210, 222
Louis Vuitton 205, 207, 209, 210, 213, 217, 221
luxury *205*, 205–206; architecture of 207–212; brands 205, 207–212; definition 205–206
luxury architecture *vs.* ordinary architecture 216
luxury brand shops 217

Manaugh, G. 180
marketing: architecture in 214; and brand identity 215; design process, role in 215
Meier, H. 156
meydan 236
Miessen, M. 33, 35–38, 181
military power 36–37

266 *Index*

movement of Cypriots 106–107
multicultural exchange 57–59

New Green Zone of Nicosia 62–63,
101–123, *103*; cosmopolitan nature
114–116; culture 105; diaspora of
105; green religion 118–121; intuitive
navigation 113–114; maximum
diversity 112–113; Pedieos river 14,
104–105, *105*, 108–110, *109*, *110*,
114; public spaces 116–118, *117*;
symbolic representation of 105–108;
vs. utopias 86–87, 103–105; vision
101–102, *101–102*, 105
Nicosia 4, 12–13, *25*, *47*, 68–69;
agriculture in 82–83; cultural identity
of 18; Green Line and 9, 13–14, 32,
62 (*see also* New Green Zone of
Nicosia); history 12; identity 12–13;
Ledras Street checkpoint 14–16; map
13; mapping of 105–108, *106–107*;
multi-colored 76–78; overview 12;
river Pedieos 14, 108–109, *109*;
scoping field 72–73; urban scenario
development 68–70; utopian urban
vision (*see* utopian urban vision for
Nicosia); visionary view of 99
'No-Man's Land'/'Dead Zone' 14

Oakley, R. 134–137
occupation 36–37
oppression 35–37, 48
Ozarisoy, B. 159
Ozarks National Organisation of
Cypriot Fighters (EOKA) 9, 12, 21n3

participant-based architectural
disseminations 49–50
participant-led co-design 39–41
participant-led design 50–53, *53*
participation 39–41
participatory-led design 37–39
Peace Hall 16, 39, 50–51, *51*
Peacock, A. 159
Pedieos river 14, 104–105, *105*,
108–110, *109*, *110*, *114*
photographic survey 4–5
Plague, The (Camus) 34
political space 35–36, 46–49
Positive Input Ventilation (PIV) system
246–247
Potsdamer Platz 231, *232*
power: of architecture 32–33, 46; of
nature 62; structures of 48

Prada 213, 221
public spaces 116–118, *117*

quality 214–215

Rabinow, Paul 35, 48
radical practices: *vs.* border 180–181;
and transgression 179–181
Rapoport, A. 132
Rehdanz, K. 156
Reichstag 231–232
reinhabit birds 85–86
Ren, G. 180
Republic of Cyprus (RoC) 9–12, 20n2,
68; agriculture in 82–83; Annan
Plan 10; buffer zone, UN 4, 9–10,
14, *15*; civilizations, ruled by 68;
Cypriots 17–18; *de facto* state 9–10,
20n1; Eastern 10; Green Line 9,
13–14; identity 17; Ledras Street
checkpoint 14–16; major cities 10;
movement of 106–107; multicultural
modality of 11; Nicosia (*see* Nicosia);
Northern 10; Peace Hall 16; urban
agglomerations in 10; Voluntary
Regrouping of Population
Agreement 10
rootedness 133
Rue des Suisses apartment
building 201

Samo, S. R. 158–159
Sassen, S. 45
scarcity 212
Scottish Housing Quality Standard 171
self-initiated projects 41–42
self-organisation 41
Shorrock, L. D. 156–160
small and medium enterprises (SMEs)
11, 21n10
social structure 134
sociocultural paradoxes 3
Sonyel, S. 140
spaces of conflict 33–35
Standard Assessment Procedure (SAP)
153–154, 173n1
state of conflict 34–35
State of Power, Kreuzberg, Berlin,
Germany (case study) 231–236
Status Anxiety 211
Sudjic, Deyan 212
suprematism 35
sustainable architecture: case studies
(*see* case studies); goals 5; New Green

Zone of Nicosia 62–63, *103*; utopian urban vision for Nicosia 34, 39, 49, 54–56, *55*, 73–90, *78*, 101–102; *see also* architecture

third-space 30, 33
transgression 2–4; architecture of 27–32, 40–42, 65–68; buffer zone, UN and 25–26; *vs.* contested urban conditions 27; for creating urban utopia 64–68; as instrument 30; learning from 56–57; between luxury brand and architecture 210–212; philosophy of 30, 35, 59, 62, 89, 123, 212, 259; and radical practices 179–181; Tschumi's ideology 32, 66–68; and utopia 178
Tschumi, Bernard 27–28, 30, 32–33, 56, 66
Turkey 9
Turkish Cypriot families/community 127–145, *130*; change/displacement, context of 133–134; critics on cultural practice/space of 141–143; cultural identity 132–133; cultural practices of 129–132, 134–137; data for research on 128–129; domestic space 127–132, *131*; home/house 132–143; hybridity as role of cultural practice 140–141; immigration/immigrants, history/reasons for 129–143, 145n11; living and their domestic space use 128–129; in London 129–140; memories of 129–132; migration and cultural practices of 129–132; poetics of space 139–140; representational space 132–133; second generation of immigrants 135–138; subject participants' interview transcripts 137–138
Turkish Cypriots 9–12, 50

Undercliffe Social Housing, Bradford, UK (case study) 238–256; construction details 241–244, *242–243*, **244**; energy consumptions 251–253, *252*; heating systems 244–245, **245**; indoor environments 249–251, *250*, **251**; monitoring study 247–249, **248**, 251; occupant survey 253–255, *254*, **255**; overview 238–241; Post Occupancy Evaluation (POE) study 239–241,

240; simplified floor plans for 238, *239*; ventilation system 245–247, **246**
unification 40, 49, 51–52, 57–59
United Cyprus Republic (UCR) 21n9
United Kingdom 5; dwellings in 152–156, *153*; Elephant & Castle regeneration development, London 219–228; energy consumption (*see* energy consumption in UK); fuel poverty in **168**, 168–169; King's Cross, London 187–202; Undercliffe Social Housing, Bradford 238–256
United Nations Peacekeeping Force in Cyprus (UNFICYP) 21n4
University of Sheffield 238
urban collectives 33
urban design 68–70; *see also* case studies
urbanism 32, 62
urban manifestos 3–5, 26–27, 33, 54, 59, 134, 258, 260
urban regeneration; *see also* case studies: New Green Zone of Nicosia 62–63, *103*; utopian urban vision for Nicosia 34, 39, 49, 54–56, *55*, 73–90, *78*, 101–102
Urry, J. 133–134
Utley, J. I. 156
utopian urban vision for Nicosia 34, 39, 49, 54–56, *55*, 73–90, *78*, 101–102; agricultural fields *111*; annual food festival 83–84, *84*; as city of birds 84–85, *85*; as city of trees 83–84, *84*; as city of watchtowers 85–86; cultural diasporas for identifying main design principles of 81–82; design scenarios 100; invisibility to 73–75; key design principles of creating 76–80, *77–80*; map of buffer zone *74*; monumental representation 110–111; New Green Zone (*see* New Green Zone of Nicosia); notion of transgression and vice versa, mapping 75–76; transgression as 64–68
utopias 32, 62–64, 97–123; architectural discourse 64–65; function of 100; futures and 98–100; *vs.* new green zone 86–87, 103–105; transgression for creating urban 64–68, 178

268 *Index*

Venturi, Robert 205, 207
violence: architecture of 32–33, 47; spaces of conflict and 33–35
Voluntary Regrouping of Population Agreement 10

Walworth Road 217–218
Warm Front programme 170–171
Warm Home Discount 171
Weizman, E. 46–47
Welsh Housing Quality Standard 171
Wenders, Wim 231

Wilford, Michael 236
Williams, R. 41–42
'Wings of Desire' 231
Winter Fuel Payments 171

zero-carbon housing 157, 160–163, *161*; building fabrics standards **165**; construction of 167–168; definition of 166; encouragement mechanisms 162–163; meaning **162**; reduction of CO_2 emissions from 162, *164*